"*When Did Sin Begin?* explores an important issue ... .
about Scripture and science. The book models integration at its best, with
serious and well-researched work on both the science side and the Scripture
side of this discussion. Even when I disagreed with some points along the way
(as one inevitably does), I could not fault the author for any failure to treat
Scripture or the theological tradition with anything less than full seriousness.
I recommend the book as a well-informed entry into many of the current
debates among Christians about creation and human origins."

—**Douglas J. Moo**, Wheaton College Graduate School

"In this timely book, Haarsma deals with the apparent dissonance between the
doctrine of original sin and the biological evolution of humanity. Throughout
the text, he systematically works through a variety of scenarios related to the
origin of sin within an evolutionary context, clearly delineating the subtle
differences between each approach and carefully working out the theological
ramifications as well. Rather than narrowing in and promoting one particular
point of view, Haarsma has laid out the parameters for a multitude of options,
setting the stage for the reader to consider various possibilities. This book
offers much food for thought and serves as a model for how we can wrestle
well with difficult questions like this in the church."

—**Ryan Bebej**, Calvin University

"This book embodies and enhances the effort to 'integrate faith and learning.'
Here a theologically-engaged scientist lays out—reverently and methodically,
from several angles—the key points at which human evolution intersects with
the doctrine of sin. The result is a valuable update on the contemporary discussion, helping theological traditionalists like me to encounter the various
alternatives and reflect on their respective implications."

—**Daniel J. Treier**, Wheaton College Graduate School

"*When Did Sin Begin?* presents a broad range of scholarship and viewpoints
with civility and evenhandedness. Whether one is a theological novice or ex-
pert, timid or bold concerning the science, Professor Haarsma's work offers
a hospitable welcome to this important topic."

—**Justin Barrett**, president, Blueprint 1543

"The subject of evolution and human origins continues to be a hot topic for
Christians wrestling with the evidence and with the implications for their
faith. Of the many books on the market, most focus on the truth or falsehood
of scientific claims or on the proper understanding of the biblical texts. Few

have focused on the potential impact of human evolution on a particular theological doctrine. Haarsma does just that with *When Did Sin Begin?*, exploring an array of possible scenarios of human origins and assessing the implications for the timing and nature of sin entering the world, the historicity of Adam and Eve, and our understanding of original sin."

—**Gregg Davidson**, University of Mississippi

WHEN
DID
SIN
BEGIN?

WHEN DID SIN BEGIN?

HUMAN EVOLUTION AND THE DOCTRINE OF ORIGINAL SIN

LOREN HAARSMA

Baker Academic

a division of Baker Publishing Group
Grand Rapids, Michigan

Published by Baker Academic
a division of Baker Publishing Group
PO Box 6287, Grand Rapids, MI 49516-6287
www.bakeracademic.com

Printed in the United States of America

Library of Congress Cataloging-in-Publication Data
Names: Haarsma, Loren D., author.
Title: When did sin begin? : human evolution and the doctrine of original sin / Loren Haarsma.
Description: Grand Rapids, Michigan : Baker Academic, a division of Baker Publishing Group,
    [2021] | Includes bibliographical references and index.
Identifiers: LCCN 2021009311 | ISBN 9781540963680 (paperback) | ISBN 9781540964267
    (casebound)
Subjects: LCSH: Sin, Original. | Human evolution—Religious aspects—Christianity. | Religion and
    science.
Classification: LCC BT720 .H33 201 | DDC 233/.14—dc23
LC record available at https://lccn.loc.gov/2021009311

21   22   23   24   25   26   27   7   6   5   4   3   2   1

Contents

Acknowledgments

I WROTE THIS BOOK for three audiences. First, it is for Christians who question scientific theories of human evolution because they appear to conflict with Christian doctrines about original sin. Second, it is for Christians who question the doctrine of original sin because they don't see how to reconcile it with the scientific evidence for human evolution. Third, it is for people of any religious view who are curious how Christians might harmonize these things.

Work on this book was supported by the BioLogos Evolution and Christian Faith program and Calvin University. I am grateful to the American Scientific Affiliation for enabling many helpful conversations on this topic over several decades. Thank you to Rachel Hekman and Amy VanZanen for research assistance. Thank you to Deborah Haarsma, John Walton, Tremper Longman, Daniel Harlow, Gregg Davidson, Lyle Bierma, Daniel Treier, John Hilber, Gerald Hiestand, Clayton Carlson, Joel White, John Cooper, Ben McFarland, Cara Wall-Scheffler, Justin Barrett, Ryan Bebej, Darrel Falk, Matthew Lundberg, Ralph Stearley, Steve Wykstra, and Steve Roels for valuable feedback on earlier drafts.

Introduction

Theology and Science
in Harmony and Counterpoint

YOU SIN. I SIN. EVERYONE SINS. Individually and collectively, we do morally wrong things and cause much suffering. Calling this "sin" is actually the start of good news. It signals that a holy and loving God wants better for us. God has a rescue plan in operation. Christianity, from its earliest days, affirmed that Jesus Christ is at the center of that rescue.

Human Evolution and the Doctrine of Original Sin Seem Dissonant

The Western church for centuries has followed St. Augustine's formulation of the doctrine of original sin. Augustine taught that God created Adam and Eve holy and righteous; they chose to sin in the garden of Eden; sin damaged them; the guilt and damage were passed by inheritance to their descendants—all of humanity. The doctrine of original sin isn't just about how the historical first sin occurred. It summarizes many things taught throughout Scripture about God's goodness, human responsibility, the pervasiveness of sin, and the need for Christ's atonement.

Theologians before and since Augustine disagreed with him on some points. But throughout church history most Christians, like Augustine, assumed that Adam and Eve were literal historical persons who were created miraculously by God a few thousand years ago in or near Mesopotamia and that all human beings are descended from just those two. So it is not surprising that many

1

Christians perceive dissonance between the theology of original sin and modern scientific theories of human evolution. Scientific evidence indicates that disease, predation, and death were in the world long before humans existed. Genetic similarities between humans and animals indicate common ancestry. Human genetic diversity points to humanity descending not from just a single pair but from a larger ancestral population probably never less than thousands of individuals.

One line of thinking is that if Augustine's interpretation of Genesis 2–3 is not true, then there was no original sin, no fall, and no need for Christ's redemption. From this perspective, it seems like the entire gospel of Christianity is at stake.

The central premise of this book is that *there are several possible ways to harmonize the doctrine of original sin and the science of human evolution*, taking seriously both what Scripture teaches and what we learn from science. The first half of this book describes a range of scenarios; the latter half discusses theological strengths and challenges of each.

Is the Doctrine of Original Sin Really Such a Big Deal?

Sin is a big deal. All of Scripture agrees on this. Sin breaks our proper relationship with God. Sin would separate us from God eternally without God's rescue.

God's shocking answer to sin is the incarnation, life, death, and resurrection of Jesus. The Word of God, "begotten from the Father before all ages,"[1] "being in very nature God, did not consider equality with God something to be used to his own advantage; rather, he made himself nothing by taking the very nature of a servant" (Phil. 2:6–7). He became an infant. He grew and lived as we do. He did not sin, but he suffered the terrible consequences of our sin— including denial and betrayal by friends, mob hatred, unjust condemnation by religious and secular authorities, and death by torture. His resurrection and ascension completed and vindicated his work of atonement. Consider how vast the problem of sin must be if God would do all that to solve it.

How did we humans find ourselves in need of such rescue? God created us. God is good. God loves us. Why aren't we sinless? Over the centuries, that question has been answered in a variety of ways.

The author of Genesis 2–3 lived in a particular cultural context and had important universal truths to communicate. The surrounding cultures of

---

1. Nicene Creed; translation from Christian Reformed Church, *Ecumenical Creeds and Reformed Confessions* (Grand Rapids: CRC Publications, 1988).

Egypt and Mesopotamia had stories of their gods creating the world, fighting one another, and forming human beings. They also had stories about a past golden age. In that context, the author of Genesis 2–3 needed to communicate some universal truths. The world was made by the one true God—the God of Abraham, Isaac, and Jacob. God created humanity. God is good. Instead of trusting God's pronouncements about good and evil, humans rebelled and tried to decide for themselves, breaking fellowship with God. But God did not leave them without hope. God had a rescue plan.

Centuries later, the apostle Paul lived in a particular cultural context and had important universal truths to communicate. Paul was taught that the Messiah would rescue Israel from political oppression and restore Israel's relationship to God through obedience to the law of Moses. But then Paul met the risen Jesus and learned some amazing truths. The Messiah had been crucified. The Messiah was for the gentiles—even without their obedience to the law of Moses! The work of the Messiah was bigger than Paul had pictured. The life, death, and resurrection of Christ were not just for Israel; they were for restoring Jews and gentiles alike to a right relationship with God. To communicate these truths, in Romans 1, Paul wrote about the knowledge of God that all human beings should have from looking at nature but that everyone gets wrong. In chapter 2, Paul wrote about how gentiles know they are sinners even without the law of Moses because of the law of God in their hearts. In chapter 5, Paul wrote about sin entering the world through the sin of Adam, the first human being.

Centuries later, St. Augustine lived in a particular cultural context and had important universal truths to communicate. Some church leaders at the time argued that infants are born sinless. Augustine believed that no one can be in a right relationship with God apart from Christ; everyone needs saving grace, even infants who have not yet sinned willfully. But this raised questions. How did humans come to be in such a state? Did God create humans sinful? If not, how was it possible that our first parents could sin? Why would the sin of our first parents affect all of their descendants, including infants? In answering these questions, Augustine and others developed the doctrine of original sin, which influenced the Eastern church and has dominated the Western church to this day.

We live today in a particular cultural context and have important universal truths to communicate. Archaeological discoveries and improved translations of ancient Near Eastern texts have taught us things about the cultural context of Genesis 2–3 that Augustine didn't know. Modern science indicates that God used evolutionary processes to create humanity. Augustine's assumption that all humans descended from just a single pair of individuals who lived a few thousand years ago does not fit with what we are learning from fossils and genetics. But in today's cultural context, we still have important universal truths to communicate. Sin is a rebellion against God's revealed will. Our sin would separate us from God eternally without God's rescue. The incarnation, life, death, and resurrection of Jesus Christ is the central point of history and the heart of God's rescue. What are the best ways to harmonize these truths in our particular cultural context today?

We Anticipate Harmony because of Our Faith in God's Character

The unity of Scripture is a guiding principle for Christian theology. This is not just a belief about Scripture; it is a statement of faith in God's character. We trust that God would not inspire one passage of Scripture to teach one thing and then inspire another passage to teach something contradictory. If two passages seem at first to contradict each other, then we do not properly understand one or both. We trust that if we interpret Scripture rightly, an overarching, coherent voice and message will emerge. We must work to discern the underlying harmony.

Scientists have a similar intuition about the natural world. If two scientific theories, each well supported by experiments, make contradictory predictions about experiments that are beyond our current ability to perform,[2] we don't simply live with the contradiction. We look for an overarching theory that incorporates both previous theories and unifies them. This procedure reflects a belief about the natural world. We believe there is a unified set of natural laws that we, at present, only partly understand. If two theories make contradictory predictions, then those theories must be incomplete. We have more work to do.

If we believe that God both created the universe and inspired Scripture, we carry this search for harmony into realms where science and theology overlap. Truths we learn from studying Scripture come from God. Likewise, truths we learn by doing science ultimately come from God. God created the world; science and philosophy are human interpretations of that world. Our human interpretations can be mistaken. God inspired Scripture; biblical scholarship and systematic theology are human interpretations of Scripture. Our human interpretations can be mistaken. If we trust God's character and believe he would not teach contradictory things, then whenever science and theology appear dissonant, we must work to find the underlying harmony.

2. Quantum field theory and general relativity are two such theories.

This doesn't mean that science and theology are equally authoritative. The natural world and Scripture are different sorts of revelation. Their complex relationship is explored in later chapters. For now, it's enough to say that we don't simply give theology authority over science or vice versa. God has authority over both.

Consensus on the *Core Doctrine* but Not on Every *Theological Theory*

Christians sometimes subscribe to a core doctrine while holding in tension multiple theological theories and not selecting one theory as superseding the others. For example, the church has developed multiple theories of atonement, which seek to explain how Christ's work answers the problem of sin. Not every proposed theory of atonement was accepted by the church; some were debated and rejected. But several complementary theories of atonement remain—still studied, preached, and compared with one another centuries after they were proposed. This is because Scripture uses numerous images for Christ's atoning work: bearing the penalty of sin as a substitute, victory over evil, ransom to free us from slavery, covenantal sacrifice, an example for us to imitate, and more. Indeed, how could a single human theory fully describe Christ's work? Christians often profess a core doctrine of the atonement while holding in tension multiple theories, each with its basis in Scripture, each recognized as incomplete. Doing so does more justice to the magnitude and mystery of Christ's atonement than any single theory could.

Christians can also agree with one another about a core doctrine while disagreeing about theological theories surrounding that doctrine. In such cases, individual Christians do not hold multiple theories in tension; rather, each one advocates for their own favorite theological theory while acknowledging that the Christian tradition includes a range of possible theories. For example, Christians generally share a core doctrine about baptism and follow Christ's command to baptize, but there is a range of theological theories regarding infant and adult baptism.[3]

Competing theological theories are part of Christian tradition. Competing theological theories can be good. They help us better understand our core doctrines and better explore their implications. There is the danger, however,

3. More examples: C. Marvin Pate, *Four Views on the Book of Revelation* (Grand Rapids: Zondervan, 1998); William V. Crockett, *Four Views on Hell* (Grand Rapids: Zondervan, 1996); Jason S. Sexton, *Four Views on the Church's Mission* (Grand Rapids: Zondervan, 2017); John Hick, Clark H. Pinnock, and Alister E. McGrath, *Four Views on Salvation in a Pluralistic World* (Grand Rapids: Zondervan, 1996); and Melvin Easterday Dieter, Anthony A. Hoekema, and J. Robertson McQuilkin, *Five Views on Sanctification* (Grand Rapids: Zondervan, 1996).

of mistaking our own favorite theological theory for the core doctrine itself.[4] A challenge to one's favorite theological *theory* might feel like an attack on the core doctrine, even when it is not.

This book first describes multiple competing theological theories about how to harmonize the doctrine of original sin with human evolution; then it examines some theological strengths and challenges of each theory.

The scenarios explored in this book disagree with one another on several significant questions. For example, they disagree about when the historical first sin might have happened, what it looked like, and what its immediate consequences were to the individuals involved. They disagree about whether we should think about the fall primarily as a concentrated historical event involving a few individuals or as spread out over time and involving many individuals. They disagree about how sin spread from some to many. They disagree about the status of the first sinners immediately prior to sin.

However, the scenarios examined here share a commitment to a core doctrine. Much of this book explores what that core doctrine is. For now, a summary: *God is good and just and holy. Sin is a rebellion against God's revealed will. The earliest acts of sinful disobedience by our ancestors had consequences both for them and for their descendants. All humans today are prone to sin and are incapable of not sinning. The incarnation, life, death, and resurrection of Jesus Christ are central to God's atonement for human sin.*

That is not a complete list; more statements could be added. In coming decades—as it has done throughout history—the church will discuss and debate what, exactly, has the status of "core doctrine" and what has the status of "theological theory." As we bring together scholarship in biblical studies, systematic theology, and evolutionary science, if we do our jobs carefully, the church will be well served by discussing the implications of these competing theological theories. The doctrine of atonement is so staggering that the

---

4. Benno van den Toren, "Distinguishing Doctrine and Theological Theory—A Tool for Exploring the Interface between Science and Faith," *Science & Christian Belief* 28, no. 2 (2016): 64, writes about the value of distinguishing our core doctrines, which Christians generally hold in common, from theological theories that seek to explain the doctrines but carry far less consensus:

> First, doctrine is crucial to the Christian life, as is the question of truth. Therefore, the church teaches who God is, how he relates to us, and how the Christian life should be lived given that this God is God. Second, not all theological reflection has the status of "doctrine" in this more narrow sense. Theological reflection can also be exploratory, or even speculative as an expression of the desire to love God with our minds, to grow in understanding or to find new ways to give account of our faith without these ideas having a similar regulative function for the Christian life and community. Third, there is a very limited range of doctrines that have the status of "dogma" in that denying them does mean undermining what is essential to the Christian understanding of salvation and would place oneself outside the orthodox Christian community.

church has found it best to hold in tension multiple theories of atonement. If the problem of sin is so vast that it requires such an astonishing solution as the atonement, perhaps we will find that we also need multiple theories of original sin. Some theories will be examined and ultimately discarded as inconsistent with God's revelation. Those that remain should deepen our understanding and appreciation of God's grace.

In Science and Theology, New Data That Challenge Old Theories Are Exciting and Important

When scientists discover new data that contradict a well-established scientific theory, they don't typically react with fear. Often, they react with curiosity. At their best, they react with humility, because they know that if the new data hold up, their current best theories will need rethinking. They have exciting work to do. They hope and trust that the new data will eventually lead to a deeper understanding of the natural world. And that gives them joy.

Of course, scientists don't simply throw out the old theory. Any new theory that explains the new data must also incorporate all the truths explained by the old theory.

Theology has had similar experiences, where it has been confronted with new data that challenged well-established theories but eventually led to deeper understandings of God's special revelation. There have been times when the Holy Spirit provided new data directly and dramatically, as when the apostle Peter's dream prompted him to go to the home of a gentile to preach the gospel of Christ (Acts 10).

At other times the Holy Spirit has done this more slowly, by challenging the church to reflect on things happening in the world. For centuries, many Christians used Scripture to justify using political and social power to oppress Jews. However, after reflecting on the suffering this caused, and ultimately witnessing the Holocaust of World War II, the church was forced to rethink how it interpreted those Scriptures.

On a few occasions, the natural sciences provided new data that helped theology improve its theories. One historical example is Galileo and other scientists finding strong evidence that the earth moves around the sun. At first the church was understandably reluctant to give up its traditional interpretations of passages like Psalm 93:1 as teaching that the earth does not move. But after significant scientific and theological work, this new data eventually moved the church to a better understanding of those Scriptures. The discovery that the earth moves did not cause the church to give up its core doctrines about the truth and divine inspiration of Scripture. Instead, it prompted the church to come up with better theological theories about whether certain scriptural passages that talk about the natural world are best interpreted literally.

For another historical example, Christians for several centuries found theological justification in passages like Genesis 1:28 ("fill the earth and subdue it") for turning wilderness wherever possible into cities and farms by clear-cutting forests, plowing up prairies, straightening rivers, and filling wetlands. Advances in science eventually illuminated some of the problems these practices created. Today, through more theological reflection, the church is developing a richer understanding of what it means to be God's stewards of the earth and why good stewardship might include maintaining some wilderness.

Of course, history has also taught Christians to exercise caution when scientific advances seem to contradict traditional theology. For example, when scientists during the last several centuries found data contradicting a literal reading of certain passages of Scripture, some people used these scientific advances to justify the rejection of core Christian doctrines such as the divinity of Christ, the inspiration of Scripture, and even the existence of God. Science provides new data for theology, and that might prompt new theological theories, but not every new theological theory preserves the truths taught by the old theories.

Theology and Science in Counterpoint, Not Compromise (Chapters 1–2)

To some, "harmony" between theology and science might sound like "compromise" in the bad sense. They fear a compromise of sound principles of interpreting Scripture, a compromise of core doctrines of Christianity, or a compromise of good science. These are real dangers to watch out for, but they are not what we seek. We seek a harmony reminiscent of J. S. Bach's counterpoint. In counterpoint, two or more melodies are played simultaneously. Each can be enjoyed independently. Although the melodies might occasionally strike notes that sound dissonant, the melodies as a whole don't clash. Each complements the other. Each draws out intricacies of the other. Played together, they form a richer whole.

Chapter 1 of this book reviews a few historical occasions when scientific discoveries prompted the church to look again at how it interpreted certain passages of Scripture. Science doesn't decide how we interpret Scripture. Theology decides. Science occasionally provides helpful information. Theology provides a conceptual foundation that helps science flourish and a biblical worldview from which to interpret the results of science. Chapter 2 discusses divine action. God is sovereign and providentially acting not only when we perceive miracles but also when the natural world is operating in regular, repeatable ways that we can describe scientifically.

Summary of Scientific Discoveries (Chapters 3–4)

Chapter 3 summarizes what science can tell us about "natural evil." The earth has a history stretching back billions of years.[5] Long before humans existed, plants and animals experienced natural disasters, death, disease, predation, and parasitism. Natural processes that we regard as pleasant and those that we regard as unpleasant occurred together throughout natural history. For example, the geological processes of plate tectonics are vital for life because they recycle to the earth's surface nutrients, but they also cause earthquakes. Biological processes involving genetic variation and natural selection can lead to symbiosis and adaptation, but they can also lead to parasitism and disease.

Chapter 4 discusses human evolution. Evidence from anatomy, physiology, developmental biology, and genetics strongly indicates that humans share a common ancestry with animals, most recently with other primates. Hundreds of fossils have been discovered that show a history of gradual changes among our ancestors over the last several million years, starting with species close to our common ancestors with other primates, through several intermediate species, eventually leading to *Homo sapiens*. During this long history, growth in brain size among our ancestors appears to have been gradual. Fossils of anatomically modern *Homo sapiens* have been found in Africa going back more than 200,000 years. *Homo sapiens* spread into Asia, Europe, and Australia in significant numbers roughly 70,000 years ago, reaching the Americas about 15,000 years ago. Genetic diversity in the human population is not consistent with what we would expect if all humans had descended from only a single pair of individuals 10,000 years ago, or even 200,000 years ago. Genetic

5. There are many mutually reinforcing lines of evidence from geology, astronomy, and biology pointing to this long age. For Christians who wish to learn more, I recommend one or more of the following: Davis A. Young and Ralph F. Stearley, *The Bible, Rocks and Time: Geological Evidence for the Age of the Earth* (Downers Grove, IL: InterVarsity, 2008); Roger C. Weins, "Radiometric Dating: A Christian Perspective," American Scientific Affiliation, 2002, https://www.asa3.org/ASA/resources/Wiens.html; Howard J. Van Till, *The Fourth Day: What the Bible and the Heavens Are Telling Us about the Creation* (Grand Rapids: Eerdmans, 1986); Howard J. Van Till, John Stek, Robert Snow, and Davis A. Young, *Portraits of Creation: Biblical and Scientific Perspectives on the World's Formation* (Grand Rapids: Eerdmans, 1990); Deborah B. Haarsma and Loren D. Haarsma, *Origins: A Reformed Look at Creation, Design, and Evolution* (Grand Rapids: Faith Alive Christian Resources, 2011); and Darrel R. Falk, *Coming to Peace with Science: Bridging the Worlds Between Faith and Biology* (Downers Grove, IL: InterVarsity, 2004). There are many other excellent books besides these.

data are consistent with models in which the most recent "bottleneck" in the *Homo sapiens* ancestral population was at least several thousand individuals more than 100,000 years ago. As *Homo sapiens* migrated out of Africa, some interbred with *Homo neanderthalensis* and other similar populations whose ancestors had migrated to Europe and Asia much earlier. So for scientific reasons, and possibly for theological reasons as well, we cannot simply equate the term "human" with *Homo sapiens*.

Some animals—especially the most intelligent and social primates—show that they have dispositions toward actions that (for humans) would be classified as selfish or immoral and also toward actions that (for humans) would be classified as altruistic or moral. Sociobiology provides hypotheses for why evolutionary processes would lead to such a mix. Neurobiology and developmental biology show that similar brain structures are involved in these behavioral dispositions in humans and other animals alike. It therefore seems likely that our earliest human ancestors also would have had such a mixture of behavioral dispositions. There appears to be some connection between the evolutionary methods that God used to create us and the genes and brain structures that push us today toward both "nasty" and "nice" behaviors.

Of course, genes alone don't determine behavior. Brain development and behavioral dispositions are significantly affected by environment. Among social animals and humans, a major part of that environment is the culture of the social group in which an individual is raised. As our ancestors evolved larger brains, it seems likely that they also developed things such as empathy, reason, and conscience that helped them understand how their behaviors hurt or helped others. They would have had moral impulses, religious impulses, and societies that could shape the content of moral and religious beliefs. Our ancestors, both as individuals and as societies, would have had impulses toward both "nasty" and "nice" behaviors and would have had the ability to receive and be shaped by divine special revelation.

Old Theological Questions Made New Again (Chapters 5–11)

Christian scholars in recent decades have proposed several scenarios for harmonizing the core doctrine of original sin and the science of human evolution.[6] Some scenarios propose that the first human sin occurred millions of years ago when our ancestors first crossed some threshold of moral awareness; others propose that our ancestors' behavior was not counted as sinful until God had specially revealed certain commands to them, perhaps as recently

6. References to specific authors, books, and articles are given throughout chapters 5–11.

as about 10,000 years ago. Some scenarios propose that Genesis 2–3 should be read as a stylized retelling of the sin of particular historical individuals chosen out of a larger population; others propose that Genesis 2–3 should be read as a literary retelling of the stories of many of our ancestors over a long period of time. Some scenarios propose that the first sin resulted in damage to our created human nature; some propose that it resulted in the loss of supernatural gifts; some propose both. Some scenarios propose that the first individuals who sinned acted as representatives of the entire population so that their individual sin resulted in a fall for the entire population; others propose that sin spread from the first sinners to the rest of the population more slowly, either genealogically or through cultural contact. Exploring the theological strengths of and challenges for these different scenarios is the work of chapters 5–11.

Church history provides a storehouse of theological reflection to help us in this work. While there is a core doctrine of original sin that the church collectively has affirmed over the centuries, the church also has a tradition of exploring a range of theological theories within and around the doctrine. Rather than starting by summarizing the answers, here we will start by summarizing the *questions* that theologians over the centuries have asked and debated. By exploring how theologians have answered these questions throughout church history, we find resources to help us appraise these modern scenarios.

Chapter 5 looks at theological questions related to human origins just prior to the fall. Does being made "in God's image" refer to our capabilities such as our intelligence, or to our personal relationship with God, or to our assignment as God's stewards on earth, or perhaps to all three? How did God create our souls? What are our souls in relation to our bodies? At some point in human history, God began to give special revelation to human beings in various ways. What other types of divine action should we consider? For example, did God at some point miraculously empower our ancestors spiritually with supernatural gifts to enable them for a time to be perfectly morally righteous? Did God miraculously physically transform our ancestors' bodies, brains, and genes? What are the theological implications of each answer?

Chapter 6 looks at how modern archaeological discoveries and biblical hermeneutics help us understand the Old and New Testament texts that refer to Adam and Eve. What do Genesis 1 and 4–11 tell us about Genesis 2–3? What can we learn from their original linguistic and cultural context? What indications are there that Adam and Eve refer to actual historical figures? What indications are there that Adam and Eve were symbolic figures? In the New Testament, the apostle Paul refers to Adam in Romans 5 and elsewhere. Does the fact that this inspired author seemed to believe that Adam was a historical person, and interpreted Genesis 2–3 that way, imply that we should as well? Does the logic of Paul's argument regarding the universal need for Christ require that Adam was a historical person?

Chapter 7 summarizes the history of the doctrine of original sin as developed in the early church and amplified by later theologians. Certain questions have occupied considerable theological reflection over the centuries. What was the state of Adam and Eve prior to their sin? What was damaged by their sin? What is passed on from generation to generation?

Chapter 8 summarizes what Scripture means by the term "sin." What are some metaphors the Bible uses? What sort of revelation from God has to be in place in order for an action to be described as sinful? Must there have been an explicit command to be violated? Or are general revelation and common grace (conscience, empathy, reason, altruistic feelings, etc.) sufficient revelation for disobedience to be counted as "sin"?

Chapter 9 discusses questions about what changed when sin entered the world. How intellectually and socially advanced were the first humans who sinned? What sort of innocence did the first human beings who sinned have? Was it an animal innocence, a human infant-like innocence, a fully adult human intelligence with moral innocence, or a legal innocence? Was a state of fully developed moral righteousness a potential state that humans might have grown into through obedience over time, or was it an actual state that some humans lived in for some period of time? Were the first humans who sinned expected to obey only simple commands they could reasonably be expected to obey, or were they expected to obey the entire moral law and live in "true holiness"? What is the connection between human physical death and the fall? Should we think of humanity's rebellion into sinfulness, the damage to our shared human nature, and the spiritual consequences for all humans as resulting primarily from that first disobedient act (or two acts) or from an accumulation of many disobedient acts over a long period of time?

Chapter 10 turns to the difficult theological questions about God's foreknowledge, human responsibility for sin, and theodicy. If God is wholly good and sovereign, why does God permit suffering? Why did God create humans capable of sinning? Why are all humans—even infants who have not yet willfully sinned—in a state in which they need Christ's atonement? Was human sin simply unavoidable? Was human sin avoidable in principle but very unlikely to be avoided in practice? Or was there a serious possibility of humanity remaining sinless?

This book does not raise every possible question, nor does it offer a complete list of all possible scenarios for harmonizing human evolution and the doctrine of original sin. It does not offer a complete list of all possible objections to the proposed scenarios or every possible good response to those objections. This book is exploratory. Think of it as a roundtable discussion of theologians, biblical scholars, and scientists—each sharing what they know, each sharing what they're not yet sure about. They've gathered together to ask tough questions. For many questions, instead of a single answer, they examine a range of answers. For each proposed answer, they discuss its theological strengths and weaknesses.

Making Charitable Assumptions about Motives

During theological arguments, Christians can be tempted to assume the worst about the motives of a person with whom they disagree. Christians who affirm evolution as God's means of creating humans have been accused of being motivated by a desire to fit in with non-Christians at secular universities and of having their theology compromised by philosophical naturalism. Christians who have been hesitant to embrace evolution as God's means of creating humans have been accused of being motivated by anti-intellectualism or of being fearful of a loss of power within their denomination.

God commands us to avoid bearing false witness. Whenever there is reasonable doubt, we should assume the best about the motives of Christians who disagree with us.[7] For example, one person might strongly prefer a scenario of human origins that includes God doing a radical act of supernatural transformation of our ancestors at some point early in human history because they believe it is theologically necessary in order for humans to have had a real chance of avoiding falling into sin. Another might strongly prefer scenarios that do not include God doing a radical act of supernatural transformation at some point in early human history because they believe this would imply that God created with an "appearance of false history."

Someone might strongly prefer an interpretation of Genesis 2–3 that downplays any attempts to derive historical information from those chapters because they believe this approach takes most seriously God's accommodation to the culture and literary styles of the original audience. Another might

---

7. The Heidelberg Catechism, Q&A 112, says this about obeying the command against bearing false witness: "That I never give false testimony against anyone, twist no one's words, not gossip or slander, nor join in condemning anyone rashly or without a hearing. Rather, in court and everywhere else, I should avoid lying and deceit of every kind; these are the very devices the devil uses, and they would call down on me God's intense wrath. I should love the truth, speak it candidly, and openly acknowledge it. And I should do what I can to guard and advance my neighbor's good name." Christian Reformed Church, https://www.crcna.org/welcome/beliefs/confessions/heidelberg-catechism.

strongly prefer hermeneutics that, while taking seriously the literary and cultural context of those chapters, maintain a more historical interpretation of Genesis because they believe that certain theological points developed in later Scriptures depend on such an interpretation.

Or someone might push for a greater freedom in scholarship on this issue, embracing a wider range of possible scenarios, because they believe that the Holy Spirit is using scientific discoveries to lead the church to new and better interpretations of Scripture. Another might prefer to start the discussion by drawing some theological boundaries, being more restrictive on the range of scenarios under consideration, because they believe that certain kinds of scenarios are clearly at odds with Scripture and potentially destructive to advancing the gospel of Christ.

On contentious theological issues, Christians can be driven to different conclusions by different valid concerns. When in doubt, we should assume the best about what motivates those with whom we disagree.

Four General Types of Scenarios

Summarized briefly here are four general types of scenarios for harmonizing original sin and human evolution. These four types correspond to specific proposals from more than a dozen authors who have recently published books on this topic. Readers might wish to bookmark these scenario types. We will refer to them throughout chapters 5–11.

1. *Adam and Eve as particular historical individuals acting as representatives of humanity.* At some point in time, God specially selected a pair (or small group) of individuals to act as representatives of all human beings. This might have been around 10,000 years ago, shortly before recorded human history began, or it might have been much further back. They received a special revelation from God. They disobeyed God and so fell into sin in a concentrated historical event. Because they sinned as representatives of all of humanity, all of humanity fell into sin. They lost the opportunity, for themselves and for the rest of humanity, to receive additional spiritual gifts and to live unmarred by sin.

2. *Adam and Eve as particular historical individuals; sin spread through culture or genealogy.* At some point in time, God specially selected a pair or small group to act as representatives of all human beings. This might have been around 10,000 years ago, shortly before recorded human history began, or it might have been much further back. They received a special revelation from God. They disobeyed God and so fell into sin in a concentrated historical

event. In the centuries following their disobedience, they and their descendants mixed culturally, and eventually genealogically, with others of their species alive at that time. In this way, the spiritual, psychological, and cultural effects of sin eventually spread to all humans.

3. *Adam and Eve as a highly compressed history referring to many individuals over a long period of time who received special revelation.* Over a long period, God from time to time selected particular individuals or groups to receive special revelation to augment general revelation, to teach them something about their relationship to God, their relationship to one another, and how they ought to live. Had they obeyed, God could have led them to greater moral and spiritual maturity over time. They chose disobedience again and again, individually and collectively. We might never know, from science or archaeology, when the first such act of disobedience occurred, although God does know. No one act of disobedience set the course for all of humanity, but consequences of each disobedience accumulated, spreading from person to person and generation to generation. Genesis 2–3 is a stylized retelling of many historical events compressed into a single archetypal story.

4. *Adam and Eve as symbolic figures referring to many individuals over a long period of time, all who became ready to be held accountable and chose sin.* Over a long period, whenever our ancestors became able, God began to hold them accountable for whatever they could understand from general revelation and whatever special revelation they had. Had they obeyed, God could have led them to greater moral and spiritual maturity over time. They chose disobedience again and again, individually and collectively. We might never know, from genetics or archaeology, when our ancestors transitioned from premoral animal self-interest to human sinful disobedience, although God does know. Genesis 2–3 is a stylized retelling of this entire history compressed into a single archetypal story.

This is not a comprehensive list of scenario types.[8] There are many possible variations on each of these four, and some of them can be blended. These four general types are intended to give an overview of a range of possible scenarios.

8. Still other types of scenarios could be considered. For example, (5) humans created miraculously and *de novo* without common ancestry with other animals yet with the appearance of common ancestry in the genetics; (6) Adam and Eve as a single pair who are the sole progenitors of all humans; (7) Adam and Eve created *de novo* amid a larger population of *Homo sapiens*, whose offspring then mixed with that larger population; and (8) humanity created by God using evolutionary processes in which the fall was necessarily built in to human nature apart from human choice, with the reality of sin and God's plan for redemption simply revealed to humanity at a later time. While these other scenarios are not the focus of this book, they are mentioned here (and discussed briefly later) to give a still broader view of the possibilities.

Such a wide range of proposals might seem troubling. It's not the case that there is no way to harmonize human evolution and the doctrine of original sin. Instead, the problem seems to be that there are too many ways! I believe this shows the richness of Christian theological tradition. The church is blessed with a treasure trove of theological reflections from over the centuries that will help us sort through the theological strengths of and challenges for each proposed scenario.

The Holy Spirit is prompting us to do this work. We can do it well, or we can do it poorly. If our work drives us to fear or resentment, or if it prompts us to make excuses for our sin, then we are doing it poorly. But if our work on this topic drives us to a deeper appreciation of God's character, God's holiness, and God's grace, then we are doing it as we should.

1

Scripture, Science, and the Holy Spirit

WHEN SCRIPTURE AND SCIENCE both speak about a topic, such as human origins, which has more authority? How might they rightly influence each other?

For centuries, most theologians understandably interpreted Genesis 2–3 in a more or less literal-historical way that implied that a specific first couple, Adam and Eve, were the sole progenitors of all of humanity. Discoveries in science and archaeology are making the church reconsider this interpretation. The church has learned not to ignore the discoveries of science simply because they challenge long-held interpretations of particular passages of Scripture. The church has also learned not to simply accept the first new interpretation of Scripture that fits with the new science.

Theology provides a foundation for doing science, and theology provides an interpretive framework for the results of science. Science by itself never dictates how we interpret Scripture. Discoveries from the natural sciences provide new data for theology and sometimes prompt consideration of new

Portions of this chapter were originally published in Loren Haarsma, "The Intersection of Science and Scripture," BioLogos, October 8, 2015, https://biologos.org/articles/the-intersection -of-science-and-scripture.

interpretations, but it is ultimately theology that decides on the best interpretation of Scripture. History has taught us that the church can maintain the
core doctrines that Scripture is inspired, authoritative, and inerrant in what it
intends to teach while adjusting—with appropriate care—its theories about
the best interpretations of particular passages.[1]

This chapter summarizes what the church has learned from history about
how theology and science can work in harmonious counterpoint to improve
our understanding of both Scripture and the natural world. Chapter 6 applies
these lessons to Adam and Eve.

How Scripture Rightly Affects Science

If we consider only those historical cases in which our interpretation of Scripture changed because of science (such as Galileo's evidence that the earth
moves around the sun or later discoveries about the great age of the earth), the
relationship between science and theology can feel like a one-way relationship
in which science steps in from time to time and "corrects" our interpretation
of some Scripture passages. But the relationship is not so one-sided. There are
many ways in which Scripture provides a lens for Christians through which
we look at the natural world as we do science.

Modern science has some foundational philosophical presuppositions that
are supported by the success of science but originate beyond science. Nearly

---

1. There are many theological theories within Christian tradition regarding the "inerrancy" of Scripture. Some Christians maintain that "inerrancy" is an important word once
suitably defined. Other Christians find the word problematic and prefer to use other words
to describe their views on the inspiration and authority of Scripture. Christians who both
affirm the inerrancy of Scripture and accept the scientific consensus regarding human evolution described in chapter 4 often have a view of inerrancy similar to that described by
Kevin J. Vanhoozer in "Augustinian Inerrancy: Literary Meaning, Literal Truth, and Literate
Interpretation in the Economy of Biblical Discourse," in *Five Views on Biblical Inerrancy*
(Grand Rapids: Zondervan, 2013): "to say that Scripture is inerrant is to confess faith that
*the authors speak the truth in all things they affirm (when they make affirmations), and will
eventually be seen to have spoken truly (when right readers read rightly)*" (207). Vanhoozer
elaborates:

> God's Word can be relied upon to accomplish the purpose for which it has been sent,
> and when this purpose is *making affirmations*, it does so inerrantly. As we have seen,
> however, texts can be "about" reality in different ways (there is more than one kind of
> map), and they can focus on different aspects of reality—from the smallest details to the
> big picture. To interpret Scripture rightly means recognizing what *kinds* of things the
> biblical authors are doing with their words. Are we reading history, story, apocalyptic,
> wisdom, science, or something else? We must not underestimate the importance of rightly
> determining the literary genre, or the challenge of rightly discerning the proposition(s)
> a narrative or parable or psalm explicitly presents. In sum: God's words are wholly reli-
> able; their human interpreters, not so much. (223)

all scientists today, regardless of their religion, hold a set of common beliefs that enable them to do science, including the following: human beings can understand the natural world, at least in part; nature typically operates according to regular, repeatable, universal patterns of cause and effect so that things we learn in the lab today will also hold true halfway around the world a week from now; simply theorizing how the world ought to work is not enough—we must test our theories; the study of the natural world is a worthwhile pursuit. These presuppositions might seem obvious to us today, but for most of human history, many people did not hold them all. For example, animists who believed that gods or spirits inhabit many aspects of the world doubted that nature operates according to regular, repeatable, universal patterns of cause and effect; instead, they believed that nature is controlled by gods and spirits who needed to be appeased or manipulated by ritual. And some brilliant philosophers of the ancient world did not see the need to do experiments, because they thought it was possible to derive from logic and first principles how the world ought to behave.

Some of the earliest scientists justified their belief in these foundational presuppositions of science because of what the Bible teaches. We are able to partially understand how the natural world works, they thought, because we are made in God's image and God has given us the gifts to study his creation. Nature operates according to regular, repeatable, universal patterns of cause and effect because nature is not filled with capricious gods but is ruled by one God in a faithful and consistent manner. God could have created in any way God chose that was consistent with his nature, but we humans are limited and sinful, so we need to test our theories with experiments. Science is worth doing because in studying the world we are studying God's handiwork.

Historically, Christian theology played an important role in bringing together these foundational presuppositions for doing science. But that does not imply that only Christians can do science. Non-Christians can also affirm those philosophical presuppositions, even when they don't accept the underlying theological beliefs held by Christians. Because of God's common grace,[2] Christians and non-Christians can do science together.

---

2. Regarding common grace, Louis Berkhof, *Systematic Theology* (Grand Rapids: Eerdmans, 1941), 432–33, writes,

> The origin of the doctrine of common grace was occasioned by the fact that there is in the world, alongside of the course of the Christian life with all its blessings, a natural course of life, which is not redemptive and yet exhibits many traces of the true, the good, and the beautiful. The question arose, How can we explain the comparatively orderly life in the world, seeing that the whole world lies under the curse of sin? How is it that the earth yields precious fruit in rich abundance and does not simply bring forth thorns and thistles? How we can we account for it that sinful man still retains some knowledge

Christians find in Scripture not only motivation to study God's creation but also teachings that support the foundational principles for doing science. Therefore, it should not surprise us that there are so few historical examples of genuine scientific hypotheses conflicting with what Scripture teaches, although there may be a few such cases. (Radical behaviorism might be one such historical case.)[3]

A far more common way that Scripture affects the way we look at the natural world is not in the scientific theories themselves but in the philosophical and religious interpretations that can be added to scientific results. Very often, Christians and non-Christians look at the same scientific results, agree about the scientific theories that best explain the data, but have very different philosophical or religious interpretations of those theories.

For example, Christians and non-Christians agree that planets orbit around the sun in stable, repeatable patterns that we can model with natural laws of gravity and motion. A deist might interpret this as saying that the solar system was set up by God, but God is now distant and no longer involved. A Christian can look at the same scientific data and theories through the lens of Scripture and come to a different interpretation. God is not absent from events

---

of God, of natural things, and of the difference between good and evil, and shows some regard for virtue and for good outward behavior? What explanation can be given for the special gifts and talents that with which the natural man is endowed, and of the development of science and art by those who are entirely devoid of the new life that is in Christ Jesus? How can we explain the religious aspirations of men everywhere, even of those who did not come in touch with the Christian religion? How can the unregenerate still speak truth, do good to others, and lead outwardly virtuous lives? These are some of the questions to which the doctrine of common grace seeks to supply the answer.

3. The scientific hypothesis of radical behaviorism became popular after the discovery of operant conditioning. Operant conditioning is a type of learning in which behavior is modified through reinforcement and punishment. It was made famous by experiments by B. F. Skinner in which animals were trained to perform complex behaviors by a gradual buildup from simpler behaviors that were learned through reinforcement or punishment. Some versions of radical behaviorism hypothesized that all human learning and decision-making were built from operant conditioning and that all human behavior was determined by this conditioning. This is a far-reaching scientific hypothesis. It could be argued that radical behaviorism was never really a scientific hypothesis, that it was only a grandiose philosophical addition to science, but that's probably not a fair criticism. Radical behaviorism deserves the status of a genuine scientific hypothesis that made testable predictions and was seriously considered by scientists for several decades. It seems difficult to reconcile Scripture and Christian theology with radical behaviorism. Most Christians would conclude that Scripture teaches against it. Several decades ago, when radical behaviorism was more prevalent, it would have been appropriate for a Christian scientist to say, "Partly for scientific reasons, but also because of my biblical beliefs about God and the natural world, I think radical behaviorism is probably a false scientific hypothesis." Ultimately, additional research led most scientists to conclude that radical behaviorism isn't true. Most scientists today conclude that, while operant conditioning does exist, it is not the case that all behavior is determined by it.

that we can explain scientifically; rather, God continually sustains creation, and natural laws describe how God usually governs creation.

Similarly, Christians and non-Christians together can conclude scientifically that many events in the natural world have outcomes that include an element of randomness. The final outcomes cannot be completely predicted in terms of initial conditions and natural laws but must be modeled probabilistically. An atheist might look at randomness in the natural world and conclude that random events are fundamentally uncaused and undirected. A Christian can look at the same randomness in the natural world and conclude that this is another means that God can use in governing the natural world. A Christian might quote Proverbs 16:33, "The lot is cast into the lap, but its every decision is from the LORD," to say that God can directly influence the outcome of events that appear random to human beings.

There are many examples in which Christians and non-Christians agree on which scientific theory best fits the data but disagree about the philosophical and religious implications of the theory. For those of us Christians who are scientists, Scripture provides a lens through which we see the natural world as God's handiwork and something for which God continually cares. Scripture helps us take scientific data and theories and fit them into a larger theological framework of God as Creator and humanity as God's image bearers.

Theology, Not Science, Determines How We Reinterpret Scripture

Science doesn't dictate how we interpret Scripture. But science does sometimes alert us to new theological problems that we had not considered before.

For example, prior to Galileo's work, there were very few theological problems with interpreting Psalm 93:1 and other passages as actually teaching that the earth is fixed in place. Galileo and others made scientific discoveries that strongly indicated that the earth moves. However, these scientific discoveries by themselves did not require the church to change its interpretation of Scripture. It is still possible today to believe that Scripture truthfully teaches that the earth is fixed in place. For someone who wants to believe that the earth is fixed, one possibility is to say that God is tricking (or permitting the devil to trick) all our measurements into giving false data about a moving earth. A second possibility is that we humans, because we are finite and sinful, simply should not trust our senses and our reasoning ability, despite the mountains of evidence that the earth is moving. A third possibility is that there is an enormous conspiracy among atheistic scientists who create false data because they want to undermine belief in God and Scripture.

Nearly all Christians reject those three possibilities because each of them carries vast *theological* problems. They are logically possible, but we judge them to be inconsistent with what we believe about God and about ourselves as God's image bearers. The evidence for a moving earth, by itself, does not require us to give up a fixed-earth interpretation of Scripture. The scientific evidence only points out that there are huge theological problems with fixed-earth interpretations. Prior to Galileo's work, the church did not face those problems.

Science provides new information, but theology decides which interpretation of Scripture is best.

Principles for Interpreting Scripture

Under the guidance of the Holy Spirit, theologians and biblical scholars have developed hermeneutical methods that might be thought of as "best practices" for interpreting Scripture. Entire books have been written on them. Seminaries teach courses about these best practices. Listed here are just a few principles that have been particularly helpful to the church on those occasions when science, in particular, prompted another look at Scripture.[4]

4. There are more good books on hermeneutics than can be listed here. Readers are strongly encouraged to seek them. For now, I restrict myself to the following recommendations. The first is Douglas Stuart, *Old Testament Exegesis: A Handbook for Students and Pastors* (Louisville: Westminster John Knox, 2009). The importance of understanding literary genre is discussed especially on pp. 12–19. Careful attention to the translation of words in grammatical context is discussed especially on pp. 8–9 and 20–21, the Scripture-interprets-Scripture principle on pp. 22–25, and cultural-historical context on pp. 9–11. A related book that discusses these principles in chapters organized around different types of biblical literature is Gordon D. Fee and Douglas Stuart, *How to Read the Bible for All Its Worth*, 4th ed. (Grand Rapids: Zondervan, 2014).

Louis Berkhof, *Principles of Biblical Interpretation* (Grand Rapids: Baker, 1950), discusses the importance of understanding literary genre especially on pp. 82–112. The careful translation of words in grammatical context is addressed especially on pp. 67–81, the Scripture-interprets-Scripture principle on pp. 133–60, and the importance of cultural-historical context on pp. 113–32.

William W. Klein, Craig L. Blomberg, and Robert L. Hubbard Jr., *Introduction to Biblical Interpretation* (Grand Rapids: Zondervan, 2017), discuss the importance of understanding literary genre especially on pp. 214–28, and with application to specific parts of the Bible on pp. 323–448. The careful translation of words in grammatical context is addressed especially on pp. 240–72, the Scripture-interprets-Scripture principle on pp. 135–67, and cultural-historical context on pp. 229–39.

Henry A. Virkler and Karelynne Ayayo, *Hermeneutics: Principles and Processes of Biblical Interpretation*, 2nd ed. (Grand Rapids: Baker Academic, 2007), discuss the importance of understanding literary genre especially on pp. 147–91. The careful translation of words in grammatical context is addressed especially on pp. 97–120, the Scripture-interprets-Scripture principle on pp. 121–46, and cultural-historical context on pp. 79–95.

We strive for the best translation of the words, phrases, and sentences in their grammatical context.

We look at the literary genre of each passage. Is it clearly poetry, song, history, parable? Is it a literary form commonly used today, or a form commonly used in ancient times but seldom used today? Understanding literary genre helps us understand what the passage intends to teach.

We look at each Scripture passage within the context of the entire Bible. We don't take one passage of Scripture and interpret it in a simplistic way that contradicts other parts of the Bible. We look at how later Scripture writers made use of earlier texts. We use all of Scripture to build, insofar as we are able, a coherent story and theology of what all of Scripture teaches. This helps us better understand individual passages.

We look at the cultural and historical context of the original author and audience. What was the original author thinking and what was the original audience hearing when the passage was written? By putting ourselves in the mindset of the original human author and intended audience, we sometimes come to a better understanding of how the message of that passage applies to us today. We also look at the cultural-historical context of when texts were added to the canon, where they were placed, and why they were added.

These principles help us understand when passages should be interpreted literally and when they should be interpreted nonliterally, and thereby help us avoid debates about slippery slopes.[5] For example, Psalm 91:2–4 says, "I will say of the LORD, 'He is my refuge and my fortress, my God, in whom I trust.' Surely he will save you from the fowler's snare and from the deadly pestilence. He will cover you with his feathers, and under his wings you will find refuge." The original author and audience did not think those feathers and wings were literal. Some of the surrounding cultures when that psalm was written did picture gods with wings and feathers, but the children of Israel were forbidden from making such images of God. They understood the wings and feathers in that passage as metaphors, and so should we.

When the prophet Nathan confronted King David after David had committed adultery with Bathsheba and killed Uriah, Nathan told a story about

---

5. Slippery slope arguments are logical fallacies. (This can be seen with the following example: "If you start by believing one slippery slope argument, you'll wind up believing all slippery slope arguments.") Moreover, slippery slopes can run in opposite directions. If we worry about a slippery slope into not enough literalism ("If you interpret Genesis 1–11 nonliterally, you're on a slippery slope to interpreting Jesus's death and resurrection nonliterally"), we could also worry about a slippery slope into too much literalism ("If you believe a literal interpretation of twenty-four-hour days of creation, then you are on a slippery slope to believing in a literal flat, fixed earth with a solid-dome firmament holding back waters above"). Good hermeneutical principles should ease our worries about slippery slopes in either direction.

a rich man who had many sheep but stole the only lamb of a poor neighbor. David, eager to dispense justice as the king, assumed that Nathan's story was a literal-historical event, and so he missed the story's message. Nathan had to correct David's interpretation. When David understood Nathan's story figuratively, he understood its message.

When we apply these hermeneutical methods to other passages, we are led to more literal-historical readings. Luke 1:1–4 reads, "Many have undertaken to draw up an account of the things that have been fulfilled among us, just as they were handed down to us by those who from the first were eyewitnesses and servants of the word. With this in mind, since I myself have carefully investigated everything from the beginning, I too decided to write an orderly account for you, most excellent Theophilus, so that you may know the certainty of the things you have been taught." That sounds to us today like something close to modern historical scholarship. The original author and audience thought that the events that Luke recorded really did happen historically. That was the intended message of the original author, that's how the original audience heard it, and that's how the church interprets it today.

Historical Examples: Discoveries about the Earth and Solar System

These hermeneutical methods helped the church through several historical episodes in which the church's traditional interpretation of certain passages conflicted with new scientific data. The most famous example is the Galileo story. Many Christians at the time interpreted passages such as Psalm 96:10, "The world is firmly established, it cannot be moved," as teaching that the earth stood still. Eventually, however, the church concluded that the literary context of Psalm 96 is teaching about God's faithfulness. The purpose of the passage is not to teach astronomy but to teach how God's promises are reliable. Moreover, the historical context of that passage is a culture in which the original author and audience really did believe that the earth didn't move.

There is no need for us today to try to "rescue" a semiliteral interpretation of this passage consistent with modern science—for example, by saying that God "fixed" the earth in its orbit around the sun. The original author and audience were not thinking about planetary orbits. They were thinking about an earth formed out of watery chaos and firmly fixed in one place, unmoving, by the power of the Creator God. When God inspired Psalm 96, he didn't use Scripture to correct the astronomy of the original audience. Instead, God used the common (although incorrect) belief that the earth was fixed in place to illustrate, through the apparent steadiness of the earth, an important *theological* truth about God's power and faithfulness.

At the time of John Calvin, astronomers were discovering that the planet Saturn must be larger than the moon, even though it appears smaller because it is farther away. Some Christians at the time argued that Scripture teaches that the "greater and lesser lights" of Genesis 1, which govern the day and night (the sun and moon), must be larger than the stars and planets such as Saturn. Calvin defended the astronomers:

> Moses described in a popular style what all ordinary men without training and education perceive with their ordinary senses. Astronomers, on the other hand, investigate with great labor whatever the keenness of man's intellect is able to discover. Such study is certainly not to be disapproved nor science condemned with the insolence of some fanatics who habitually reject what is unknown to them. . . . Moses did not wish to keep us from such study when he omitted details belonging to the science, but since he had been appointed a guide of rude and unlearned men rather than the learned, he could not fulfill his duty except by coming down to their level. If he had spoken on matters unknown to the crowd, the unlearned could say that his teaching was over their heads. In fact, when the Spirit of God opens a common school for all, it is not strange that he should choose to teach especially what could be understood by all. When the astronomer seeks the true size of stars and finds the moon smaller than Saturn, he gives us specialized knowledge. But the eye sees things differently, and Moses adapts himself to the ordinary view.[6]

From the time of the church fathers through the Reformation, some Christians argued that Scripture teaches that there are waters above the sky and waters below the earth. Science of that time had shown that the earth is spherical and that the natural place of water is above earth and below air. Science said that there should not be waters above the sky, nor should there be waters below the earth. Yet because many Old Testament passages talk about waters above the sky and below the earth,[7] some Christians argued that Scripture teaches literally that there are waters above the sky and below the earth. For example, Martin Luther wrote, "Scripture simply says that the moon, sun and stars were placed in the firmament of the heaven below and above which are heaven

---

6. Joseph Haroutunian, *John Calvin: Commentaries* (London: SCM, 1958), 356.

7. E.g., Gen. 1:1–22; 7:11–20; 8:1–5; 11:4; 49:25; Exod. 15:8; 20:4; Deut. 5:8; 28:12; 33:13; 2 Sam. 22:8–17; 2 Kings 7:2, 19; Job 9:6; 22:12–14; 26:8–14; 36:27–30; 37:18; 38:4–38; Pss. 19:4–6; 74:13–17; 75:3; 89:9–12; 93:1–4; 102:25; 104:1–9; 135:6–7; 136:5–9; 139:8–9; 146:6; 148:1–7; Prov. 3:19–20; 8:22–29; 25:3; Isa. 14:12–15; 24:18–19; 40:21–26; 42:5; 45:18; 48:13; 51:13; 65:17; 66:1–2; Jer. 4:23–28; 10:11–13; 51:16; Ezek. 32:7–8; Dan. 4:10–11; Zech. 12:1; Mal. 3:10.

and the waters. . . . It is likely that the stars are fastened to the firmament like globes of fire to shed light at night. . . . We Christians must be different from the philosophers in the ways we think about the causes of things and if some are beyond our comprehension, like those before us concerning the waters above the heavens, we must believe them rather than wickedly deny them or presumptuously interpret them in conformity with our understanding."[8]

Because of the many passages that talk about waters above the sky and below the earth, it is understandable that Luther and other Christians interpreted those passages literally. However, Augustine (centuries before Luther) knew the science of his day, and he insisted forcefully that Christians should not interpret Scripture as teaching that there literally are waters below the earth and above the sky. Augustine had sharp words for Christians who said that Scripture teaches things in contradiction of well-established scientific knowledge. "Usually, even a non-Christian knows something about the earth, . . . and this knowledge he holds to as being certain from reason and experience. Now, it is a disgraceful and dangerous thing for an infidel to hear a Christian, presumably giving the meaning of Holy Scripture, talking nonsense on these topics; and we should take all means to prevent such an embarrassing situation, in which people show up vast ignorance in a Christian and laugh it to scorn."[9]

Hermeneutics Informed by Knowledge of Ancient Cultures

Geologists of the eighteenth and nineteenth centuries amassed convincing evidence that the earth is very old. This prompted the development of several old-earth "concordist" interpretations of Genesis 1. The "gap interpretation" proposes a long period of time between verse 1 and verse 2, with the earth being re-created starting in verse 2. The "day-age interpretation" tries to make the order of events in Genesis 1 match scientific natural history by stretching each day (Hebrew: *yôm*) into a long period of time (millions or billions of years).

While the scientific discoveries of geology alerted the church that Genesis 1 might be a stylized, compressed account of creation, they didn't give any clear understanding of the "vault" (Hebrew: *rāqîaʿ*), the "water under the vault," or the "water above it" (1:6–7). For that, the church benefited from the work of historians studying ancient Near Eastern cultures.

8. Martin Luther, *Luther's Works*, ed. Jaroslav Pelikan, vol. 1 (St. Louis: Concordia, 1958), 30, 42–43.
9. John Hammond, *Augustine: The Literal Meaning of Genesis*, vol. 41 (New York: Newman, 1982), 42.

Archaeological discoveries have improved our understanding of the cultural and historical contexts of the Old Testament era. The cultures surrounding the ancient Hebrews—the Egyptians, Assyrians, and Babylonians—did not know that the earth was spherical. They pictured a flat earth with a primeval ocean—a dark, watery chaos—split into waters below the earth and waters above the sky, with something (*rāqîaʿ* in Hebrew, translated in the King James Version as "firmament") holding back the waters above the sky.[10] In this picture of the cosmos, the sun, moon, and stars moved along the firmament. The floodgates of heaven could open if God commanded, releasing waters held above the firmament.

After summarizing studies of ancient Near Eastern literature and archaeology and a linguistic study of the Hebrew word *rāqîaʿ*, Paul Seely concludes that ancient Hebrews shared with their surrounding cultures this belief about the physical structure of the world. "We have every reason to think that both the writer and original readers of Genesis 1 believed the *rāqîaʿ* was solid. The historical meaning of *rāqîaʿ* in Gen 1:6–8 is, accordingly, 'a solid sky.' . . . The *rāqîaʿ* was for them a literal physical part of the universe, just as solid as the earth itself. Solidity is an integral part of its historical meaning."[11] Denis Lamoureux, in *Evolutionary Creation*, likewise summarizes several Old Testament uses of the word *rāqîaʿ*:

> The root of this noun is the verb *rāqaʿ* which means "to flatten," "stamp down," "spread out," and "hammer out." That is, the Hebrew verb carries a nuance of flattening something solid rather than opening a broad empty space. Exodus 39:3 and Isa 40:19 use *rāqaʿ* for pounding metals into thin plates, and Num 16:38 employs *riqqûaʿ* (broad plate) in a similar context. The verb *rāqaʿ* is even found in a passage referring to the creation of the sky, which is understood to be a firm surface like a metal. Job 37:18 asks, "Can you join God in spreading out the skies, hard as a mirror cast of bronze?"[12]

There is some discussion among scholars of the ancient Near East regarding the extent to which people of these cultures actually believed in a literal,

10. Pictures of this can be found with an internet image search of the word "firmament."

11. Paul H. Seely, "The Firmament and the Water Above," *Westminster Theological Journal* 53 (1991): 227–40. The second paragraph of this article summarizes: "The historical evidence, however, which we will set forth in concrete detail, shows that the *rāqîaʿ* was originally conceived of as being solid and not a merely atmospheric expanse. The grammatical evidence from the OT, which we shall examine later, reflects and confirms this conception of solidity. The basic historical fact that defines the meaning of *rāqîaʿ* in Genesis 1 is simply this: all peoples in the ancient world thought of the sky as solid" (227–28).

12. Denis O. Lamoureux, *Evolutionary Creation: A Christian Approach to Evolution* (Eugene, OR: Wipf & Stock, 2008), 123.

physical solid dome holding back primeval waters above the sky and the extent to which this language and mental model were used more analogically and phenomenologically.[13] Because this ancient literature is drawn from several cultures and languages over several centuries, it seems likely that many ancient people assumed these things referred to literal physical structures, while others thought of them more analogically.

Archaeologists' discovery of this ancient cosmological picture helps us understand why there are so many references to waters above the sky and waters below the earth throughout the Old Testament. Whether all the ancient writers believed these things were real physical structures, or whether some of them used this common way of speaking analogically and phenomenologically, it is clear that when we read these Scriptures today, we are not expected to throw out our modern scientific understanding. We are not expected to interpret these passages as teaching that this ancient picture is literally true today. Thanks to archaeological discoveries, we understand that in these Scriptures, God was speaking to the original audience in a way that they could easily understand in order to teach them important theological truths about God's relationship to humans and to the world.

When the inspired psalmist wrote about God, "He stretches out the heavens like a tent and lays the beams of his upper chambers on their waters" (Ps. 104:2–3), the poet was not thinking about the earth's blue sky, nor about the expansion of space due to dark energy, which astronomers have recently discovered. The psalmist was celebrating God's power by pointing to the firmament stretching over the entire world and capable of holding back the primeval, chaotic waters above the sky. The poet was saying that God could stretch out that firmament as easily as a human could stretch out a tent, thereby making a roof under which his creatures could dwell.

The ancient Egyptians, Babylonians, and Assyrians believed that these physical structures of the world had particular gods associated with them.

---

13. I agree with scholars who conclude that the original authors and audiences of several Old Testament passages really did believe in a literal solid firmament and that this was part of God's accommodation when inspiring Scripture. Several scholars argue that the Old Testament language was more analogical and phenomenological: Othmar Keel and Silvia Schroer, *Creation: Biblical Theologies in the Context of the Ancient Near East*, trans. Peter T. Daniels (Winona Lake, IN: Eisenbrauns, 2015); Noel K. Weeks, "Cosmology in Historical Context," *Westminster Theological Journal* 68 (2006): 283–93; C. John Collins, *Reading Genesis Well: Navigating History, Poetry, Science, and Truth in Genesis 1–11* (Grand Rapids: Zondervan, 2018); and Richard E. Averbeck, "Ancient Near Eastern Mythography as It Relates to Historiography in the Hebrew Bible: Genesis 3 and the Cosmic Battle," in *The Future of Biblical Archaeology: Reassessing Methodologies and Assumptions*, ed. James K. Hoffmeier and Alan Millard (Grand Rapids: Eerdmans, 2004), 328–56. For a recent analysis of this discussion, see John W. Hilber, *Old Testament Cosmology and Divine Accommodation: A Relevance Theory Approach* (Eugene, OR: Wipf & Stock, 2020), chap. 2.

Egypt had gods and goddesses of the firmament (Nut), earth (Geb), sky (Shu), sun (Re), and underworld (Osiris).[14] The theology of Genesis 1 is strikingly different from the polytheism of the surrounding cultures. Genesis 1 speaks of one God who created all these physical structures. The proper names of the sun and the moon are not even used in Genesis 1. Instead, they are called greater and lesser lights, emphasizing that they are not divine beings. They are things created by the one true God. For the original author and audience, the message of Genesis 1 was obvious: the gods of the surrounding cultures are not true gods at all. The earth, sky, sun, and moon are not to be worshiped because they are not gods; they are only physical things made by the one true God, the God of the children of Israel.

When God inspired Genesis 1 and other passages that talk about a *rāqîaʿ*, waters above the sky, and waters below the earth, God was speaking to the original audience in ways they could understand. God didn't need to correct their false picture of the physical structures of the world. God didn't need to teach them about evaporation and condensation as the source of rain. God didn't need to teach them that the earth is spherical or that it moves around the sun. Doing so would have confused the original audience and detracted from the message. Because God spoke to them in a way they could understand, the theological message of Genesis 1 came through more clearly. This helped the people of Israel share their story with the surrounding cultures. They could communicate the essential truths of Genesis 1 to the Egyptians, Assyrians, and Babylonians in a way that those cultures, too, could easily understand.

Calvin's Principle of Accommodation: God Speaks "Baby Talk" to Us

John Calvin noted that Scripture often ascribes to God a mouth, ears, eyes, hands, and feet. But we should not therefore conclude that God has a material body. Calvin wrote, "For who is so devoid of intellect as not to understand that God, in so speaking, lisps with us as nurses are wont to do with little children? Such modes of expression, therefore, do not so much express what kind of a being God is, as accommodate the knowledge of him to our feebleness."[15] God uses common language so that many people can understand

14. Images of this can be found with an internet image search of those names. A helpful discussion is found in John H. Stek, "What Says the Scripture?," in Howard J. Van Till, John Stek, Robert Snow, and Davis A. Young, *Portraits of Creation* (Grand Rapids: Eerdmans, 1990), 226–32, with an image taken from Othmar Keel, *The Symbolism of the Biblical World: Ancient Near Eastern Iconography and the Book of Psalms* (New York: Crossroad, 1985).

15. John Calvin, *Institutes of the Christian Religion* 1.13.1 (Beveridge trans.), https://www.ccel.org/ccel/calvin/institutes. The principle of God's accommodation to human limitations

the message. This demonstrates God's graciousness. Also, this leaves people without excuse. (If God always used technical language, it would be easy for people to excuse themselves with, "This is too hard to understand.") J. I. Packer further describes the principle:

> For clarity's sake, God in giving Scripture accommodated Himself to our capacity, condescending not only to talk man's language but to do so in an earthly and homespun way, sometimes "with a contemptible meanness of words." "God lowers himself to our immaturity. . . . When God prattles to us in Scripture in a clumsy, homely style, let us know that this is done on account of the love he bears us." It is a sign of love for a child to accommodate to his language and to be willing to use baby talk in conversing with him, and so it is, said Calvin, when God in Scripture speaks to us in a simple, not very dignified way. It helps us to understand Him, and the very fact that He does it assures us of His affection and goodwill.[16]

Calvin referred to this principle of accommodation primarily when discussing God's revealed truths about God himself, since God's full nature is far beyond our human understanding. But as noted earlier, Calvin also used this principle at least once when discussing debates about interpreting Scripture in light of scientific discoveries of his time (the size of Saturn). Since Calvin's time, many have found this principle helpful when dealing with other scientific discoveries.

Two recent authors, John Walton (in *The Lost World of Adam and Eve*) and Denis Lamoureux (in *Evolutionary Creation*), disagree with each other on some aspects of interpreting Genesis 2–3 and agree with each other on others (see chapter 6 of this book). Both write compellingly that reading the Bible with this hermeneutical principle in mind does not undercut the Bible's authority; rather, it respects where God chose to vest the authority. Walton writes:

> The authority of the text is not respected when statements in the Bible that are part of ancient science are used as if they are God's descriptions of modern scientific understanding. When the text talks about thinking with our hearts or intestines, it is not proposing scientific ideas that we must confirm if we wish

---

and sinfulness is a broad topic. For a historical overview, see Glenn S. Sunshine, "Accommodation Historically Considered," in *The Enduring Authority of the Christian Scriptures*, ed. Donald A. Carson (Grand Rapids: Eerdmans, 2016), 238–65. Sunshine's summary of Calvin's use of the principle is on pp. 252–55; as it relates to the natural world and the science of Calvin's day, see pp. 254–55.

16. J. I. Packer, "John Calvin and the Inerrancy of Holy Scripture," in *Inerrancy and the Church*, ed. John D. Hannah (Chicago: Moody, 1984), 166.

to take the biblical authority seriously. We need not try to propose ways that our blood-pumping organs or digestive systems are physiologically involved in cognitive processes. This is simply communication in the context of ancient science. In the same way, when the text talks about the water below the vault and the water above the vault (Gen. 1:6) we do not have to construct a cosmic system that has waters above and waters below. Everyone in the ancient world believed there were waters above because when it rained water came down. Therefore, when the biblical text talks about "water above" (Gen. 1:7), it is not offering authoritative revelation of scientific facts. If we conclude that there are not, strictly speaking, waters above, we have not thereby identified an error in Scripture. Rather, we have recognized that God vests the authority of the text elsewhere. Authority is tied to the message the author intends to communicate as an agent of God's revelation. God has accommodated himself to the world of ancient Israel to initiate that revelation.[17]

Lamoureux states:

This approach contends that in order to reveal spiritual truths as effectively as possible to the ancient peoples, the Holy Spirit used their ancient phenomenological perspective of nature. That is, instead of confusing or distracting the biblical writers and their readers with modern scientific concepts, God descended to their level and employed the science-of-the-day. . . . Therefore, passages in the Bible referring to the physical world feature both a Message of Faith and an incidental ancient science. According to these interpretive principles, biblical inerrancy and infallibility rest in the Divine Theology, and not in statements referring to nature. Qualifying ancient science as "incidental" does not imply that it is unimportant. The science in Scripture is vital for transporting spiritual truths.[18]

The "Plain Lesson" of Scripture (Not Necessarily the "Plain Reading")

When God inspired the Old Testament, the original authors and audience pictured the stars and planets moving along a firmament above a flat earth. God didn't correct that picture with modern scientific ideas. Instead, God told them what they needed to learn in a way they could understand. They needed to learn that the sun, moon, and firmament weren't the gods worshiped in Egypt or Canaan; rather, they were just objects created by the one true God.

17. John H. Walton, *The Lost World of Adam and Eve* (Downers Grove, IL: InterVarsity, 2015), 18–19.
18. Denis O. Lamoureux, *Evolutionary Creation: A Christian Approach to Evolution*, 110. Lamoureux calls this the "Message-Incident" principle.

In the centuries that followed, science advanced. By the fourth century BC, Greek natural philosophers had demonstrated that the earth was spherical rather than flat. So for a while, people pictured each planet moving on a different crystal sphere around the earth. Later, we found evidence that the earth orbits the sun. After Isaac Newton, we described the motion of planets using laws of motion and gravity. Today we have Einstein's theory of general relativity. But with each scientific advancement, the message of Scripture has stayed the same.

Languages and cultures change over the centuries. Science advances. A "plain reading" of a passage of Scripture might change from century to century. But the "plain lessons" of Scripture—the lessons that God intended for the original audience and intends for us today—stay the same.

By accommodating his message in Genesis 1 to the historical-cultural understanding of ancient times, God helps us today. All future generations can learn the message of Genesis 1 regardless of their scientific advancement. The message of Genesis 1 does not depend on it matching up with fifth-century science, fifteenth-century science, twenty-first-century science, or twenty-sixth-century science.

Celebrating God's Accommodation

We should be comforted by the idea that God communicated the authoritative message of Scripture in ways that accommodated the sometimes-mistaken cultural beliefs of the original authors and audience. It's another example of God's grace. But this can be a scary idea at first. A Christian might hear that, in Scripture, God claims credit for creating a firmament and ask, "Did God lie in Scripture then?"

Our modern, scientific culture is not the culture of the original audience of Genesis. We cannot avoid the influence our modern culture has on us as we read Scripture. The following story is meant to illustrate how pervasive that influence is.

> Once upon a time, there was a small nation in a remote, mountainous region. They had their own language and culture. One of their rules was that *any story involving human characters must accurately describe what really happened to real people.* Because the rule was strictly enforced, this culture had very little malicious gossip or bearing false witness in legal matters. Also, this culture had no fictional stories with human characters. But they knew the usefulness of having fictional morality tales, fictional stories that explore human motivations, and simply entertaining fictional stories to share with friends and family.

So this culture had another rule: *fictional stories must have talking animal characters*. If you lived in this culture, you immediately knew if a story was fictional (although it might still be a story with an important lesson). And if you heard a story involving human characters, you were assured that it accurately described real events.

One day the gospel of Christ came to this nation. Many received it with joy. The Bible was translated into their language, and believers studied it.

When these believers discussed Jesus's parables, they were amazed that Jesus knew so many stories with human characters that also perfectly illustrated the spiritual lessons he was teaching. How did Jesus know so many perfect stories? They all agreed that Jesus must often have been listening for and remembering such stories. Some people speculated that many other teachers of Jesus's time had done this as well, and perhaps they shared collections of such stories. And Jesus was God's Son, so of course nothing was too hard for him.

Decades later, the leaders of this nation sent some of its brightest young people to the best seminaries of the world to learn all they could about the Bible and church history. These young seminarians then returned to their nation to teach.

One day, as the people were discussing Jesus's parables and speculating as usual about how Jesus came to learn all these stories, some of the seminarians said, "Actually, we learned something interesting in seminary about the customs and culture of the Jewish people in Jesus's day. In that culture, in that time and place, it was not considered wrong for them to make up fictional stories involving human characters, provided all the listeners knew that it was a fictional story involving fictional humans rather than a false story about real humans. It was common practice in that culture for religious teachers to make up fictional stories about fictional humans in order to teach a true spiritual lesson. Everyone at the time knew this. Jesus probably did the same thing when he told his parables."

You can imagine the shock and horror as the listeners exclaimed to the seminarians, "Are you saying that Jesus told lies?"

We are that fictional nation. We inherited, from the Enlightenment, cultural expectations about what sorts of literature are appropriate, and inappropriate, for teaching certain sorts of truths. In our culture, scientific truths and historical accuracy are held in high esteem. Like the cultural rules of that fictional nation, our high esteem for scientific truths and historical accuracy are not bad things. They have served us well over the centuries. Much good has come from them. But we must remember that our cultural practices were not the practices when Scripture was written.

When people recovered from the horror of their first reaction, some of them began to ask, "We understand what you're saying about the culture of Jesus's time. We can accept that maybe it was okay for people at that time to tell fictional stories about fictional humans, as long as everyone understood what was going on, and that even the human religious leaders did this. But why do you insist that Jesus did it too? Isn't it possible that Jesus's parables were also true stories about real people? Even if some of Jesus's listeners at that time thought he was making up fictional stories to make a spiritual point, like other religious teachers of the time, Jesus wasn't limited like those human teachers. Couldn't Jesus's parables also have been true stories about real people?"

The seminarians answered, "Yes, it's possible that Jesus's parables could have been true stories about real people. But they probably weren't. That wasn't the cultural practice at that time."

And the people asked, "Wouldn't it have been better if Jesus's parables, in addition to teaching spiritual truths, were also true stories about real people rather than fictional stories about fictional people? Ever since we received the Bible, we interpreted Jesus's parables one way. Now, decades later, you would have us change our interpretation based on this so-called historical scholarship. Aren't you subjecting the authority of Scripture to the authority of human scholarship?"

The seminarians replied, "If we insist on our traditional interpretation—if we insist that it would be unworthy of Jesus to tell fictional stories about fictional people—we are subjecting Scripture to the authority of our own particular cultural practices. Our cultural practices are not wrong; they serve us well. But our practices were not the cultural practices in place when Jesus taught his parables. We can celebrate that Jesus taught his lessons while accommodating the cultural practices of the original listeners. But whether you accept our new interpretation or stay with your traditional interpretation, the fundamental messages of Jesus's parables haven't changed."

Good Reinterpretations of Scripture Are the Work of the Holy Spirit

Jesus promised that the Holy Spirit would "guide [us] into all the truth" (John 16:13). One implication of that promise is that, on those occasions when a scientific discovery prompted the church to reexamine an interpretation of Scripture, and the new interpretation proved sound, ultimately this was the work of the Holy Spirit.

The Holy Spirit prompts the church to reinterpret Scripture in a variety of ways. One way is through the giving of spiritual gifts. Acts 11 tells the story of the apostle Peter and the centurion Cornelius. After Peter's visit to Cornelius, the other apostles criticized Peter for going into a gentile's house and breaking the law of Moses. Peter told them about his prophetic dream, and then he told them how the Holy Spirit came upon Cornelius and his household even before they were baptized. This stopped the argument (11:18). Through the clear giving of spiritual gifts to many individuals, the Holy Spirit led the church to understand that Jesus, the Messiah of the Jews, was also granting gentiles repentance of sins and new life in Christ. Similarly, the church council in Jerusalem several years later was debating whether new gentile believers scattered all over the Roman Empire should follow the law of Moses. We can imagine the scriptural arguments made by both the traditionalists and the nontraditionalists. Acts 15:12–15 tells us that the arguments stopped when Paul and Barnabas described the miraculous signs God was doing among the gentiles. God gave the gift of the Holy Spirit to gentile believers without them first having to obey the law of Moses. This helped convince the assembly. The church's interpretation of an extremely important theme throughout the Old Testament Scriptures—the importance of obeying the law of Moses— changed to follow the leading of the Holy Spirit.

At times, the Holy Spirit has used the suffering caused by social evils to prompt the church to reinterpret Scripture. Consider slavery. For many centuries, some Christians quoted Scripture to justify the practice of slavery.[19] But the Holy Spirit confronted the church again and again with the suffering caused by slavery and forced the church to rethink its interpretation of those passages. Likewise, for several centuries before and after the Reformation, some churches tortured and killed people they judged to be heretics. Some churches encouraged political leaders to use violence and warfare to suppress theological disagreements. At the time, these practices were justified by interpretations of Scripture. Today most Christians look back with abhorrence on using torture and murder as means to maintain theological correctness within the church. Until a few decades ago, it was common for some Christians in North America to use Scripture to justify racial segregation. Through witnessing the courageous actions of those who opposed segregation and the violence inflicted on them, many Christians finally saw the injustice and suffering caused by institutionalized racism. While racism is still a problem, far fewer Christians today interpret Scripture to justify it.

At times, the Holy Spirit has used the good caused by social innovations to prompt the church to reinterpret Scripture. For centuries, many Christians justified monarchy as a divinely instituted means of government and quoted Scripture to support it. Yet reflecting on the abuses of power that often occur under monarchy and on the social goods that come with democracy eventually led many Christians to decide that democracy is a form of government more in line with what Scripture teaches about human nature. Today, few

19. E.g., Eph. 6:5; Col. 3:22; Titus 2:9.

Christians would say that monarchy is a more biblical form of government than democracy. Or consider banking practices, specifically giving and receiving interest on loans. Several passages in the Bible speak against charging interest on loans.[20] No passages speak favorably about it. For centuries, the church said that Scripture clearly teaches that Christians should never charge interest. But eventually the church saw that when banks are allowed to set modest interest rates to attract savings and give loans, tremendous social good can be generated by allowing people to buy houses, gain education, start businesses, and save for old age. Today, few Christians believe that Scripture teaches that banks should never be allowed to give loans and receive savings at modest interest rates.

Of course, just because a reinterpretation of Scripture fits well with modern scholarship on a topic does not mean that it is a correct reinterpretation. Church history offers a long list of interpretations of Scripture that arose, became popular for a long while, but were ultimately rejected by most of the church. The ultimate standard for a good reinterpretation cannot be simply each individual interpreting Scripture for themselves the way they *think* the Spirit might be guiding them. We need each other. In addition to the guidance of the Holy Spirit, the church needs good human scholarship. Indeed, good scholarship is one means that the Holy Spirit uses. A good reinterpretation must follow the principles of sound hermeneutics that the church has learned over the centuries.

These historical examples should remove the fear that scientific discoveries motivating reinterpretations of Scripture amount to compromises with or capitulations to science. Within church history, scientific discoveries are one of several ways that the Holy Spirit has prompted the church to reinterpret certain passages. The work of reinterpretation should be done under the guidance of the Spirit using all the resources the Spirit gives us, including science, the entirety of Scripture, and centuries of theological scholarship. Ultimately, it's not about science having authority over our interpretation of Scripture or our interpretation of Scripture having authority over science. It's about God having authority in all our endeavors.

20. E.g., Exod. 22:25; Lev. 25:36–37; Neh. 5:10–11; Ps. 15:5; Ezek. 18:8, 13, 17; 22:12.

2

Creation, Evolution, and Divine Action

IF THE SCIENTIFIC EVIDENCE for human evolution is correct, what does it imply about God's actions in creating humans?

Scripture describes God's creation and governance of the natural world in ways appropriate to ancient cultures. It uses metaphors of kingly decrees, handiwork, God's breath, and even the "finger of God."

As discussed in the previous chapter, the foundational presuppositions of science are compatible with Christian theology. But science describes natural processes in ways that don't explicitly mention God. Science describes chains of natural cause and effect. So it is not surprising that these two kinds of description seem, at first, dissonant.

Scripture teaches that God sends rain on the righteous and the unrighteous (Matt. 5:45). Many passages proclaim that God causes rain and drought,[1] and several refer to God's storehouses of snow and rain.[2] Atmospheric scientists explain rain in terms of evaporation and condensation, high- and low-pressure systems, and cold and warm fronts. Scripture teaches that God feeds the birds of the air (Matt. 6:26); ornithologists can describe scientifically how robins

---

1. E.g., Deut. 11:14–17; 1 Kings 8:35–36; Job 5:10; 37:6; Jer. 14:22.
2. E.g., Deut. 28:12; Job 38:22; Ps. 135:7; Jer. 10:13.

hunt for worms. Scripture teaches that God created the sun and the stars (Gen. 1:14–16); astrophysicists mathematically model the formation of stars via gravitational collapse of interstellar clouds of dust. The psalmist praises God for knitting him together in his mother's womb (Ps. 139:13); developmental biologists describe the processes of embryonic and fetal development in terms of cell growth, gene regulation, signaling molecules, morphogenesis, and cell differentiation.

It can be tempting to simply let the modern scientific description replace the theological description. Alternatively, if the descriptions in Scripture are dear to us, and if we have always pictured God accomplishing these things in one particular way, it's tempting to accuse science of trying to take something away from God. We shouldn't do either.

By letting Scripture guide our interpretation of what science discovers, listening for counterpoint, the church has learned to harmonize what science discovers with what Scripture teaches about God's governance. This chapter focuses mostly on God's ongoing governance of the natural world in the present and during the long period of natural history prior to humanity's first appearance. Chapters 4 and 5 apply this to God's creation of humanity.

A Summary of Natural History Using Scientific Language

This section summarizes the consensus of scientists[3] regarding the natural history of our world, noting where scientists have considerable certainty and where there are still open questions. It refers to these events and processes in terms of natural causes and effects. The rest of the chapter explores ways that these processes reflect God's actions.

Act 1: The big bang (13.79 ± 0.02 billion years ago). All the matter, energy, and space of our universe was compressed in a tiny volume. Temperatures and densities were so high that our current best theories of physics cannot

3. This section summarizes the consensus of scientists regarding which theories are well established by multiple lines of data and which are less established. Among the general public, there isn't always consensus even when there is consensus among scientists. For example, a 2014 Associated Press-GfK poll of 1,012 American adults found that 51 percent were "not too confident" or "not at all confident" that the statement "the universe began 13.8 billion years ago with a big bang" was correct. "The AP-GfK Poll," AP-GfK Public Affairs & Corporate Communications, March 2014, http://surveys.associatedpress.com/data/GfK/AP-GfK%20March %202014%20Poll%20Topline%20%20Final_SCIENCE.pdf. Among scientists with advanced degrees in physics or astronomy, however, there is nearly complete consensus that the big bang happened (99.9 percent among members of the National Academy of Sciences). Alexis C. Madrigal, "A Majority of Americans Still Aren't Sure About the Big Bang," *Atlantic*, April 21, 2014, https://www.theatlantic.com/technology/archive/2014/04/a-majority-of-americans -question-the-science-of-the-big-bang/360976/.

describe what was happening. Scientists can extrapolate the history of the universe backward in time to just slightly after the big bang, but the actual start of the big bang is currently unexplainable in terms of any known physical laws.

Act 2: Formation of atoms, galaxies, stars, and planets (13.79 billion years ago to the present). As space expanded, the initial hot, dense mixture of unstable particles cooled to become the familiar stable particles we know today—protons, neutrons, electrons, and a few others.[4] These combined to form hydrogen, helium, and small amounts of a few other atoms. By gravitational collapse, these combined to form galaxies and stars and planets. Over billions of years, nuclear fusion in stars created atoms in the lighter half of the periodic table. Supernovae (and more exotic processes such as colliding neutron stars) created the heavier atoms and triggered new generations of star and planet formation. Scientists understand a great deal of this natural history, although there are many details yet to discover, some of them potentially quite important.

Act 3: Formation of the earth's oceans, atmosphere, and land (about 4.54 billion years ago to the present). Many physical and chemical processes are involved in this story. An interstellar cloud of material, including atoms and molecules left over from an earlier generation of stars, underwent gravitational attraction. Some of the material formed our sun. Some material in orbit around the forming sun came together to form the earth, the other planets, and the smaller objects of the solar system. As material accreted onto the forming earth, it heated up, resulting in separation of the earth's metallic core, rocky mantle, and initial crust. This heat caused outgassing, which helped produce the atmosphere and liquid ocean. Initially, there were no true continents; the first tiny continents were formed by magmatic processes on a hot early earth. Ongoing processes of plate tectonics and volcanism continue to reshape the continents, create and submerge islands, form new mountains and ocean trenches and river deltas, recycle minerals, and create new soil. Scientists understand a great deal of this natural history, although, again, there are many details yet to discover.

Act 4: First life on the earth (somewhere between 4.2 and 3.8 billion years ago). Scientists have a pretty good idea of the physical and chemical conditions of the early earth and of some of the chemical reactions that were happening. Scientists know a few things about the earliest single-celled life forms for which we have fossil evidence. In between are many, many steps that scientists don't

---

4. Protons and neutrons are not fundamental particles but are made out of particles called "up" and "down" quarks. Neutrons are not stable by themselves but are stable when combined with protons in atomic nuclei.

yet understand. How life first formed on the earth is perhaps second only to the start of the big bang on the list of scientific open questions.[5]

Act 5: Biological evolution (roughly 3.8 billion years ago to the present). Once life began on the earth, life forms evolved and spread. Evolution is sometimes defined as changes in the heritable characteristics in a biological population over generations. One important natural mechanism of evolution is random genetic mutation. In every living cell, the DNA molecules act as instructions for the cell to manufacture and regulate the chemicals it needs. When a mutation occurs, there can be a change in the DNA passed from parents to offspring. Saying that mutations are "random" means that scientists cannot predict when a mutation will happen or what form it will take and that the actions of the parents do not determine what sorts of mutations their offspring will have. Mutations increase the genetic variability in a population of organisms. A second important natural mechanism of evolution is differential reproductive success. Some organisms are better suited to their environment than others. Organisms that are less suited might still survive, thrive, and reproduce, but those that are better suited tend, on average, to have more offspring. This process is not random; it sculpts the variety produced by mutations. Over time, this can result in populations that are better adapted to a particular niche of the environment. Biological evolution is sometimes summarized simply as random genetic mutation plus differential reproductive success. While these two mechanisms are centerpieces, they are not the whole story. Many other important natural mechanisms play roles in biological evolution.[6] Through these mechanisms, over billions of years, the diversity and complexity of single-celled life increased. Multicelled organisms evolved. Interrelated webs of interacting organisms formed ecosystems. Scientists understand a great deal of this natural history, although, again, there are many details yet to discover.

Act 6: Gene-culture coevolution (roughly 2 million years ago to the present). Many of the most neurologically complex animals live not just in family groups but in social groups bigger and more important than their immediate families. Individuals in these social groups not only share the tasks of survival

5. A minority of scientists say that the formation of first life is "unexplainable" in terms of known natural laws. Some of them would say this points to a supernatural miracle taking place; others would say that some as-yet-undiscovered natural law is awaiting discovery. A majority of scientists, however, would say that the formation of life is not "unexplainable" in terms of known laws and physics and chemistry but rather "partially explainable," although we are still very far from explaining all the steps scientifically. The distinction between "unexplainable" and "partially explainable" is discussed later in this chapter.

6. For an excellent summary of some of these mechanisms and their importance, see Dennis Venema, "Evolution Basics," BioLogos, October 30, 2018, https://biologos.org/blogs/dennis -venema-letters-to-the-duchess/series/evolution-basics.

with one another but also pass on knowledge and skills from one generation to the next. At some point starting around two million years ago, our ancestors developed so many novel tools, communication skills, teaching and learning skills, and social practices that they changed their environment. Each generation inherited both genes and cultural practices from their ancestors, and both were important for survival and reproduction. Both genes and culture coevolved as our ancestors' neurological and social complexity increased. (This is discussed in more depth in chapter 4.)

God Designed the Fundamental Laws, Raw Materials, and Initial Conditions

Before matter or energy or the laws of nature existed, God had a plan for how all the acts of natural history would accomplish his intentions. Think of this as "act zero."

One of the most remarkable things that scientists have discovered about God's design is the vast variety of things that can be made out of just a few simple parts. Consider just three particles: protons, neutrons, and electrons. The mathematical formulas that model how they move and exert forces on one another can be written on approximately a single sheet of paper. These three types of particles combine into roughly one hundred different types of atoms. Those one hundred types of atoms combine into a tremendous variety of molecules. Look around the room you're in and think about every different solid, liquid, and gas present. Then think about the thousands of different biological molecules in your body. Each has unique properties. Each is made from a different arrangement of just those three kinds of particles. Molecules, in turn, combine to form almost everything we see: mountains and lakes, living cells, trees and beetles and people. The vast variety of things in this world—plus the moon, asteroids, planets, stars, nebulae, and galaxies—are all made from different arrangements of just three kinds of particles.

When God designed the properties of protons, neutrons, and electrons, and the laws that describe their interactions, God had in mind all the possible things that could be made by combining them in different ways. More than that, God had in mind all of natural history. God designed their properties so that clouds of hydrogen and helium would come together under gravity to form the first stars (act 2), so that light nuclei would fuse to create heavier nuclei, so that terrestrial planets with liquid water oceans and gaseous atmospheres would form in orbits around long-lived and stable stars (act 3). God designed not only what forms these particles could combine into but also how they would naturally form these things by interacting the way they were created to interact. The mathematical structures of the laws of nature, the properties of the fundamental particles, and the initial conditions of the universe must all be finely tuned to make natural history happen this way.

One particularly amazing thing that protons, neutrons, and electrons can combine to form is the DNA molecule. DNA molecules are strings of just four kinds of molecules called nucleotides (typically labeled C, G, A, and T). But they can be combined in almost any order into long strings. The DNA in mammalian cells has about a billion nucleotides strung together. There are about $10^{500,000,000}$ possible ways to put together a DNA string that long. God designed the laws of nature to make living creatures and DNA possible, and in doing so he also created a vast array of possibilities—what we might call a "possibility space" consisting of all creatures that could, in theory, be generated by all those combinations. Living organisms, over the history of life on earth, through processes of evolution (act 5), have explored only an extremely tiny portion of that enormous possibility space that God designed.

God Gives Existence to Matter, Energy, Space, and Time

Matter, energy, space, and time are not coeternal with God. God created them out of nothing (*ex nihilo*). They do not now exist independently from God. God continually sustains the natural world in existence moment by moment.

It is tempting to identify the theological idea of God creating this universe *ex nihilo* with the scientific description of the big bang (act 1). As far as we know, that might be the case. It's possible that the moment of the big bang corresponds to God creating this universe out of nothing, miraculously. Of course, just as God today creates new stars and new trees through natural mechanisms, it's also possible that God created a natural mechanism—one we have yet to discover—to start our particular universe with a big bang. One version of this theory is called the "multiverse hypothesis."[7] If scientists

7. The multiverse hypothesis proposes that some natural process in some preexisting universe gave rise to our big bang (all the matter, energy, space, and time of our particular universe) and to many other universes as well. This idea is speculative, but there are some sound scientific reasons for thinking it might be true. Atheists sometimes present the multiverse hypothesis as an alternative to God. For Christians, if the multiverse hypothesis turns out to be scientifically valid, it will not replace God but instead tell us more about the means God used to create our particular universe. For more on this topic, see Deborah Haarsma, "Universe or Multiverse, God Is Still the Creator," BioLogos, May 3, 2018, https://biologos.org/blogs/deborah-haarsma-the-presidents-notebook/universe-or-multiverse-god-is-still-the-creator; and Deborah Haarsma, "God and the Multiverse," Trinity Forum Lectures, September 13, 2016, https://www.youtube.com/watch?v=KTS_8B0CNeU.

one day discover a natural mechanism that could have caused our big bang, that will not threaten the theological teaching of creation *ex nihilo*. It will simply lengthen the chain of natural causes and effects that science can study. Ultimately, God gives existence to and sustains the entire chain of causes and effects, from beginning to end. God is the ultimate reason that matter, energy, space, and time exist.

God Sustains Natural Laws

When scientists observe regular patterns in nature—such as rainstorms and their connection to high- and low-pressure centers and warm and cold fronts— they try to understand the underlying patterns of cause and effect. In some cases, the patterns are so basic and universal that scientists call them "natural laws." For example, the gravitational force between two objects is so predictable that scientists model it with a mathematical equation. It is so regular and universal that scientists call it a law of nature. They might even say something like, "The law of gravity governs the motion of planets."

Scripture tells us that this isn't the whole story. Natural laws don't govern; God governs. God speaks of his "covenant with day and night" and the fixed "laws of heaven and earth" (Jer. 33:25).

Psalm 104:19–24 celebrates God's governance.

> He made the moon to mark the seasons,
>   and the sun knows when to go down.
> You bring darkness, it becomes night,
>   and all the beasts of the forest prowl.
> The lions roar for their prey
>   and seek their food from God.
> The sun rises, and they steal away;
>   they return and lie down in their dens.
> Then people go out to their work,
>   to their labor until evening.
>
> How many are your works, Lord!
>   In wisdom you made them all;
>   the earth is full of your creatures.

This psalm describes the same events both as natural events (the sun goes down, lions hunt) and as divine actions (God brings darkness, lions receive their food from God). While this psalm was written centuries before modern science, the psalmist knew the difference between miracles and ordinary natural events like the sun going down. The Psalms are full of praise to God for acts of miraculous deliverance in Israel's past. Yet this psalm and many other passages insist that even when it comes to ordinary natural events, God is fully in charge. Nothing takes place in the created world apart from God's will or without God's cooperation with the created world.[8]

Although God can create new stars and new species miraculously, he often chooses to create through cooperation with his creation, a type of divine action called "mediated creation." He calls nature itself to be a partner in his creative and providential work. New stars form through gravitational collapse of interstellar clouds. Thus, God creates new stars by drawing on materials he created previously and in partnership with natural processes. Similarly, God formed the carbon and oxygen in our bodies through natural processes of fusion in the cores of stars. God made the earth's ocean, atmosphere, and dry land through processes of gravity and chemistry acting on the raw materials of the early solar system. All the "acts" of natural history described earlier in this chapter can be described using both the scientific language of natural cause and effect and the theological language of God's acts. The scientific descriptions take nothing away from the theological ones.

Philosopher and physicist Robert Bishop describes God's mediated action in creation as God calling one part of creation to minister to another:

> Some parts of creation are called and empowered to serve as mediators or ministers to other parts of creation, so that creation participates in becoming what God calls it to be. For example, in Genesis 1, "God said, 'Let the earth grow grass, plants . . .'" (Gen. 1:11) and "God said, 'Let the earth bring forth living creatures . . .'" (Gen. 1:24). . . . The great creation psalm, Psalm 104, is filled with examples of creation ministering to creation under divine call, guidance and enabling: trees and mountain crags providing shelter for animals, grass and water providing sustenance and refreshment for plants and animals, cycles of day and night and the seasons for sustaining the livelihoods of plants

8. There are at least two ways of understanding the status of natural laws that are within the tradition of Christian orthodoxy. One view is that created things have real creaturely cause-and-effect powers granted by God, but they do not operate independently of God. They depend on God for their continued existence, and God "concurs" with natural cause and effect. This view, often called "concurrence," is probably the most common view among scientists who are Christians. Another traditional Christian view, less commonly held, called "occasionalism," says that created things do not have their own cause-and-effect powers; whatever happens is always directly caused by God. Creaturely actions are merely the occasions of divine activity. This chapter assumes concurrence rather than occasionalism. One broader survey and analysis of theological options on this topic is C. John Collins, *The God of Miracles: An Exegetical Examination of God's Action in the World* (Wheaton: Crossway, 2000).

and animals, lions looking for their food from God by hunting for it, etc. Or think of Jesus' Sermon on the Mount during which He says, "Look at the birds of the air; they do not sow or reap or store away in barns, and yet your heavenly Father feeds them" (Matt. 6:26). The diets of birds are quite varied, as various species eat seeds, plants, insects, worms and more. Different species deploy different strategies for finding food, but all of these feeding behaviors are described by Jesus as the Father feeding them by being active in creation so that creation provides the foods needed by birds (compare with Job 38:39–41).[9]

God used scientifically understandable natural processes to grow each one of us from a single cell at conception to a newborn baby nine months later, yet each of us can join the psalmist, proclaiming that God "knit me together in my mother's womb" (Ps. 139:13). God used scientifically understandable evolutionary processes when forming our species, yet we can still proclaim that God created us. When scientists explain some part of the natural world in terms of natural laws, this does not remove God from the picture. Rather, science helps us to partially understand the patterns of God's governance. Scripture teaches us to interpret God's mediated action in the cosmos not as a sign of God's distance but as a sign of God's gracious partnering with his creatures to accomplish his goals.

God Uses Natural Processes That Include Randomness

It is said that no two snowflakes are identical. Snowflakes are made of water molecules. Each water molecule is identical, so how can each snowflake be unique? The answer lies in the interplay between natural laws and chance. The regularity of natural laws makes each snowflake a six-sided crystal. Randomness makes each snowflake unique—the random motion of the flakes through the air and the random motion of individual water molecules as they accumulate onto the growing crystals.

God designed the laws of physics and chemistry that give water molecules their properties, and in doing so he also (among other things) created the possibility space for snowflakes—that is, the vast array of possible shapes that snowflakes might take. If you tried to count all the *possible* arrangements of water molecules into snowflakes, the number would be absurdly large—much larger than the number of particles in the visible universe. If you could collect every snowflake made during the earth's lifetime, the total would amount to only a tiny fraction of all possible snowflake shapes. As each snowflake forms through random motions, we can think of it as exploring narrow paths through the vast array of all snowflake possibilities.

As God works in partnership with his creation, we see him using processes that look random to us. In everyday speech, "random" is often used to mean "without meaning" or "purposeless." But when scientists use the word "random" in a scientific context, they simply mean "unpredictable."[10]

"Random" need not imply purposelessness. In fact, humans often deliberately employ randomness. Referees toss a coin at the start of a football game because we consider this the fairest way to determine which team receives the ball first. Casinos use games of chance as sources of entertainment and as a way for a few customers to win more than they lose, even though the odds are set so that the casinos profit in the long run. Video game designers add some randomness to games to make them more fun. An artist could program a computer to display a sequence of beautiful pictures based on mathematical equations and then have the computer randomly alter variables in the equations in order to display a whole new sequence of different beautiful pictures.

Many natural processes employ randomness: from flowers diffusing scent into the air, to protons colliding and fusing in the sun's core, to oxygen diffusing from your lungs into your bloodstream. Particularly relevant to us in this chapter is how evolutionary processes use randomness to allow species to change and adapt (act 5).

Imagine a species of bird thriving in a forest. If the climate becomes drier or wetter over time slowly enough, the mechanisms of evolution allow that bird species to adapt to the changes. The unpredictable aspects of DNA replication occasionally lead to random mutations. Each mutation passed to offspring increases the genetic variation within a species. Some individuals have variations that make them better adapted to the changing environment, and these individuals tend to have greater reproductive success.

---

10. Sometimes scientists use the word "random" for processes that are predictable in principle but unpredictable in practice because the final outcome is very sensitive to slight changes in the initial conditions. Consider the roll of a pair of dice. We can calculate the probability that the roll will yield a 7 or a 9, but we can't predict what any particular roll will be. Each time the dice are rolled, they follow exactly the same natural laws of gravity and motion, but they land differently each time because of how they bounce and spin. If the dice are tossed even slightly differently from one time to the next, that slight difference is magnified by each bounce, and after several bounces, the final outcome is changed. Scientists also use the word "random" for processes that are, as far as we can tell, unpredictable in principle. Quantum mechanics, the physics used to describe the behavior of molecules, atoms, and elementary particles, appears to work this way. If a million identical atoms are placed in exactly the same unstable state, each one will decay at a different time. We can predict the probabilities and the distribution of decay times, but the exact decay time of each particular atom is, as far as we know, unpredictable in principle.

But random mutations do not only enable greater diversity *within* species; they can also contribute to greater diversity *of* species and even ecosystems. Once again, imagine a species of bird thriving in a forest. Suppose to the south of the forest there is a swampy region, to the east there are sandy grasslands, and to the west there are mountains. Birds living on the edges of the forest can evolve subspecies adapted to those crossover regions. With enough time, their offspring can adapt further to live entirely in those neighboring environments as new, separate species. Where once there was one species, now there are two or three or four. And each time a new species arrives in an ecosystem, it can create niches and opportunities for still more species to move in.

God created the laws of physics and chemistry that give DNA its properties, and in doing so he also (among other things) created a vast possibility space consisting of all possible forms life might take. If you tried to imagine all the life forms that could be made from 3 billion base pairs of DNA, every possible arrangement of the pairs, the number of possible life forms would be absurdly large—much larger than the number of particles in the visible universe. If you could catalog every living being that has existed in the earth's history, you would have only a tiny fraction of all possible life forms. As species evolve over the earth's history, we can think of them as exploring paths through the vast possibility space that is all possible forms of life.

God Might Have Selected the Outcomes of Particular Random Events

Events that appear random from a human perspective might be fully determined by God. Consider Proverbs 16:33: "The lot is cast into the lap, but its every decision is from the Lord." Centuries before modern science, ancient people knew that some things, like casting lots and the weather, are unpredictable. This passage from Proverbs and other Scriptures proclaim God's sovereignty over events that scientists today would describe using probabilities.

Did God guide biological evolution in general, and human evolution in particular, by selecting particular mutations to happen at particular times? That is primarily a theological question—although, as we will see, there is also a scientific question that helps inform the answer.

Let's start with a broader theological question. Does God directly control every event in nature that appears random from a scientific standpoint? Or did God build true randomness into natural processes and allow his created systems, through randomness, to explore options within the bounds he set? Christian scholars have offered several answers. They agree that God is sovereign over natural laws and over events that are scientifically described as random. They don't agree on how best to describe this sovereignty.[11]

According to one theological view, God determines the activity of all material objects from moment to moment, including the outcome of each event that appears scientifically random. God determines the exact placement of each water molecule in each snowflake. God determines the exact moment that each unstable atom decays. God determines precisely when and where each mutation happens in every population of organisms over the entire history of life. Advocates of this view point out that it maintains a high view of God's sovereignty. Critics sometimes argue that this view makes God something like a puppeteer who gives his creatures only an illusion of freedom.

A second theological view is that God gives material objects the freedom to explore a range of possibilities allowed by the laws of nature, which God sustains. God does not determine the outcome of any scientifically random event but instead governs randomness by setting the range of possible outcomes and the probability of each outcome. God then allows particles, systems, and organisms to interact according to natural laws within those boundaries, producing a wide range of beautiful and complex results. Although God gives material objects some freedom, they still depend on God for their continued existence. (And in addition to God's usual governance using natural laws with random elements, God can still choose to perform miracles outside of those natural laws.) Advocates of this view argue that randomness is one way God graciously gives real cause-and-effect powers to his creatures, allowing them to explore the range of possibilities God has created for them. Critics sometimes argue that this view weakens God's sovereignty too much.

A third theological view, intermediate between the two just mentioned, is that God doesn't directly choose the outcome of *every* scientifically unpredictable event but does for *some* at strategically important points to ensure that certain things happen. For example, God might not determine every single random mutation in the history of life, but God might direct some particular ones to guide the evolution of certain species along certain paths. Advocates of this view argue that it gives real cause-and-effect power and real freedom to God's creatures while also ensuring that God's will is always accomplished. Critics sometimes argue that this view makes questions of

11. Some helpful books by Christian scholars with differing views on this topic include Donald MacKay, *Science, Chance and Providence* (Oxford: Oxford University Press, 1978); John Polkinghorne, *Quarks, Chaos, and Christianity* (New York: Crossroad, 1994); John Polkinghorne, *Science and Providence* (Boston: Shambhala, 1989); and Robert John Russell, Nancey Murphy, and Arthur Robert Peacocke, *Chaos and Complexity* (Notre Dame, IN: University of Notre Dame Press, 1995).

theodicy (why God permits evil) more difficult. Why does God select the outcome of random events to accomplish good or prevent suffering sometimes but not other times?

Scientific tests cannot determine which of these views is correct.[12] Whether God selects the outcomes of random events always, never, or sometimes is one of a larger set of theological questions about God's sovereignty, creaturely freedom, and theodicy. Each of the views discussed here falls within the bounds of most Christian traditions. More theological arguments can be made for and against each, but summarizing them would take us beyond the needs of this book. We are most interested in how these views impact our thinking about human evolution.

As I mentioned above, there is also a scientific question that might influence our answers to this theological question: To what extent is evolution highly *contingent* on particular historical events, and to what extent is evolution *convergent* to essentially the same outcomes regardless of the particular historical paths taken?

Mutations are contingent events. From a scientific standpoint, they are random. And some mutations seem to be key events that allow a species to develop one way rather than another. Other contingent events can also affect evolutionary history, such as the exact time and location of earthquakes, volcanoes, or meteor strikes that wipe out entire species or ecosystems. Some scientists conclude that evolution is so dependent on contingent events that its outcome is entirely unpredictable. Perhaps the most famous version of this claim is from Stephen Jay Gould's *Wonderful Life*.[13] He states that if we were to rewind the "tape of life" back to a time before multicellular life, and then

12. Some people, when they use the phrase "God guided evolution," mean something like the following: "The natural mechanisms of evolution by themselves can produce only small-scale changes in species. They cannot explain large-scale changes in the history of life, especially increases in complexity and intelligence. Those changes are extremely improbable by the ordinary mechanisms of evolution. Therefore, God must have been guiding evolution by providing just the right mutations at just the right times, through biological history, to produce those large-scale changes." If this view were correct, then God's guidance of random events would be scientifically detectable in practice—perhaps not at the level of any one individual mutation, but by their accumulation to achieve such an extremely improbable result over time. However, I do not think that this view is correct. I believe, along with most scientists, that the natural mechanisms of evolution are capable of producing not only small-scale changes but also large-scale changes in species, including increases in complexity and intelligence. See Deborah B. Haarsma and Loren D. Haarsma, *Origins: Christian Perspectives on Creation, Evolution, and Intelligent Design* (Grand Rapids: Faith Alive Christian Resources, 2011); and Loren Haarsma and Terry M. Gray, "Complexity, Self-Organization, and Design," in *Perspectives on an Evolving Creation*, ed. Keith B. Miller (Grand Rapids: Eerdmans, 2003), 288–309.

13. Stephen Jay Gould, *Wonderful Life: The Burgess Shale and the Nature of History* (New York: Norton, 1990), 14, 238, 317, 323.

replay it, the history of life on earth would be entirely different. Human-like creatures might never evolve.

Other aspects of evolution are not random. Natural selection acts on the diversity within species and shapes species to be better suited to particular environments. As a result, very different species with different evolutionary histories sometimes independently converge on very similar solutions to the challenges posed by their environments. Paleontologist Simon Conway Morris has written several books describing data supporting this conclusion.[14] Some famous examples of convergent evolution include the wings of birds and bats; the camera-like eyes of vertebrates (fish, amphibians, reptiles, birds, and mammals), cnidarians (certain jellyfish), and cephalopods (squid and octopus); echolocation in bats and dolphins; and the streamlined body shape of fish, seals, penguins, and whales. Some scientists conclude that while contingency plays a role in evolution, the large-scale outcomes of evolution are largely convergent. If we replayed the tape of life over again, very similar life forms would evolve again.

Scientists have not yet reached consensus on the extent to which evolution is highly contingent on particular historical events and the extent to which it is convergent. How does this scientific question inform our theological question about God's governance of randomness?

If God selects the outcome of every scientifically random event, or even just some random events, then the scientific question becomes unimportant theologically. It doesn't matter whether evolution from a scientific standpoint is highly contingent or highly convergent. Either way, by selecting the outcome of random events, God guided evolution, including the evolution of humanity, into the particular outcome he wanted.

On the other hand, if God does not select the outcome of scientifically random events, then the scientific question has a greater theological impact. If it turns out that evolution is highly convergent, then the evolution of something very much like humanity was built in by God from the beginning, destined to happen regardless of what random events happened along the way. But if it turns out that evolution is highly contingent, then the evolution of something like humanity on the earth was not inevitable. Someone who takes this view might still conclude that this is no barrier to God achieving his will, however, because there are a vast number of planets in the universe, and God would know that the evolution of something like humanity was eventually inevitable somewhere.

14. See Simon Conway Morris, *The Crucible of Creation: The Burgess Shale and the Rise of Animals* (Denver: Peterson's, 1998); and *Life's Solution: Inevitable Humans in a Lonely Universe* (Cambridge: Cambridge University Press, 2003).

God Might Have Acted Miraculously during Natural History

God is sovereign over natural events that we can describe scientifically. The Bible also talks about miracles. A "miracle" does not always imply a violation of natural cause and effect. Miracles can be ordinary events with extraordinary timing, such as the famine that began and ended with the prophet Elijah's proclamations.[15] Such miracles are not scientifically impossible or even improbable, but the timing was specially arranged by God and accompanied by special revelation explaining its significance. Miracles can also be highly improbable events with special timing, such as some miraculous cures of illnesses. Some miracles in Scripture, such as Jesus's resurrection, defy explanation on the basis of natural laws. When the term "miracle" is used in science-and-religion contexts, people are usually thinking of events that include a supernatural break in ordinary, natural chains of cause and effect—so that is how the term is being used in this book.

If natural laws are the way God normally oversees his creation, then God can supersede that ordinary governance in special instances. Humans sometimes behave in unexpected ways for good reasons. For example, you might know a friend so well that you could predict how she would act in most situations. If one day she did something highly unusual, you might be bewildered by her actions until you investigated the special circumstances of that day. Given those special circumstances, you would then understand that she had good reasons for taking that surprising action on that day—reasons that are consistent with her character. In the Bible, that's often how miracles are depicted. God does something unexpected (based on how God ordinarily governs creation), but it turns out to be entirely appropriate considering the special circumstances.

Science excels at discovering the ordinary patterns of cause and effect in nature. When the unexpected happens, science can tell us whether the unexpected event was highly improbable or impossible given our current understanding of natural laws. That's helpful, but science cannot tell us the spiritual significance of an unexpected event. And natural laws do not constrain God.[16]

Scripture records a number of miracles performed during human history as part of God's revelation. Most of these happened at special times in salvation

15. Some theologians prefer to call events like this "extraordinary providence"; they reserve the term "miracle" for things that God causes to happen without secondary cause. However, because it is common to call events such as these "miracles," I do so in this book.

16. For more about this, see Loren Haarsma, "Does Science Exclude God? Natural Law, Chance, Miracles, and Scientific Practice," in *Perspectives on an Evolving Creation*, ed. Keith B. Miller (Grand Rapids: Eerdmans, 2003), 72–94; and Haarsma and Haarsma, *Origins*, 44–53.

history, especially around the times of Moses, Elijah, and Jesus. It is tempting to extrapolate from these and conclude that God also did a few miracles in prehuman natural history at special times, such as the formation of the earth, or the formation of first life, or increasing the mental abilities of our prehuman hominin ancestors. It is possible that this is what God did. But we should note a significant difference between these kinds of miracles. Miracles during salvation history were performed in contexts where the spiritual message was explicitly taught (or should have been obvious) to the witnesses. Miracles in prehuman natural history, if they occurred, would have been performed when there were no human witnesses, and presumably they were performed because the natural laws and processes that God created were incapable of achieving something that God wanted to happen unless God supernaturally augmented those processes.

Consider the formation of the first life on earth (act 4). Scientists do not have a detailed and testable scientific explanation for how it could have formed via known natural processes. Most scientists who study the problem believe that they are making progress and eventually will find an explanation. However, a few scientists believe that any explanation in terms of known natural processes can already be judged to be vastly improbable. The scientific community does not yet have consensus on this issue. Theologically, both options are acceptable. It is possible that God designed and created the laws of physics and chemistry so that the first life on earth formed via natural processes, and that this is just one of the many puzzles that scientists have yet to unravel. It is also possible that God performed a miracle to create the first life on earth because God designed and created the laws of physics and chemistry so that it would have been vastly improbable that first life could have formed via natural processes. If our theology sees God as sovereign over both natural events and supernatural miracles, we don't need to feel theologically threatened by scientific research into the question of first life.

Since God can perform miracles, it is also possible that God performed miracles at the dawn of the human species to give our ancestors special mental, social, moral, and spiritual abilities that God could not have created in them through evolutionary processes. Some pros and cons of these options are discussed in chapters 5 and 9.

Avoiding a Theological Problem: False Apparent History

False apparent history can be illustrated with an extreme example. Imagine that God created the world two weeks ago, including false memories of events in our brains, wear and tear on buildings, textbooks full of history that never happened, fossils buried in the ground, and so forth. God has the power to do this. Science could not disprove it. Nevertheless, most Christians reject this idea for theological reasons, seeing it as inconsistent with God's revealed character.

Now consider a less extreme example. Imagine that someone tells you that a full-grown tree appeared miraculously last week in a nearby forest grove. Even if this person was normally reliable and trustworthy, you might think they were mistaken, and you might investigate the tree scientifically. Suppose you take a sample from the tree trunk and find each of the seventy-seven rings to be exactly equal in width, and you find that the leaves are distributed perfectly symmetrically around the crown (something plant biologists tell you does not normally happen when trees grow), and you find no evidence of insects ever living in the bark (a surprise to any entomologist), and you find that each leaf is genetically identical without any somatic cell mutations (geneticists would say that is highly unlikely), and you find that the isotopic ratios of hydrogen to deuterium in the tree do not match those of the surrounding trees (a surprise to any chemist). Because this tree, in all these details, is so different from what you would expect if the tree had grown there normally, you would probably conclude that the scientific evidence supports the claim that the tree was miraculously created.

But suppose the scientific investigation showed something else. Careful study of the bark and trunk show evidence of insect and woodpecker activity from the oldest rings to the youngest. The leaves are distributed in typical patterns expected from growth on sunny and shady parts of the tree. Tree ring widths vary in patterns matching surrounding trees and meteorological records of past droughts and rainy seasons. Every isotopic ratio measured in every ring of the tree exactly matches those of surrounding trees, including the ratios during a five-year period twenty years ago after a falling of volcanic ash. Genetic analysis shows that leaves on different branches show the small number of somatic cell mutations expected during normal tree growth. In short, every scientific test you conduct is consistent with what you might expect if the tree had grown in that location over the last seventy-seven years. There is a rich, detailed apparent history written into every part of the tree.

In this second case, you would probably believe that the tree was not miraculously created last week. Why not? It is certainly possible for God to have done so. No scientific test could determine whether the tree grew over a long period or whether God miraculously created it *de novo* and made it appear to every scientific test as if it had grown in place. The difficulty with the claim that the tree was created miraculously is not a scientific one but a theological one. Based on what we know about God's character revealed in Scripture, it seems unlikely to us that God would miraculously create an adult tree but then make it appear to every scientific test that the tree had a long, intricate, richly detailed but *false* history. God has the power to do this, but it does not seem like something the God of Scripture would do. (Unless perhaps there was some accompanying special revelation that both affirmed the miraculous creation of the tree and also explained a theological purpose for the richly detailed apparent history.)

When scientists study the natural world, they don't see evidence for just great age. They see evidence for a richly detailed history. When astronomers look at distant galaxies, they don't merely calculate that the light was traveling for millions or billions of years. They see, in the patterns of the photons and gravitational waves, a fascinating story of changes over time—changes in the composition of stars over the history of the universe, evidence of repeated galaxy mergers, nebulae slowly expanding from supernovae, supernovae exploding and dimming with light curves that correspond to the half-lives of known radioactive elements, luminosity-temperature correlations in star clusters indicating that nearly all of them formed at roughly the same time, momentary signals of black hole and neutron star mergers detectable only via recently built gravitational wave detectors, and literally dozens of other independent, mutually reinforcing indications of a long, detailed history going back billions of years. If the universe was created just a few thousand years ago, and the light and gravitational waves from objects billions of light years away were created just a few thousand years ago, in transit toward the earth, then that light and those gravitational waves were created carrying information about a richly detailed history of events that never actually happened.

Geologists could also give an equally impressive list of dozens of lines of evidence telling a rich, detailed history of the earth going back billions of years. Paleontologists could tell a similar story with fossils. Geneticists could tell a similar story written into the DNA of every living (and some extinct) species.

For this reason, few Christians advocate for a false apparent history interpretation of Genesis 1.[17] We'll discuss how this might apply to God's creation of human beings in chapter 5.

---

17. This is why young-earth creationist organizations, while advocating a literal-historical interpretation of Genesis 1–11, do not typically advocate a false apparent history interpretation and instead dispute the claim that scientists are correctly interpreting the scientific data as pointing to a billion-year history.

Avoiding a Theological Problem: Deism

Deism is a philosophical or religious view that affirms that God created the universe and got it started but does not affirm that God providentially oversees it, performs miracles, or reveals himself in any other way. Deism can be a tempting philosophy if one rejects what Scripture teaches and looks only at what science has learned, but deism is not biblical. Christian theology affirms both what science has learned about natural cause and effect and also what Scripture teaches about God's providential oversight of the natural world and miracles.

Avoiding a Theological Problem: Episodic Deism (God of the Gaps)

Our modern culture tries to put scientific study of the natural world and worshipful praise of the Creator into entirely separate mental and cultural categories. As a result, when we discover scientific explanations for important things like the formation of stars, or the evolution of new species, or the development of babies in the womb, we might feel as if we have made God less involved. To make matters worse, some atheists use scientific advances to argue against any belief in God. Christians sometimes respond by looking for evidence of God's miraculous acts in the present gaps in scientific understanding, in those things that science cannot (yet) explain.

There are many gaps in our scientific knowledge. As we study God's world scientifically, our discoveries close some gaps and often open our eyes to new ones. The more we study God's world, the more wonderful mysteries we find. Some exciting examples of this are the metamorphosis and migration of monarch butterflies. The Project Creation website summarizes the gaps in our scientific knowledge and then draws conclusions about God's actions.

> The first thing that the caterpillar does inside its chrysalis is to release chemicals stored in its body and dissolve itself into a liquidy mush. . . . Out of this liquidy mush the body, head, wings and internal organs are formed. In only 8 days a full size Monarch butterfly emerges. The question that has intrigued humanity for centuries is this, how does the mush organize itself into the incredible complexity that is a butterfly? . . . Entomologists have studied this mystery for years, but have no answers as to how it happens.
>
> The transformation from caterpillar to butterfly is only part of the amazing story of the Monarch. Most Monarchs are born in the northern United States or Canada, but they can then migrate up to 3000 miles to spend the winter in Mexico. What is amazing about this migration is that butterflies never meet

their parents, but they are able to fly to the same tree in Mexico their parents or grandparents wintered at the year before. There have even been documented cases where it has taken three generations of butterflies to complete the round trip. How they are able to find the same tree is another of the mysteries of the Monarch butterfly.

Monarch butterflies are one of the best examples of design in God's Creation, for none of the stages of caterpillar/butterfly development occur by chance, the central principle of the religion of evolutionism.[18] The facts show that God programmed every stage of the caterpillar/butterfly life cycle. If there were no other evidence of design in God's Creation than caterpillars and butterflies, this alone would be enough to show the fact of His design in His Creation.[19]

It is certainly true that God created monarch butterflies, but should Christians use these gaps in our current scientific knowledge as evidence that God created monarch butterflies through supernatural miracles? Given the research being done,[20] it seems likely that scientists will eventually figure out explanations for not only how these butterflies metamorphose and migrate but also how those abilities could have evolved.

If God's status as Creator and Designer is proclaimed only in the gaps in current scientific explanations, then God's role seems to shrink as scientific knowledge grows. A better approach is to proclaim God's design and governance both in the things science cannot explain and in the things it can. Scientific explanations should not make God feel more distant. We should be grateful that God is governing his creation in ways that permit us to study and partially understand what is happening. We should rejoice that God chooses to act in mediated ways, calling parts of creation to minister to other parts, as a reflection of how God calls us to minister to one another. When scientists eventually figure out how monarch metamorphosis and migration happen, and how these abilities could have evolved, it will be amazing. Whatever scientists learn, their discoveries won't detract anything from God. This knowledge should increase our awe of and our praise for God as designer and sustainer.

18. The Project Creation website uses the terms "chance" and "design" differently than I use them in this chapter. By "chance" and "religion of evolutionism," they mean an atheistic interpretation of evolution in which mutations happen without any involvement from God. By "design," they mean God creating miraculously and de novo rather than through concurrence with evolutionary processes.

19. "Butterflies—the Miracle of Metamorphosis," Project Creation, https://projectcreation .org/butterflies-the-miracle-of-metamorphosis/.

20. A survey of research literature shows that considerable progress has been made toward scientifically understanding metamorphosis in Drosophila (small fruit flies).

It is tempting to think that we are more faithful to God if we look for evidence of miracles in every scientific puzzle. But hunting for God's fingerprints is not necessarily the most faithful approach to studying God's creation. Hunting for new scientific explanations, in terms of natural laws that God created and sustains, can be equally God glorifying—and in some cases may be more defensible theologically. Every time we solve a new scientific puzzle, we are not taking territory away from God's control; rather, we are learning more about how God typically governs his creation. Our discoveries should prompt us all the more to worship the Creator.

What Theology and Science Can Each Contribute to Unresolved Questions

How did the big bang happen (act 1)? How did first life arise on the earth (act 4)? How did humans become intelligent, self-conscious beings with a moral and spiritual sense (act 6)? God can do miracles. God is equally sovereign over events that are scientifically explainable and those that are not. We should avoid God-of-the-gaps thinking, but there might be theological reasons for thinking that God performed miracles in these particular cases.

Here is what science can contribute. When faced with a puzzling event or process, science can neither prove nor disprove that natural laws were superseded. Science tries to build quantitative, empirical models of the event using its understanding of natural laws plus information about the physical conditions before, during, and after the event. Attempts to build empirical models meet varying degrees of success. Scientists can reach three general types of conclusions:

1. *Explainable event.* Good empirical models predict that known natural laws can explain the event. Some puzzling features might remain, but most of the event is well understood.

2. *Partially explainable event.* The best empirical models are not sufficient to explain significant elements of the event. However, based on what we have so far, we believe that known natural mechanisms are sufficient to account for the event. We believe that future improvements in knowledge, more elegant models, or more computing power will eventually allow us to prove that the event is explainable.

3. *Unexplainable event.* No known natural laws can explain the event. In fact, there are good, empirical reasons for ruling out any model that relies only on known natural laws.

Scientists spend most of their time trying to move things from the second category into the first, and occasionally from the third category into the second. Often, scientists have consensus about how much progress they've made; however, scientists don't always agree. For any particular event, there may be debates in the scientific community as to whether it is explainable, partially explainable, or unexplainable. Yet even when there are debates, the majority of scientists usually do agree. For example, most scientists agree that supernovas are explainable events (although some mysteries remain to be investigated). Most agree that the development of animals from single-celled zygotes into mature adults falls into the category of partially explainable. A few scientists argue that the origin of first life on earth (act 4) is unexplainable in terms of known natural laws, but most scientists argue that it should be considered partially explainable. Most agree that the source of the big bang (act 1) is unexplainable in terms of known natural laws.

Scientific conclusions are tentative. Events that today are deemed explainable or unexplainable could tomorrow be reclassified with the discovery of new natural laws or better empirical models.

That is about as far as science goes on its own. Beyond this point, philosophical and religious considerations make significant contributions to the discussion.

If scientists conclude that an event is scientifically unexplainable, individual scientists can reach (at least) five different conclusions about its cause: (1) an as-yet-unknown natural law is responsible for the event; (2) a supernatural event occurred; (3) superhuman technology brought about the event—that is, the event was caused by intelligent beings who are contained in and limited by our universe but with superior technology; (4) a very improbable event simply happened; or (5) a very improbable event happened, but this isn't so surprising because there are many universes and we just happen to live in the one where it happened.

A search through popular books and articles written by scientists turns up examples of each of these five types of conclusions. Although these five conclusions are very different from one another philosophically and religiously, they play virtually identical roles in *scientific* studies. Empirical science cannot distinguish among these five possibilities. Each scientist reaches conclusions based in part on their philosophical and religious preferences.

Theology tells us that God can perform miracles. Theology also warns us against too quickly reaching for God-of-the-gaps explanations. Church history and theology can push us either toward or away from explanations in terms of miracles, depending on the cases in question. Consider four examples.

John 11:1–44 tells the story of Jesus raising Lazarus from the dead. It is possible to try to explain what happened in terms of natural processes. (Perhaps Lazarus fell into a coma and was mistaken for dead.) Yet the story, taken in context, is meant to tell us about Jesus's divine authority even over death. The event occurs just before Jesus's own death and resurrection. So in this case, we have compelling theological reasons to conclude that this was a supernatural miracle.

Now consider a hypothetical example in experimental science. Suppose a scientist claims that a particular laboratory effect—for example, a 5 percent alteration in the electrical resistance of a sample of a new material—is evidence of God superseding natural laws. Few Christians would rush to embrace this claim. No matter how thoroughly and convincingly all the known natural mechanisms affecting the sample were accounted for, we would still believe that the scientist had made a mistake, or perhaps we would believe that some as-yet-undiscovered natural mechanism was at work causing the resistance change. Even if the scientist could demonstrate that the alterations in resistance occurred whenever a certain prayer was said, we would still be skeptical that it was evidence of a supernatural break in natural laws. We might believe that an intelligent agent was involved in producing the resistance change, but we would strongly suspect that this agent was the scientist or an accomplice. Theologically, we do not expect God to perform miracles on demand in the laboratory. Such behavior seems out of character for the God of the Bible. (We also note the history of charlatans performing tricks like this, giving us even more reason to be skeptical of this particular claim.)

Consider a third example. There is still a great deal we do not understand about how humans grow from single-celled fertilized zygotes, through fetal development in the womb, to babies ready to be born. The process is very complex. So many different steps have to happen in the right order for newborn babies to be healthy, with all their different organs working properly and their nervous systems and brains functioning and ready to go. We have some scientific understanding of how these things happen. We have not found any evidence that these events are, in principle, scientifically unexplainable, indicating that something miraculous happens. However, there are plenty of gaps in our knowledge. We could propose that God performs some miracles during these processes each time a new human is made, provided these miracles are subtle enough so that they do not leave evidence detectable to scientists today. Yet Christians are cautious about making such a claim. Why? One reason is that we have a sense that science will continue to advance and fill in the gaps in our current understanding. Another reason is that we do not have a strong reason from biblical exegesis to conclude that God must be doing miracles to create the body of each new human baby. Many passages talk about God's care and oversight. Psalm 139:13 praises God, "You knit me together in my mother's womb." But as we interpret these passages, we consider the type of literature of these passages, their cultural-historical context, the prescientific assumptions of the original author and audience, and the principle of God's accommodation. We have good reason to conclude that God cares for each person during their conception and development, but we do not have a strong theological reason to conclude that God must be acting *miraculously*. So although there are still many gaps in our scientific understanding of fetal development, theologically we do not expect that God has to perform supernatural miracles to aid the development of each new infant.

Finally, consider a fourth example: the formation of first life on earth (act 4). God might have chosen to design the laws of chemistry and biology so that under the conditions of the early earth, it would have been impossible for life to arise without God miraculously superseding those laws. If that is what God did, then scientific research into the origins of life should eventually come to the consensus that the formation of first life on the earth is scientifically unexplainable in terms of natural laws. However, just because scientists today do not have a detailed scientific model for the formation of first life, that does not mean that Christians ought to embrace this as potential evidence for a miracle. Just as in the hypothetical example of the resistance change in the lab, we ought to consider several scientific, theological, and experiential factors. How much scientific progress has already been made on the question of first life? What are the prospects for future scientific breakthroughs in this area? In this particular instance, do we have strong theological reasons to expect that God acted via natural laws? Alternatively, do we have theological reasons to expect that God superseded them? And on this question, we can admit to having some conflicting theological intuitions. Some Christians argue that the formation of first life is a special event, so it makes sense that God might act in a special, miraculous way. Other Christians note that the creation of living plants and animals is described in Genesis 1 in a similar manner as the creation of the sun, moon, stars, and the earth's oceans, atmosphere, and dry land—all of which we have good reason to believe God created over time using his ordinary governance of natural processes.

In cases like Lazarus being raised from the dead, theology has strong reasons for believing that a supernatural miracle occurred. In other cases, such as the hypothetical electrical resistance change in the laboratory, theology has strong reasons for being skeptical that miracles are occurring. And in cases such as first life on earth, theology can offer reasons to embrace either answer.

At Some Point, God Began to Give Special Revelation to Our Ancestors

At some point during act 6, God began a new kind of relationship with our ancestors. At some point in history—before Isaiah, before Moses, before Abraham, and perhaps even long before humans began writing things on papyrus or clay—God began giving "special revelation" to our ancestors. Special revelation is knowledge about God and spiritual matters that comes through God's supernatural activity. God can communicate through audible words and visible signs, as he did with Moses and the burning bush. God can communicate with visions, as he did with Abram in Genesis 15. God can communicate through inspired words and actions of humans accompanied by the inner testimony of the Holy Spirit, as he did with prophets and priests throughout history. As the Old and New Testament show, special revelation can come in many forms. We don't know exactly when or how God began to communicate in this way with our earliest ancestors. Several scenarios, and their theological pros and cons, are discussed in chapters 4, 5, and 9.

3

Suffering and Death
before Humans

WAS THERE ANIMAL SUFFERING AND DEATH before humans sinned? If so, how do we fit that into a biblical understanding of God creating the world "very good"?

Theologians make a distinction between moral evil and natural evil. Moral evil can be defined as evil that results from people making sinful moral choices that hurt others and themselves. Natural evil is a name for things like earthquakes, parasites, and diseases—things that hurt, destroy, and kill but are not caused by an individual's choices.

Not Everything That Annoys or Hurts Us Is a Result of the Fall and the Curse

When considering the origin of suffering, one place Christians look is Genesis 3. Adam and Eve eat of the fruit of the tree of the knowledge of good and evil in disobedience to God's commands. The "curse," as it's sometimes called, comes immediately after, in verses 14–19:

The Lord God said to the serpent,

> "Because you have done this,
>   cursed are you among all animals
>   and among all wild creatures;
> upon your belly you shall go,
>   and dust you shall eat
>   all the days of your life.
> I will put enmity between you and the woman,
>   and between your offspring and hers;
> he will strike your head,
>   and you will strike his heel."

To the woman he said,

> "I will greatly increase your pangs in childbearing;
>   in pain you shall bring forth children,
> yet your desire shall be for your husband,
>   and he shall rule over you."

And to the man he said,

> "Because you have listened to the voice of your wife,
>   and have eaten of the tree
> about which I commanded you,
>   'You shall not eat of it,'
> cursed is the ground because of you;
>   in toil you shall eat of it all the days of your life;
> thorns and thistles it shall bring forth for you;
>   and you shall eat the plants of the field.
> By the sweat of your face
>   you shall eat bread
> until you return to the ground,
>   for out of it you were taken;
> you are dust,
>   and to dust you shall return." (NRSV)

These verses have stimulated much speculation regarding how much the created world changed at the time of the fall and the curse. With the development of modern science, Christians have sometimes asked this question using scientific language. Were the fundamental laws of nature radically changed when humanity rebelled against God? Or were the fundamental laws of nature left the same, with the effects of humanity's rebellion limited primarily to changes in human beings—changes in how we relate to God, how we relate to one another, and how we relate to the natural world?

Many things in the world annoy or hurt us. It's tempting to believe that God created the world as a place where humans would be utterly free of any harm or even annoyance. If so, then anything that annoys or hurts us today could be blamed on the fall and the curse. For example, there's a low spot in my garage. When snow melts off my car, it drains to that low spot and makes a big puddle exactly between the car and the door into the house. More often than not on winter days, I must walk around a big puddle in the most inconvenient place in the garage. Why is there an annoying low spot in my garage floor? Is it due to the fall? Maybe the person who poured the concrete was sinfully lazy. Maybe, but probably not. It's more likely that the dirt underneath that particular spot was just a bit softer than the surrounding dirt, it therefore sank a little more after the concrete was poured, and the person who poured the concrete couldn't have known. That low spot in my garage floor is just part of the natural operation of creation. Maybe the puddle in my garage isn't a result of the fall. Maybe the fact that the puddle annoys me so much, however, is a result of the fall.

What about earthquakes? What about mosquitoes? What about pain? What about parasites and disease? Theology raises these questions. Science not only helps us understand how the natural world operates today; it also gives us information about natural history. Therefore, science can provide theology with some useful information regarding these particular questions.

Entropy

Imagine watching a movie of sixteen billiard balls moving and colliding on a table. Assuming there was no friction to slow the balls, they would just keep moving and colliding, and you wouldn't be able to tell if the movie was running forward or backward. The laws of nature that describe those collisions look the same forward and backward in time. But if the movie ever showed the fifteen numbered balls meeting in a triangular shape at rest at one spot on the table, with the cue ball moving rapidly away, you would strongly suspect that the movie was running backward. You're not surprised if a cue ball hitting fifteen stationary balls causes those fifteen balls to change from an orderly state, all sitting at rest in a neat shape, to a disorderly state, all moving around in many speeds and directions. But you would be very surprised if collisions caused fifteen balls to spontaneously change from a disorderly state to an orderly state, with all sitting at rest in a neat shape.

Natural systems often change from an ordered state (low entropy) to a disordered state (high entropy); however, it is extremely improbable for them spontaneously to go the other way. "Entropy" is a mathematical measure of the disorder of matter and energy. (More technically, it is a measure of how many distinct ways a set amount of particles and energy can be arranged.) The second law of thermodynamics says that the entropy of the universe or any closed subsystem of the universe doesn't decrease but only remains constant or increases.

Even living systems, which can become more complex and orderly over time, follow the second law of thermodynamics. Plants take in orderly sunlight energy and simple molecules from the air and soil, build more complex molecules, and expel disorderly waste heat and molecules. Cells in our bodies do something similar using the orderly chemical energy stored in food molecules. Some open systems, like cells, can become more ordered locally, but only by increasing the total entropy of the universe as a whole.

At first impression, the second law of thermodynamics sounds like a bad thing. It implies that closed natural systems (and the universe as a whole) are always changing from order to disorder. But the second law of thermodynamics is an inevitable statistical result of the fact that there are many particles moving and interacting with one another. Consider the billiard ball example. If sixteen balls are moving around and colliding randomly, statistically, it is extremely unlikely that they will all collide in just the right way to make an orderly pattern. However, it is statistically very likely that such collisions will turn an orderly arrangement into a disorderly one. The second law of thermodynamics is connected to the simple statistical fact that when there are many different particles interacting, there are many more disorderly ways to arrange them than orderly ways. We depend on this fact with every breath we take. Right now, supposing that you're indoors, the air molecules in the room with you are distributed randomly and evenly. They are moving randomly in every direction. In other words, the air molecules in the room are in a state of high entropy. It is extremely unlikely that, by randomly colliding with one another, all the air molecules will suddenly wind up together in the western half of the room. And that's a good thing if you're sitting in the eastern half of the room.

The second law of thermodynamics plays a vital role in many natural processes that we would call good. When heat spontaneously flows from a hot object to a cold object, entropy increases. When a flower opens and its scent diffuses into the air so that the whole area is perfumed and bees can be guided to the blossom, entropy increases. When our sun converts nuclear energy into sunlight, entropy increases. When ice melts, entropy increases. When winds blow and rain falls, entropy increases. When oxygen passes from our lungs into our bloodstreams, entropy increases. When we see and hear things and store memories in our brains, entropy increases. The second law of thermodynamics appears to be part of God's good creation and God's original intention for the world.

Entropy can't increase forever. After a very long time, all the energy in the universe will be converted to disorderly energy. Our sun should burn for a few billion years, but eventually it will burn out. If the laws of nature keep on working the way they always have, eventually all the stars will burn out and it won't be possible for any new stars to be born. Eventually, all the hot parts of the universe will come into equilibrium with the cold parts. Everything will be the same temperature. No more change in any meaningful sense of the word will be able to happen. If the universe keeps going on long enough the way it has been, eventually it won't be able to support life. Entropy will be at a maximum, and the universe will grind down to a very boring conclusion. This is sometimes called the "heat death" of the universe.

Does science's prediction of the heat death of our universe create a theological problem? If we think that this universe is all there is, we seem to have a theological problem. However, Scripture doesn't teach that this universe was meant to be a permanent dwelling for humanity. Christians place their ultimate hope in the promises God makes in Scripture about a resurrection and a renewed creation. Christians have always believed that this world isn't permanent. All of God's creatures are finite. We are finite in space and finite in time. The second law of thermodynamics tells us that this whole universe is also finite in time, just like all of God's creatures. But God promises that the end of life in this universe, or the end of this universe itself, is not the end for us. A new creation awaits.

The Fundamental Laws of Physics Haven't Changed Since Creation

Entropy and the second law of thermodynamics are inevitable consequences of the basic laws of nature as they now operate. But what if the basic laws of nature changed with the fall and the curse? Some Christians have supported this idea with references to Genesis 3:14–19 and Romans 8:20–21. The latter reads, "For the creation was subjected to frustration, not by its own choice, but by the will of the one who subjected it, in hope that the creation itself will be liberated from its bondage to decay and brought into the freedom and glory of the children of God."

But another possible interpretation is that the effects of the fall and the curse are not broadly applied to the basic functioning of all creation but are limited primarily to humanity and our relationships to God, one another, and the rest of creation. The surrounding context of Romans 8 shows that the passage is about human beings—about our transformation through Christ, from being in bondage to sin to becoming children of God. Creation is frustrated now because humans are not playing their proper role of sinless image bearers of God and stewards of creation. C. John Collins argues on the basis of other Old Testament blessings and curses (e.g., Deut. 28:16–17) that Genesis 3 does not teach that the properties of the ground or plants changed because of humanity's sin; instead, God uses the properties he gave the ground and plants to discipline sinful humans.[1] Other Bible passages support the idea that the fall and the curse did not radically rewrite all the laws of nature. Jeremiah 33:20–26 talks about God's "covenant with day and night and . . . the laws of heaven and earth" (v. 25). God appears to be keeping this covenant with the natural world today in the same way that he did before the fall and the curse. And Psalm 19:1, "The heavens declare the glory of God; the skies proclaim the work of his hands," teaches that creation today still proclaims God's glory.

So did the fall and the curse cause a radical rewriting of the laws of nature, or were their effects more limited, confined more or less to a human scale? We have at least two interpretations of Genesis 3:14–19; each can find support in other parts of Scripture. Since this is a question about the natural world, it's the sort of question on which science may be able to give some useful information to theology. And in this case, scientific data points in a clear direction.

Astronomers have found that the light from each star contains detailed information about the natural laws at work in the star, including laws for gravity, pressure, the quantum mechanical behavior of atoms, electromagnetism, and the speed of light. When scientists compare the light from our sun, nearby stars, and the most distant stars, they see exactly the same fundamental laws of nature in operation in every case. This is an amazing discovery, one worth celebrating. By carefully studying the light from distant stars, astronomers have discovered that everything in the universe, including even the most distant galaxies, is made of exactly the same atoms obeying exactly the same laws of nature that operate here on Earth.

Because light takes time to travel, the light we see today left those distant stars millions or even billions of years ago. The light we see today shows us what the fundamental laws of nature were like in the distant past when the light was emitted. Since all distant stars show the same laws of physics as nearby stars, this is clear evidence that the laws of nature did not radically change at some point in the past.

1. C. John Collins, *Science and Faith: Friends or Foes?* (Wheaton: Crossway, 2003), 150–51.

Geologists have similar evidence. When they study rocks, they are also studying the fundamental laws of nature that were in operation when those rocks were made. They can compare rocks made recently with the oldest rocks on earth. These comparisons show that exactly the same laws of nature were in operation in every case. Like astronomers, geologists also see clear evidence that the laws of nature have not radically changed in the past.

Could the Fundamental Laws of Nature Be Different because of the Fall?

Some Christians suggest that when humans fell into sin, God caused the effects of the fall to propagate backward in time, in some sense changing the laws of nature back to the beginning of time, so that the laws of nature operating in the universe are different from what they would have been had humanity not fallen into sin. Another, similar, suggestion is that the fall of Satan is somehow responsible for changing the laws of nature operating in the universe since its beginning. Neither of these ideas can be disproven scientifically, but both raise some significant theological and scientific difficulties.

Theologically, these proposals suggest that the force of evil had tremendous influence in shaping creation, down to even the most fundamental levels, almost making evil a cocreator with God. It is conceivable that God, in order to achieve some higher good, might permit such a radical influence of evil at all levels of creation going back to its beginning. While skirting the edges of Manichaeism,[2] these proposals do not necessarily fall outside the scope of orthodox Christian theology. However, as this chapter discusses later, these proposals are difficult to reconcile with numerous verses in the Psalms and in the book of Job in which God takes credit for creating things in the natural world that sometimes harm humans.

Scientifically, it is difficult to imagine how the laws of physics in our universe could be subtly altered in a way that would eliminate destruction and suffering. Scientists have learned that the laws of physics are very finely tuned to make possible the formation of stars and planets and the growth of trees, flowers, insects, and all sorts of beautiful things. Simply tweaking the laws of physics a bit—maybe changing the mass of hydrogen atoms or the strength of gravity—will not produce a universe that keeps all those beautiful things but eliminates things like entropy, earthquakes, or mosquitoes. In particular, the second law of thermodynamics appears to be a statistically inevitable result in any system

2. The early church rejected the religion and philosophy of Manichaeism, which teaches that good and evil are both eternal powers, both involved in shaping the creation of this world.

in which large numbers of particles move and interact. Having a creation in which the fundamental laws of nature wouldn't allow for entropy, earthquakes, or mosquitoes but would allow for all the things we like about stars, planets, and life would require not just a few tweaks to the laws of nature—it would require a complete rewrite of the laws of nature on a different basis.

Earthquakes

In 1755, a great earthquake near Lisbon killed nearly 50,000 people. It happened on a Sunday at a time when many were in church, which probably greatly increased the death toll. Terrible destructive events have prompted theologians over the centuries to wrestle with difficult questions about the relationship between God, sin, and natural disasters. Looking scientifically at the natural causes for such disasters provides some helpful information for theologians.

Earthquakes are caused by tectonic plates bumping into and rubbing against one another. These plates move because of the motion of the mantle underneath them. The mantle rock moves in convection cycles. These convection cycles are a result of the basic laws of thermodynamics and the material properties of the mantel. Given how the earth is constructed and the basic laws of nature, earthquakes are inevitable.

The motion of tectonic plates is part of a good system. It creates a wide variety of ecological niches—deep oceans, shallow oceans, shores, flat plains, hills, and mountains. All of these different ecological niches allow a vast variety of plants and animals to exist. Moreover, rain and wind are constantly washing fertile soil and nutrients into the ocean. Over time, this would turn all ground into barren rock that couldn't support life. The motion of the tectonic plates constantly brings new nutrients up from below ground to the surface. This motion, while causing earthquakes, is also necessary for life to exist on land.

Physicist and theologian John Polkinghorne, writing in 2011, affirmed the answer of theologian Austin Farrer (1904–68) in response to a question about what God's will could have been in the 1755 Lisbon earthquake. "The will of God in the event [earthquake] is his will for the elements of the earth's crust or under it: his will that they should go on being themselves and acting in accordance with their natures."[3]

Earthquakes, like entropy, are an inevitable result of matter simply doing its thing, behaving according to the fundamental laws of nature that God

---

3. Austin Marsden Farrer, "A Science of God?," in John C. Polkinghorne, *Science and Providence: God's Interaction with the World* (Conshohocken, PA: Templeton Foundation Press, 2011), 67.

ordained. Earthquakes, like entropy, are part of a bigger system that, it turns out, is necessary for life to exist. In order to have life on earth and not have earthquakes, God would continually have to override the laws of nature or else change the laws of nature entirely.

In light of this, instead of looking for answers to the question "Why did God directly cause the 1755 Lisbon earthquake?" we are prompted to look for answers to a different question: "Why didn't God miraculously prevent the 1755 Lisbon earthquake or the suffering it caused?" Because of the devastation, pain, and death caused by that earthquake and other disasters, this is still an important theological question. Some possible answers are explored in the remainder of this chapter and in chapter 10, although we might never have an answer that fully satisfies us.

Mosquitoes, Weeds, Mutations, and Disease

Mosquitoes annoy us. They are, however, well adapted to their ecological niche, just like the insects we enjoy, like butterflies and ladybugs. Weeds growing through the sidewalk might annoy us and make our property look ugly. But consider lichen, which can cling to bare rock on cliffs and grow where nothing else can. As lichen grows, it slowly turns bare rock into fertile soil that can support other plants. Whenever I see lichen growing on otherwise bare rock, I celebrate how robust life can be, fitting into all sorts of ecological niches, holding on and growing tenaciously. Crabgrass and dandelions spoiling our sidewalks and lichen turning rock into fertile soil are following the same laws of nature. They are displaying the same hardiness and robustness of life. They are all part of a package.

The symbiosis between flowering plants and pollinating insects seems beautiful to us. Each provides the other with something it needs to survive. But what about parasites, such as the wasps that lay their eggs inside other animals so that their larvae can eat the host animal from the inside? That seems ugly. But again, when we study these systems scientifically, they seem to be part of a package deal. The same laws of nature that allow beautiful symbiosis to develop between two species also allow parasitism to develop. Given the laws of nature that God designed, if we're going to have one, it seems like we're also going to have the other.

When we study biology microscopically, the same package deal appears. Some bacteria, such as the bacteria that allow termites to digest wood, are symbiotic and helpful to their host animals. Some bacteria are neutral to their host animals. And some bacteria cause harmful diseases that sicken and sometimes kill their hosts. It looks like it's been this way throughout the history of life on earth. The fossil record tells us that there were diseases and parasites and predators on the earth long before humanity existed.

There is a similar package deal when it comes to genetic mutations. Some genetic mutations cause animals to be born deformed, unable to survive. However, as we saw in the previous chapter, mutations also allow species to adapt to changing or new environments. Mutations allow the diversity of living organisms to increase. Over time, mutations allow for the development of complex, beautiful ecosystems. And at a fundamental level, a certain frequency of mutations is an inevitable result of the laws of physics and chemistry acting on DNA molecules.

When a living cell in a body is working properly, it has mechanisms for repair and reproduction. Those very same processes are at work, obeying the very same laws of nature, when a few of those mechanisms subtly change and a cell becomes cancerous. Again, our scientific understanding of the fundamental laws of nature seems to imply that we have a package deal.

So mutations allow for adaptation and diversity, and mutations allow for deformity and disease. With symbiosis, we also get parasitism. With mechanisms for living cells to repair and reproduce, we have the possibility of cancer. Given the fundamental laws of nature in the universe, it seems that we can't have one without the other—unless, of course, God were to constantly and miraculously intervene whenever something might hurt us. But the idea that God would create the universe to operate under a set of laws and then constantly intervene miraculously to fix anything hurtful would raise some serious theological questions about what it means to say that God created the world "very good" in the first place.

Pain

There is abundant scientific evidence that animals experience pain. The similarities in the nervous systems of mammals, birds, reptiles, and other animals suggest that animal experience of pain goes far back in evolutionary history. Our ancestors, even before they could sin, knew and experienced pain in some fashion.

Genesis 2–3 does not suggest that humans had an utterly pain-free existence prior to sin. In Genesis 3, after Adam and Eve sinned, God said to Eve, "I will greatly increase your pangs in childbearing; in pain you shall bring forth children" (3:16 NRSV). The word "increase" implies that Adam and Eve already understood what pain was.

Philip Yancey has written about pain as a good and necessary system that God created. In his book *Where Is God When It Hurts?*,[4] Yancey describes how pain alerts us to parts of our bodies that are in danger or need attention. Animals and humans who can't feel pain (for example, patients suffering from leprosy) injure themselves and are not aware of the injuries, leading to further medical complications. Yancey concludes that pain was created as part of a finely crafted system to help us avoid injury and treat illness. Yancey wrote the following for *Christianity Today*:

> Pain is good. Pain is bad. Pain can be redeemed. . . . My work with leprosy specialist Dr. Paul Brand has convinced me beyond doubt that the pain system is one of the most remarkable engineering feats in the human body. Take away its exquisitely tuned warnings, and you get people who destroy themselves— the problem of leprosy, precisely. Yet pain is also bad, or "fallen." Working in a hospice, my wife sees daily the ravaging effects of pain that no longer has a useful purpose; to the dying patient, pain warnings may seem like the jeers of a cosmic sadist. Even so, pain can be redeemed. The dying, individual leprosy patients, and people like Joni Eareckson Tada who live with permanent afflictions have demonstrated to me that out of the worst that life offers, great good may come.[5]

Animal Death prior to Human Sin

Even before there was scientific evidence that the earth was billions of years old, theologians discussed, purely on the basis of Scripture, the question of whether there was animal death before the fall. Scripture passages that discuss death as a consequence of sin (Gen. 2:16–17; 3:19, 22; Rom. 5:12–21; 1 Cor. 15) clearly refer to humans, but it is unclear whether they also refer to animals. Some proposed that animals would have been immortal if Adam and Eve had not sinned, pointing to prophetic passages such as Isaiah 11:6–7 and 65:25 that refer to predatory animals like bears and lions living peacefully with cows and lambs. These passages clearly point to future messianic times, and in the New Testament period they are thought of as pointing to the new heaven and the new earth, referred to in Revelation, that are to appear with Jesus's second coming. Some argued, however, that these passages also describe life on earth before human sin.[6]

4. Philip Yancey, *Where Is God When It Hurts?* (Grand Rapids: Zondervan, 1997).
5. Philip Yancey, "Back Page," *Christianity Today*, September 11, 1995, 96.
6. Among church fathers, see Irenaeus of Lyons (c. AD 130–202), *Adversus haereses* 5.33; and Theophilus, bishop of Antioch (Syria) (died c. AD 183), *Ad Autolycum* 2.17.

Others argued that these verses of Isaiah should be applied only to the new heaven and the new earth. They argued that a limited life span and physical death are a natural part of animals' creaturely existence on this earth.[7] Job 38:39–40 and Psalm 104:21 refer to God providing prey for predatory animals, implying that God intended from the beginning for animals to die and make way for new generations. Moreover, the new heaven and the new earth described in Revelation 21–22 are not simply a restoration of this creation to its state prior to human sin. For example, marriage is considered a good part of this creation, but Jesus taught that those "taking part in the age to come and in the resurrection from the dead will neither marry nor be given in marriage" (Luke 20:35). Revelation 21:23 describes the new Jerusalem as a place that does not need the sun or the moon, "for the glory of God gives it light, and the Lamb is its lamp." Revelation 21:1 describes the new earth as no longer having a sea. Recall that in the minds of biblical writers, the sea was connected to the primeval "watery deep"—dark, formless, and empty (Gen. 1:2)—which God structured to make this creation. To the original readers of Revelation 21:1, no longer having a sea probably implied, like the rest of chapters 21–22, God's presence permeating every part of the new heaven and the new earth.

Since Scripture is unclear on the subject of animal death prior to humanity's sin, and since theologians have offered competing interpretations that can be reconciled with the rest of Scripture, this seems to be another situation in which we can look to God's revelation in nature to see if it can provide useful information. It can. The abundant scientific evidence for an old earth and the long history of life on earth clearly indicate that death was a natural part of both animal and plant existence from the beginning.

The death of animals and plants is part of a larger system. If animals and plants didn't die, there wouldn't be room for new generations to grow and thrive. Reproduction would have to stop, or the earth would soon be overfull. Without death and reproduction, animal and plant species couldn't genetically adapt to environmental changes. Evidence from the natural world implies that God has created animals and plants to be finite, not eternal. Thus, animal and plant death plays a role in a good system in which one generation gives way to another, species adapt, and ecosystems can become more complex and filled with a greater variety of creatures over time.

Centuries before modern science, Augustine summed up the argument that God chose to create animals and plants to be finite in time. Change, decay, and death are natural for earthly creatures.

---

7. Among church fathers, see Basil of Caesarea (329–79), *Hexaemeron* 9.2; and Augustine, *The City of God* 12.4, https://www.ccel.org/ccel/schaff/npnf102.iv.XII.4.html.

But it is ridiculous to condemn the faults of beasts and trees, and other such mortal and mutable things as are void of intelligence, sensation, or life, even though these faults should destroy their corruptible nature; for these creatures received, at their Creator's will, an existence fitting them, by passing away and giving place to others, to secure that lowest form of beauty, the beauty of seasons, which in its own place is a requisite part of this world. For things earthly were neither to be made equal to things heavenly, nor were they, though inferior, to be quite omitted from the universe. Since, then, in those situations where such things are appropriate, some perish to make way for others that are born in their room, and the less succumb to the greater, and the things that are overcome are transformed into the quality of those that have the mastery, this is the appointed order of things transitory. Of this order the beauty does not strike us, because by our mortal frailty we are so involved in a part of it, that we cannot perceive the whole, in which these fragments that offend us are harmonized with the most accurate fitness and beauty. And therefore, where we are not so well able to perceive the wisdom of the Creator, we are very properly enjoined to believe it, lest in the vanity of human rashness we presume to find any fault with the work of so great an Artificer.[8]

"Natural" Mortality of Our Human Ancestors

Our prehuman primate ancestors, like other animals, would have been naturally mortal. How does this relate to what Scripture teaches about the relationship between sin and human death? This is discussed in more detail in chapter 9, but we should address it briefly here.

On the subject of human death, the Bible talks in many places about death as a consequence of sin, but even on this topic, there are several interpretations. One interpretation is that the passages that name death as a consequence of sin, such as Romans 5:12–21 and Genesis 2:17, refer only to "spiritual death" (spiritual separation from God), not to physical death. In Genesis 2:17, God tells Adam and Eve, "But you must not eat from the tree of the knowledge of good and evil, for when you eat from it you will certainly die." Adam and Eve did not physically die shortly after disobeying God, although they were separated from God spiritually. This interpretation can be supported by passages such as Colossians 2:13 and Ephesians 2:1–3, where the apostle Paul tells his readers that they were "dead in their sins" before being made alive in Christ through the forgiveness of sins.

But another common interpretation of Scripture is that human physical death, as well as spiritual death, is a consequence of sin. In 1 Corinthians

---

8. Augustine, *The City of God* 12.4, https://www.ccel.org/ccel/schaff/npnf102.iv.XII.4.html.

15:21–22, Paul states that death (physical death is strongly implied) came through the sin of Adam. Verse 26 speaks of physical death as "the last enemy to be destroyed." For those holding this interpretation, there is still potential disagreement about the original physical state of humans. Was physical immortality built in to human bodies from the beginning and taken away when they sinned, or were humans created mortal but with physical immortality a potential gift that humans could have received if they had chosen not to sin? If the first humans were created physically immortal, they would have had bodies that didn't age and could overcome all disease and injury. If they had only the potential for immortality, the first humans could have had bodies similar to our own, bodies that could become immortal only by God's miraculous action. In Genesis 2–3, the presence of the tree of life in the garden of Eden favors the second interpretation. The tree of life was in the garden before Adam and Eve sinned (Gen. 2:9). If Adam and Eve were naturally immortal before the fall, then the purpose of the tree of life in the garden is not obvious. The presence of the tree of life makes the most sense if Adam and Eve were mortal and needed something else to grant them immortality. However symbolically or literally we interpret the garden and the tree, the tree of life seems to represent a potential for physical immortality, as a gift that was lost when they sinned. The tree of life appears again in Revelation 22 on the new earth, where death has been abolished. This implies that, through Christ, God's ultimate plan of human immortality will be fulfilled in the new creation.

We will return to this theological discussion in chapter 9. For now, consider what additional information we can get from studying the natural world scientifically. From studying our bodies, it is difficult to imagine how human bodies would function if they had built-in physical immortality. Our bodies today grow old and respond to disease and injury much like those of other creatures. The human immune system for fighting disease is very similar to that of other animals. Humans and animals have only a limited ability to repair injury. A physical body that could recover from any injury or disease would have to be constructed on principles entirely different from those governing our current bodies. Aging itself is built in to our DNA; our very cells wear out and die. To make human bodies immortal would require more than a few minor changes to our present bodies; it would require a complete reconstruction with fundamentally different processes in place. In fact, there seems to be no physical object in this created universe that is built to last forever. Mountains erode, continents shift, and the sun does not have enough fuel to shine forever. The natural processes God designed do not seem to support immortality in this creation. True immortality seems to be something for the next creation. Immortality, in this creation or the next, is possible only by God's miraculous and gracious action.

The Fall, Natural Evil, and Romans 8

Our scientific study of the natural world has told us some important things about earthquakes and disease and parasites—things we might call "natural evils." First, they were part of the created world long before humans existed or sinned. Second, they seem to be an inevitable consequence of how the laws of nature operate. Third, those fundamental laws of nature have not changed during the history of the universe. Fourth, although individual earthquakes and diseases and parasites cause pain and death, they are results of a larger system that on the whole is beautiful, complex, and life sustaining.

This implies that the fall is not to blame for their existence. It appears that the fall has much more to do with our attitude toward and response to these things. When something annoys or hurts us, how do we react toward God or toward one another? Does natural evil drive us to be more loving or more selfish? Does it drive us closer to God or away from God? If we examine ourselves—how we react toward others and toward God when things annoy or hurt us—we will certainly see evidence of our sinfulness.

What, then, does it mean that creation "was subjected to frustration" (Rom. 8:20)? There is, of course, the sinful human abuse of creation. We harm the environment, selfishly and unnecessarily destroying species and ecosystems. In addition, humans, as the most powerful and intelligent beings on the earth, are supposed to be the voice of creation. The rest of creation is our home, and we are supposed to be God's image bearers within creation, personally praising God and living in right relationship with God. We are not doing our job. Therefore, the rest of creation cannot praise and serve God as it was intended to do.

Natural Evil and the Book of Job

In Job 1–2, Job suffers attacks caused by both moral and natural evil. Thieving raiders, natural disasters, and disease take Job's possessions, children, and health. What Job doesn't know—but we, the readers, do know—is that Job is being attacked by a spiritual enemy. An accuser has told God that human beings cannot be good just for the sake of being good. The accusation claims that humans are good only because God is good to them—in other words, that humans are good only for selfish reasons. At stake is the very idea that humans are redeemable and that we can be good for the right reasons instead of just for what we get out of it. It appears that God chooses to refute the accusation by allowing Job to suffer evil in order to show that a human can be good even when getting nothing out of it.

When a righteous person suffers undeserved attacks, caused by both moral and natural evil, how should they respond? The next chapters show three responses. First, Job's wife says that Job should stop being righteous. "Curse God and die," she says. Job rejects that idea. Second, Job's friends tell him, "If you're suffering, you must have done something wrong. That's how God always works. If you do good, you prosper; if you do evil, God makes you suffer." Both Job and God reject that idea. Job himself gives a third response to suffering. Job essentially says, "God is attacking me unjustly, and I can't do anything about it." After this goes on for a while, God finally replies to Job in chapters 38–41.

Interestingly, God doesn't tell Job about the original accusation. God doesn't tell Job that he's suffering in order to prove a spiritual point, that humanity can be redeemed. What does God say to Job? God points to the chaotic, primeval waters of creation and the boundaries that God set on those waters. God then asks Job, "Can you do that?" God points to the places of darkness under the earth—the springs of the sea and the gates of death—and says, "Have you been there?" God points to lightning and storm, to the desert wilderness, and to wild and untamable animals like mountain goats and ostriches and predatory eagles and lions, and God says, "Do you understand these things? Can you take care of them?" God points to land and sea monsters called behemoth and leviathan and says, "Can you handle them?"

In the ancient worldview of Job's time, these things—the edges of the earth, the dark places, the desert wilderness, wild animals, and primeval monsters like behemoth and leviathan—were considered not only physically dangerous but also spiritually dangerous. In pagan religions of that time, these things were literally gods-forsaken, spiritual figures or forces in opposition to the gods. In contrast, both the book of Job and Genesis 1 say that these wild things are under God's control. In the book of Job, God makes another point. While these wild things are under God's control, they are not under Job's control. Dangerous, wild, chaotic things are not gone. They exist, and they are dangerous to humans, but they are under God's control.[9]

9. For more discussion on these themes in Job, see Tremper Longman III, *Job*, Baker Commentary on the Old Testament (Grand Rapids: Baker Academic, 2012); Tom McLeish, *Faith and Wisdom in Science* (Oxford: Oxford University Press, 2014); and Richard F. Carlson and Jason N. Hine, "Two Interlocking Stories: Job and Natural Evil and Modern Science and Randomness," *Perspectives on Science and Christian Faith* 66, no. 1 (2014): 23–35.

Job accused God of attacking him unjustly and causing his suffering. God responds by pointing to all the powerful, wild, and dangerous places in creation and saying, "These things are under my rule, but not yours. They serve my purposes, not yours." After hearing this, Job stops accusing God.

Themes of Order and Non-order in Genesis

Old Testament scholars have noted that when God brings order out of non-order in Genesis 1, some non-order remains. John Walton writes:

> In Genesis 1:2, the state of the cosmos at the beginning of the story is that nothing is yet functioning as it should. This non-ordered state serves as the canvas for the creative acts that bring a semblance of order to the cosmos. . . . God's creative work is defined as bringing order to this non-ordered existence. This will be carried out in stages through a process. Even as God brought order, there were aspects of non-order that remained. There was still a sea (though its borders had been set); there was still darkness. There was an outside the garden that was less ordered than inside the garden. . . . This initial ordering would not have eliminated natural disasters, pain, or death. We do not have to think of these as part of the ordered world, though they are not beyond God's control, and often they can be identified with positive results. All non-order will not be resolved until the new creation. In Revelation 21 we are told that there will be "no longer any sea" (Rev. 21:1), no pain or death (21:4) and no darkness (21:23–25). There is no temple because God's presence will pervade all of it (21:3, 22).[10]

Why Would Creation Include Things That Can Hurt and Destroy?

We might ask, "Why would God create a world with wild and dangerous things?" Scripture doesn't give us a simple answer. Theologians and philosophers have offered some possible explanations.

In answer to a related question, "Why does God permit moral evil?" some offer what is called the "free will defense."[11] God hates moral evil, but God values human free will. God chooses not to interfere with the free will of people when they choose to do harmful evil. Human free will is so important that God is willing to tolerate morally evil actions. God's ultimate answer to

10. John H. Walton, *The Lost World of Adam and Eve* (Downers Grove, IL: InterVarsity, 2015), 149–50.
11. For example, see Alvin Plantinga, *God, Freedom, and Evil* (Grand Rapids: Eerdmans, 1977), 30.

moral evil is not to crush our free will; rather, it is found in the incarnation, life, death, and resurrection of Jesus.

If the free will defense is a reasonable answer to the question of why God permits *moral* evil, the "free process defense" has been offered by some theologians as an answer to the question of why God permits *natural* evil.[12] God loves creation enough to give it the freedom to do what it was created to do, without God continually overriding it. God created the good processes of tectonic plate motion that foster life on earth, and God lets the plates move even though the resulting earthquakes sometimes hurt and kill. God created a wonderful living world full of amazing biological processes of life, reproduction, and adaptation, and God lets them do their thing, even though they sometimes result in parasites and disease.

And perhaps a certain amount of natural evil is necessary in this world if it is to be the home of human beings who have free will. Perhaps in order to have the ability to choose between good and evil, humans have to see good things and bad things happen in the world and understand how their own free choices can have good or bad consequences for other people. Perhaps God's choice to create humans using evolutionary processes (discussed in the next chapter) required the amount of natural good and natural evil we see in the world today and throughout natural history. This idea is discussed further in chapter 10.

Job didn't get a complete answer from God that explained all of his suffering, and neither do we. However, because Scripture tells us in many more ways, and in many eloquent ways, that God is merciful and has our best interests at heart, we take the rest on faith. We believe that God has all the processes that cause natural evil under his control and that these processes serve his purposes, even if they don't serve our human desires. And we are reminded that the ultimate hope for justice and peace comes not in this world but in God's promise of a resurrection and a new creation.

Wildness and "Subduing the Earth"

Should we simply resign ourselves to living with natural evil? Does all of this make natural evil "good"? And does this mean we should expect natural evil to be part of God's new creation after the resurrection?

First, even if natural evil is a natural part of this creation, it won't necessarily be part of God's new creation. Even some good things that are part of God's created order now (such as marriage) won't be repeated in the new

---

12. For example, see Polkinghorne, *Science and Providence*.

creation. Moreover, the imagery of the new creation in Isaiah and Revelation suggests a new creation that ends violence and death, with the tree of life and the close presence of God at all times.

As for our present world, even if we conclude that parasites, harmful mutations, disease, and earthquakes are a natural part of this world, we don't need to be resigned to them. They don't seem to have been caused by humanity's sin, and they may be parts of a very good system, but we don't need to call them "good" in and of themselves.

Genesis 1:28 offers another theological category for these things. Before humanity's fall into sin, God gave humanity what is called the "cultural mandate." God commands humans to "be fruitful and multiply, fill the earth and subdue it." Biblical scholars tell us that the Hebrew word translated "subdue" is not a wimpy word. D. C. Spanner writes,

> The mandate given to man in Genesis 1:28 which reads, "Be fruitful and multiply, and fill the earth and subdue it; and have dominion . . . over every living thing" . . . charged man with "subduing" the earth. The Hebrew word for "subdue" is *kabas*, and in all its other occurrences in Scripture (about twelve in all) it is used as a term indicating strong action in the face of opposition, enmity or evil. Thus, the land of Canaan was "subdued" before Israel, though the Canaanites had chariots of iron (Josh. 17:8; 18:1); weapons of war are "subdued," so are iniquities (Zech. 9:15; Mic. 7:19). The word is never used in a mild sense. It indicates, I believe, that Adam was sent into a world where *not* all was sweetness and light, for in such a world what would there be to subdue? The animals, it suggests, included some that were wild and ferocious; and Adam was charged to exercise a genuinely civilizing role and to promote harmony among them.[13]

To get a sense of how the word "subdue" is used elsewhere in Scripture, we can survey how it is translated in other passages. In the King James Version, the Hebrew *kabas* is translated as "bondage" (Neh. 5:5), "force" (Esther 7:8), "subdue" (Gen. 1:28; Mic. 7:19; Zech. 9:15), "subdued" (Num. 32:22, 29; Josh. 18:1; 2 Sam. 8:11; 1 Chron. 22:18), "subjection" (Jer. 34:11, 16), and "under" (2 Chron. 28:10).[14]

Genesis 2 speaks of a garden. Today we think of gardens as open places, but in the ancient Near East, gardens were usually walled enclosures, places of refuge from the outside world. God created a world with a lot of *wildness*

---

13. Douglas Clemant Spanner, *Biblical Creation and the Theory of Evolution* (Milton Keynes, UK: Paternoster, 1987), http://www.creationandevolution.co.uk/the_primal.htm.

14. See the online King James Bible Hebrew concordance entry, under "kabash," at www.htmlbible.com/sacrednamebiblecom/kjvstrongs/CONHEB353.htm#S3540.

in it. This might not be how we humans would have created the world for our own comfort, but it is what God chose to create and call good. God made a world that is a good and fitting home for humanity, and God commissioned us as stewards over it. This home includes challenges to subdue.

Perhaps earthquakes, mosquitoes, and disease—things we call natural evil because of the suffering they cause—we should neither call good in and of themselves nor blame on the curse but instead classify as a third kind of thing: a natural part of creation that we are meant to be subduing. Not subduing in the sense of arrogantly destroying everything in nature that annoys us nor arrogantly using everything in nature purely for our own comfort and convenience. That would not be stewardly. Rather, subduing in a way that, in the face of real challenges and opposition, works to ease and prevent suffering.

Following Christ's Example

We can look at natural evil as scientists and as theologians, but we must deal with it pastorally. All of us, at various times in our lives, must help people who are suffering from natural disasters and disease. The suffering is real, and a scientific or theological lecture about how these things fit into a bigger pattern might be very unhelpful.

When we help someone who is suffering, we don't usually try to comfort them with complicated theological arguments. In the midst of their suffering, we suffer with them, we empathize, and we do what we can to ease their suffering.

At the end of the book of Job, God eased Job's suffering. God restored Job's health, wealth, and family. Unlike with Job, we know that many people today suffer from natural evil and never recover from it in this life. But we know more about what comes next than the author of the book of Job knew.

Today we have the hindsight of seeing the life, death, and resurrection of Jesus, and we know about Jesus's promises regarding our resurrection and the new creation. For Christians, new creation is the final answer to natural evil. Whatever the source of natural evil, Jesus is the ultimate example for what we should do about it. Jesus healed sick people. Jesus even calmed a dangerous storm on occasion. Jesus eased the suffering of others, whether that suffering was caused by moral evil or natural evil. We can do the same.

At the dawn of human history, God gave humanity the mandate to subdue the earth. In God's later revelations, and above all in the person of Jesus, God gave us the mandate to ease the suffering of others.

4

Human Evolution

WHAT IS THE EVIDENCE for human evolution? How much does it tell us about what our ancestors were like before they began to sin?

Chapter 5 discusses theological topics of the soul, the image of God, and possible divine action beyond God's governance of natural processes. This chapter focuses on what science can tell us. God designed and sustains all the natural mechanisms discussed here. I use the phrase "what science can tell us" as shorthand for "what the evidence in God's creation can tell us about the natural mechanisms God used."

Since there isn't space to discuss all the mutually reinforcing lines of scientific evidence for human evolution, this chapter focuses on a few scientific issues that are especially relevant for the question "When did sin begin?" Readers who want to study the scientific evidence in greater detail should consult other books.[1]

1. For Christians who are not scientists and who wish to learn more about this scientific evidence, I recommend one or more of the following: Francis S. Collins, *The Language of God: A Scientist Presents Evidence for Belief* (New York: Simon & Schuster, 2006); Denis O. Lamoureux, *Evolutionary Creation: A Christian Approach to Evolution* (Eugene, OR: Wipf & Stock, 2008); Scot McKnight and Dennis Venema, *Adam and the Genome* (Grand Rapids: Brazos, 2017); Deborah B. Haarsma and Loren D. Haarsma, *Origins: A Reformed Look at Creation, Design, and Evolution* (Grand Rapids: Faith Alive Christian Resources, 2007, 2011); Darrel R. Falk, *Coming to Peace with Science: Bridging the Worlds Between Faith and Biology* (Downers Grove, IL: InterVarsity, 2004); Gregg Davidson, *Friend of Science, Friend of Faith: Listening to God in His Works and Word* (Grand Rapids: Kregel, 2019); and Agustin Fuentes, *The Creative*

This chapter focuses on what we can learn from science. Later chapters discuss how this evidence fits into possible scenarios for Adam and Eve. By the end of this chapter, we will see that much of what science tells us about human evolution is fairly easy to connect with traditional theological teachings about original sin, but some things science tells us will take more work.

In most of this book, the word "human" is not precisely defined. This is intentional. Even if we were to identify the word "human" with the *Homo sapiens* species, there is no sharp demarcation point for when that species began. Some scholars prefer to use "human" more broadly: to include all species of the genus *Homo*, or even those of the earlier genus *Australopithecus*. Other scholars, concerned with particular theological or philosophical questions, would use the term "human" more narrowly: to refer only to a subset of *Homo sapiens* who had crossed over some threshold of intelligence, rationality, self-consciousness, or spirituality. In later chapters, when discussing specific scenarios for the entrance of sin into the world, it will be important to define "human" more carefully within each scenario. For this chapter, however, it's best to leave the word loosely defined.

Humans Share Common Ancestry with Animals

Imagine you went to a family reunion of several hundred people. If you took DNA samples from each individual, scientists could reconstruct the entire tree of family relationships using only that information. Siblings have more similar DNA than first cousins, first cousins have more similar DNA than second cousins, and so forth, in predictable nested patterns.

Scientists can do something similar with all living species. Looking only at the nested patterns of similarity of DNA among different species, they can reconstruct a tree of common ancestry and estimate how long ago any two species shared a common ancestor. The tree reconstructed using DNA can be compared to trees constructed from other lines of evidence—fossils, comparative anatomy, developmental biology, biogeography—for confirmation and small corrections.

Human DNA is more like chimpanzee DNA than that of other primates. Human and other primate DNA are more like each other than that of other mammals. Other mammals' DNA are more like each other than that of lizards and fish. Human DNA, like the DNA of all living species, fits into a larger pattern that ties all living organisms together in a tree of common ancestry.

Spark: How Imagination Made Humans Exceptional (New York: Penguin, 2017). This is not a comprehensive list; there are other excellent books besides these.

Current estimates from all the lines of evidence listed above are that the lineages leading to modern chimpanzees and to modern humans fully diverged between four and seven million years ago.

It is sometimes suggested that different species have similar genes not because they share a common ancestor but because the genes have a common function. Perhaps humans, chimpanzees, orangutans, and other apes have similar genes, so the argument goes, only because the genes perform very similar functions in species with similar body plans. This "common function" theory is sometimes presented as an alternative, competing theory to "common ancestry" to explain the nested pattern of genetic similarities among all species. But the two theories are not actually competing. Rather, common ancestry theory is one particular, more specific version of common function theory. There is a lot of redundancy in the DNA code; many different versions of a DNA string can encode for the same function. (For an analogy, think about how a company might have multiple spellings of a web address all go to the same web page.) Of all the possible DNA sequences that are consistent with the theory of common function, only a tiny subset of DNA sequences is also consistent with the theory of common ancestry.

Genetic evidence pointing to common ancestry is seen in at least four independent and mutually reinforcing lines of evidence: there is redundancy in how the amino acids that make up proteins are encoded in the DNA,[2] there is redundancy in how some amino acids in proteins can be replaced by similar amino acids without changing the function,[3] there is repetition in noncoding regions of DNA,[4] and there is similarity in how genes are arranged on

2. Each amino acid that goes into a protein is encoded by a DNA triplet. For example, the amino acid methionine is encoded by the DNA triplet "ATG" (adenine + thymine + guanine). Many amino acids can be encoded by two or four or six different DNA triplets. Functionally, almost any DNA encoding for the same amino acid would do. But, as common ancestry predicts, in closely related species, we find that the same amino acid encoded in the same locations on the same proteins is encoded by identical DNA triplets far more frequently than would be necessary for common function alone.

3. This is sometimes called "conservative amino acid replacement." In proteins, many amino acids can be replaced with other amino acids with very similar biophysical properties without changing the protein's function. Functionally, many conservative amino acid substitutions could be made throughout each protein without changing their functions. But, as common ancestry predicts, in closely related species, we find that the exact same amino acids are used in the same locations on the same protein far more frequently than would be necessary for common function alone.

4. Some noncoding regions of DNA include introns, pseudogenes, and retroviral insertions. While these regions of DNA might sometimes have functions, their functions typically are very insensitive to point mutations, or even to large insertions or deletions. But as common ancestry predicts, in closely related species, we find sequence similarities in these noncoding regions far more frequently than would be necessary for common function alone.

chromosomes.[5] These four lines of evidence are independent of one another—any one or two or three could be true without the others being true. Each line of evidence holds redundantly, on every chromosome, throughout the genome. Moreover, the nested patterns of similarities across multiple species fit the "tree of life" of common ancestry constructed by other methods that don't involve DNA (fossils, anatomical comparisons, developmental biology, and biogeography). The nested patterns of similarity fit common ancestry even when there is convergent evolution to similar body types.[6]

When we compare human DNA to that of chimpanzees and other primates, we find that the data are consistent not only with common function theory but also with the much more restrictive common ancestry theory.[7]

Fossils Show Evolutionary Changes from Earlier Primates to Modern Humans

Thousands of fossils have been discovered that provide data regarding the evolutionary history of humans. Many of them are only fragments of skeletons, some consist of multiple fragments found together, and some include many parts of the skull or the entire skeleton. Most are thought to be not from

5. This applies not only to the arrangement of genes but also to the arrangements of pseudogenes and retroviral insertions. Chunks of chromosomes can often be cut out and inserted elsewhere on the same chromosome (or a different chromosome), sometimes inverted, without hurting function. But as common ancestry predicts, in closely related species, we find that the sequence ordering of genes (and pseudogenes and retroviral insertions) on the chromosomes is far more similar than would be necessary for common function alone.

6. For example, among placental mammals there are lynxes, wolves, anteaters, moles, flying squirrels, groundhogs, and mice. There are marsupial mammals with body types and lifestyles similar to their placental mammal counterparts. If common function was the only explanation for DNA similarities, we might expect that the genes that encode for, say, muscle growth and muscle attachment would be most similar between placental wolves and marsupial wolves, compared to all others. Likewise, we might expect that the genes that encode for claws and snouts and tongues would be most similar between marsupial anteaters and placental anteaters, compared to the others. (Although common function wouldn't require this to be true, we might expect it.) Common ancestry, however, predicts that those genes would be closer to one another among all marsupials than they would be to the genes of any placentals, including their placental counterparts. This is what we find in the data. In addition, when we compare related species' genomes to one another, the rate of change of nonselected point mutations is consistent with their time to last common ancestor as determined by the fossil record.

7. To use a detective mystery analogy, common function theory is like saying, "Evidence indicates that the thief was right-handed." Common ancestry theory is like saying, "Evidence indicates that the thief was right-handed, was taller than 6′2″, was about 260 pounds, had light brown hair at least three inches long, walked with a limp in his left foot, wore size 11 hard-soled shoes, and recently stepped in a mud puddle with red clay and maple tree pollen." These are not competing theories. The second theory makes a much more restrictive prediction than the first.

direct ancestors of *Homo sapiens* but from species closely related to direct ancestor species, and they therefore provide important data. Species that arose after the split with the chimpanzee lineage are collectively called "hominins." Some of the oldest hominin fossils, dated from 5.6 to 4 million years ago and given the genus name *Ardipithecus*, have brain sizes similar to those of modern chimpanzees. They have anatomical features indicating that they probably belong on the hominin lineage, but they are similar in many ways to species on the chimpanzee lineage in that same time period. Various *Australopithecus* fossils, dated to around 4 to 2 million years ago, have slightly larger brains than *Ardipithecus*, and their skeletons imply that they walked upright much of the time. Fossils of *Homo habilis*, dated from 2.4 to 1.5 million years ago, show that they had still larger brain sizes, but their brains were still only half the size of modern human brains. Stone tools are sometimes found with *Homo habilis* fossils (and there is some evidence of stone tool use even earlier associated with *Australopithecus*). *Homo erectus* fossils, dated from 2 million to about 200,000 years ago, are still more modern looking. They had brains ranging from *Homo habilis* size up to nearly modern human size. (The largest fall within the range of modern humans, but their brain structure was somewhat different.) There is archaeological evidence that some *Homo erectus* controlled fire and cooked food. Fossils are found not only in Africa but also in parts of Europe and many parts of Asia, indicating that this was a very successful species that spread widely. *Homo heidelbergensis* fossils are still closer to people alive today. They are found simultaneously across Europe and Africa from around 700,000 to 600,000 years ago and have brains, on average, only a little smaller than those of modern humans. They also spread into parts of Asia and are thought probably to have given rise to Neanderthals (Europe), Denisovans (Asia), and *Homo sapiens* (Africa).

"Archaic" *Homo sapiens* fossils, dated from 300,000 years ago to less than 100,000 years ago, look like modern humans but have some features closer to those of late *Homo erectus* and *Homo heidelbergensis*. Their brain sizes fall within the range of modern human brain sizes but are, on average, smaller. *Homo neanderthalensis* (Neanderthals), dated from about 440,000 years ago to around 30,000 years ago, were generally shorter and more heavily built than modern humans, but their brain size was like that of modern humans. Archaeological evidence shows that they made stone tools and other tools, controlled fire, and buried their dead. Fragmentary bones and DNA from another group, called Denisovans, who lived around the same times as Neanderthals, have been found in central Asia. The last common ancestor of Neanderthals, Denisovans, and *Homo sapiens* is thought to have lived about 500,000 years ago, though some research groups push this date back quite a bit. Fossils of nearly modern-looking *Homo sapiens* have been found as far back as around 300,000 years ago in Africa. Some of these *Homo sapiens* spread from Africa into Asia and Europe, on various occasions, as early as 200,000 years ago. Although these early *Homo sapiens* migrations left some archaeological evidence, they did not seem to leave significant populations of descendants. A major migration out of Africa into Europe and Asia of at least several thousand *Homo sapiens* occurred about 70,000 to 60,000 years ago. This migration produced descendants that spread around the rest of the globe, reaching Australia more than 50,000 years ago and the Americas more than 15,000 years ago. Throughout the last 100,000 years, tools became gradually more sophisticated, with some musical instruments and small statues dated as old as 35,000 years ago.

Fossils can tell us a great deal about the anatomy of hominins, and the fossil record is consistent with gradual evolutionary change. For example, when the brain size of hominin fossils is graphed as a function of time, it does not show abrupt jumps but rather a gradual increase from *Ardipithecus* to modern humans. However, fossils cannot tell us as much about behavior. Though fossils are extremely useful for telling us how early hominins walked and climbed, and how tall or short they were, it is harder to use bones to tell us other things, such as how much these hominins communicated verbally. There is still a wide range of opinions among scientists about the language abilities of *Homo erectus*, archaic *Homo sapiens*, and Neanderthals. Similarly, there is a range of opinions on whether the paintings and sculptures created by modern-looking *Homo sapiens* more than 15,000 years ago or Neanderthal burial practices, from even earlier, held any religious significance. However, a significant amount of artwork has been discovered going back tens of thousands of years. Most of it is by *Homo sapiens*, but some paleoanthropologists argue that the earliest currently known cave paintings, dating around 65,000 years ago, are by Neanderthals.

The Human Ancestral Population Was Probably Never Just Two Individuals

One of the most challenging scientific findings for traditional interpretations of Adam and Eve is genetic evidence that the first *Homo sapiens* were a larger group, not just two individuals.

Species typically don't start from just a single pair. Speciation usually happens at the population level, when a larger reproductively interbreeding group splits into two or more subpopulations reproductively isolated from each other. Each subpopulation is usually more than two individuals. The larger the size of the founding subpopulation, the more genetic diversity it is likely to have.

Imagine someone put two dogs, one male and one female, on an island. Two hundred years later, we find that one thousand descendants fill the island. If we took genetic samples from all of them, we would find very little genetic diversity. All the genetic information in that population, apart from a handful of mutations along the way, would have come from that first pair. Now imagine repeating the experiment on another island, this time starting with fifty males and fifty females. Two hundred years later, if we took genetic samples from their one thousand descendants, we would find much greater genetic diversity. With computer modeling, using only the genetic diversity information of the final population, it's possible to estimate both the population size at that original "population bottleneck" and how long ago the bottleneck occurred.

Scientists have studied human genetic diversity using several techniques:[8] counting the number of different versions of each gene in the human population,[9] noting the amount of statistical correlation between different versions of neighboring genes on the same chromosome,[10] and comparing the patterns by which similar versions of the same genes are found in species with close common ancestry.[11] These different lines of evidence point to the most recent

8. For an excellent and readable description of these methods, see McKnight and Venema, *Adam and the Genome*. See also BioLogos Editorial Team, "Adam, Eve, and Human Population Genetics: Signature in the SNPs," BioLogos, November 12, 2014, https://biologos.org /articles/series/genetics-and-the-historical-adam-responses-to-popular-arguments/adam-eve -and-human-population-genetics#signature-in-the-snps.

9. Specific versions of a gene are called "alleles." The "allele diversity" of a gene refers to the number of different versions of that gene existing within a population. If we start with only two individuals, all of their offspring initially would have at most four different alleles of each gene, although later mutations could increase that number. The "allele frequency spectrum" is the distribution of allele diversity across all genes over the entire population.

10. Barring mutations, each parent can pass one of two versions of each gene to its offspring. If each gene were inherited randomly, then there would be no correlation between which version of a gene is found in one location and which version of another gene is found in another location. For the most part, that is what we see. But genes that are close to each other on the same chromosome tend to be inherited in clusters. Therefore, there tends to be some correlation between versions of a gene found in one location and versions of another gene found in a neighboring location. This is called "linkage disequilibrium." Computer modeling of this data can sometimes determine how recently a species went through a population bottleneck and roughly the size of that bottleneck.

11. This is sometimes referred to as "incomplete lineage sorting" of alleles. Imagine a population has four versions of a gene (A, B, C, and D). It splits into two subpopulations. One has three versions (A, B, and C), and the other has a different subset of three (A, B, and D). The offspring species of each subpopulation will show that pattern. Incomplete lineage sorting can

population bottleneck in *Homo sapiens* occurring around 100,000 to 200,000 years ago, with an interbreeding population size of about 10,000 individuals. (In computer models, this number is called the "effective population size" of reproducing individuals. The actual population size was probably somewhat larger than this number.)

The question is sometimes asked, "Could the genetic diversity of human beings today be consistent with all of us descending from only a single pair of individuals, provided they lived sufficiently long ago?" For a single pair less than about 500,000 years ago (well before the first appearance of anatomically modern *Homo sapiens*), the answer is no. For a single pair more than 500,000 years ago, the answer is "More research is needed."[12] Given the data we have so far, the general consensus of scientists is that the ancestral bottleneck shrinking to a single pair in the very distant past (somewhere between half a million and several million years ago) might be possible, but it's unlikely. The most likely explanation for the genetic diversity data we currently have is that our ancestral population never fell below several thousand individuals throughout the last several millions of years.

Combining fossil, genetic, and other data, our current understanding points to *Homo sapiens* evolving out of a subset of *Homo erectus*, primarily in Africa, with a population size that probably never fell below about 10,000 individuals. Starting about 70,000 years ago, a significant subset of *Homo sapiens* spread to the Middle East, Europe, and Asia, and from there to the Pacific islands and the Americas. (There is evidence of earlier, probably smaller, migrations out of Africa.) As they spread out of Africa, *Homo sapiens* encountered other descendants of *Homo erectus*. Neanderthals were already living in the

---

be used to reconstruct portions of common ancestry trees to check against other methods, and with enough data, it can estimate the number of generations since two species shared a common ancestor and roughly estimate population bottleneck sizes. See Dennis Venema, "Evolution Basics: Incomplete Lineage Sorting and Ancestral Population Sizes," BioLogos, July 29, 2013, https://biologos.org/articles/series/evolution-basics/incomplete-lineage-sorting.

12. There isn't, at the time this chapter was written, a good estimate *using multiple methods* indicating how long ago such a pair would have had to live to account for *all* the genetic diversity we see in humans today. Some recent, unpublished work suggests that it is possible to fit the data on one of those three methods, the allele frequency spectrum, if that pair lived 500,000 years ago or more. Similar work modeling the linkage disequilibrium data and incomplete lineage sorting data has not yet been done. When that work is done, those other two methods might also be consistent with the human genetic diversity we see today arising from only a single pair of ancestors roughly 500,000 years ago; alternatively, those methods might indicate that such a pair would have had to have lived several million years ago—possibly even before our last common ancestor with chimpanzees. It should also be noted that while this work might *allow* for the possibility that all humans descended solely from a single pair of individuals (if that pair lived long enough ago), the most probable interpretation of the data would still point toward a bottleneck population size of several thousand individuals.

Middle East and Europe. Genetic evidence now shows that *Homo sapiens* and Neanderthals interbred to some extent. Non-African humans today have 1 to 4 percent Neanderthal DNA in their genomes, while Africans have a smaller percentage. In central Asia, *Homo sapiens* encountered a population known as Denisovans. Genetic evidence indicates that Denisovans and Neanderthals shared a common ancestor roughly 300,000 years ago. Some *Homo sapiens* and Denisovans also interbred, and their descendants colonized southeastern Asia, Oceana, and Australia. Modern Melanesians (in a region of Oceana including New Guinea and smaller islands) have about 5 percent Denisovan DNA. This story is incomplete and is complicated by the fact that most genetic studies to date have a dearth of African samples, given that living Africans have more genetic diversity than the rest of the world combined. Genetic studies over the next several decades will make the story more interesting and detailed.

Humans Share Genetic and Genealogical Unity

Humans today share a genetic unity. We all get the majority of our genetic sequences from a common interbreeding population that lived in Africa around 200,000 years ago.

Humans today also share a genealogical unity. Imagine if you could write down the names of all your ancestors: two parents, four grandparents, eight great-grandparents, and so on. By the time you reached back thirty generations, which is only about 750 years, you would be writing just over one billion names. But the entire world population at that time is estimated to be less than half a billion. How can that be? Once you go back several generations, some people start appearing in multiple slots in your genealogy tree. Most strangers you meet share at least one common ancestor with you if you go back just ten or fifteen generations. If we go back far enough in history, we begin to find individuals who are common ancestors of *every* human living today. How far back in time do we have to go to find *a* person who is a common genealogical ancestor of *every* human alive today? Some recent scholarship estimates only about 3,000 years.[13]

If we ask the same question about all humans living 2,000 years ago, or all humans living 10,000 years ago, the time back to their most recent common ancestor is probably longer than 3,000 years, because humans were less mobile back then. Even so, at any point in the history of *Homo sapiens*, if we ask, "How far back do we have to go to find *a* common ancestor of every

13. Douglas L. T. Rohde, Steve Olson, and Joseph T. Chang, "Modelling the Recent Common Ancestry of All Living Humans," *Nature* 431, no. 7008 (2004): 562–66.

Homo sapiens alive at that time?" the answer would be "Just several thousand years."[14] If we ask the question "How much further back do we have to go before every *Homo sapiens* alive at that time shares an identical list of all common ancestors?" the answer would be "Just a few thousand more years."[15] Everyone alive today has an identical list of ancestors in their family tree (albeit arranged differently) if we go back enough generations. So if we went back far enough, perhaps just 20,000 years or so, every individual alive at that time who is an ancestor of *anyone* living today would, in fact, be an ancestor of *everyone* living today.

The Human Ancestral Population Probably Never Lived All in One Location

Back when the *Homo sapiens* population was at its smallest—probably about 10,000 or more individuals roughly 100,000 to 200,000 years ago—*Homo sapiens* lived in small hunter-gatherer groups of at most a few dozen individuals. These groups were likely spread over large areas of Africa and slightly beyond. They did not have agriculture or other technologies that would have permitted several thousand individuals to live together in one location with relatively close proximity.

We know from human history, and from observing other primates, that it's common for individuals or small subgroups who grow up in one social group, upon reaching adulthood or later, to migrate to join neighboring or more distant groups. In this way, both genes and cultural innovations spread through the entire population. However, depending on how spread out the groups were geographically, it probably took at least hundreds of years for cultural information to spread throughout the species, and at least a few thousand years for genealogical family connections to spread from one end of the population to the other. (Some theological implications of this are discussed in chapter 9.)

14. The exact number of thousands of years is difficult to estimate from archaeology and DNA because we don't know how isolated some subpopulations were. It is possible that the first *Homo sapiens* settlers of Australia were isolated from *Homo sapiens* in Asia for several tens of thousands of years. Likewise, it is possible that the first *Homo sapiens* settlers of the Americas were isolated from *Homo sapiens* in Asia and Europe for about 10,000 years. But in both cases, it is also possible that a few immigrants going in either direction during the periods of relative isolation would have resulted in reducing the time to most recent common ancestor. So there is some possibility that all *Homo sapiens* alive, say, 2,000 years ago would have had a common ancestor of just a few thousand years previous.

15. The addition of Neanderthal and Denisovan DNA to *Homo sapiens* subpopulations does not substantially change this conclusion.

There Is No Sharp Demarcation for When the *Homo sapiens* Species Began

An everyday useful definition of the term "species" is that two organisms are the same species if they can interbreed, and they are different species if they cannot. This definition helps us understand why, when species evolve, there is no specific time when we can say that a species "begins." A useful analogy to illustrate this is how languages often change over time.

Imagine a regional population of humans all speaking the same language. For whatever reason—migration, social isolation, war, or politics—they split into two groups that have very little communication with each other. (Something like this has happened many times in human history.) The languages of the two groups diverge. After a century or two, the groups still have a common language and understand each other, but they have noticeably different dialects. After four or five centuries, communication between the two groups might be difficult. After seven or eight centuries (based on examples from history), the languages might have diverged so much that they would be considered different languages—and neither would be the same as the original language. While the speaker of one might recognize some words of the other, normal written or spoken communication would be very difficult or impossible.

Something similar happens when even a single language changes over time without splitting into multiple languages. Compare modern English to English from 1800, or 1600, or 1400, or 1200. Written and spoken English from eight centuries ago is incomprehensible to modern English speakers who are not trained in ancient languages. The changes to the language were gradual. An English speaker in any given century would be able to understand speakers from a century before or a century later. But the English of 1200 is, by most definitions, a different language than modern English.

The evolution of languages, while not a perfect analogy for biological evolution, illustrates several aspects of the evolution of species (though the evolution of species takes longer). A common way for new species to "start" is for one interbreeding population to split into two or more subpopulations that no longer interbreed. This could happen due to migration, geographical changes, behavioral changes, new ecological niches opening, or other factors. At first the subpopulations are nearly identical and are considered the same species. Over time, changes accumulate in each subpopulation as it adapts to its particular environment. After a while, each subpopulation is noticeably different, although they are still capable of interbreeding. (At this point, each might be called a subspecies.) After a while longer, differences are more noticeable, although interbreeding is still possible with some difficulty. After enough time, interbreeding is impossible. Initially, there was unambiguously one species; eventually, there are unambiguously two or more species. But the changes were gradual, and it is somewhat arbitrary to pick a particular point in time as the start of new species.

A similar story can be told when one species changes over time without splitting. A modern animal might be easily distinguishable from its ancestor from 7 million years earlier, and—were they alive at the same time—they would be incapable of interbreeding. They would be considered different species. But changes from the ancient to the modern occurred gradually throughout the entire population, and it is somewhat arbitrary to pick one point in time as the transition from the ancient species to the modern.

Considering the lack of sharp demarcation between species, we might revise the earlier summary of our ancestors as follows. The species that was the last common ancestor between humans and chimpanzees gradually gave rise to several species, including several *Ardipithecus*-like species. The fossils we have today might be from a human ancestral species, or they might be from a closely related sibling species. One of these species gradually gave rise to *Australopithecus*-like species. One of these gradually gave rise to *Homo habilis* and other related species. From one of these eventually came *Homo erectus*, which spread throughout Africa, Europe, and Asia. A subset of late *Homo erectus* or *Homo heidelbergensis* around 500,000 years ago was the last common ancestor of Neanderthals, Denisovans, and *Homo sapiens*. The ancestors of Neanderthals and Denisovans migrated to the Middle East and spread from there, while some of those who remained in Africa eventually gave rise to modern-looking *Homo sapiens* between 200,000 and 300,000 years ago. Some of these migrated to the Middle East, Europe, and Asia and, sometime around 70,000 to 40,000 years ago, encountered Neanderthals and Denisovans. While many differences had accumulated during those nearly 500,000 years of relative isolation, some interbreeding was still possible when they encountered each other again. We might decide to call Neanderthals, Denisovans, and *Homo sapiens* different subspecies, or we might choose to call them distinct sibling species that still allow limited interbreeding.

This illustrates the difficulties with defining the word "human" from a scientific standpoint. One useful definition is this: all members of the genus *Homo*, starting around 2 million years ago, including multiple hominin groups now extinct, some of which are not ancestors of modern *Homo sapiens*. Another useful definition, depending on context, is this: starting around 600,000 years ago, the common ancestors of Neanderthals, Denisovans, and *Homo sapiens*, and all their descendants. Another useful definition is this:

all anatomically modern *Homo sapiens*, starting somewhere around 300,000 years ago. Another potentially useful definition, depending on context, is this: "behaviorally modern" *Homo sapiens* (modern human behavior is discussed later in this chapter) beginning somewhere around 100,000 to 50,000 years ago. Another possible definition is this: all *Homo sapiens* beginning around 15,000 years ago, concurrent with the rapid growth of agriculture and cities.

Scientifically, there is no sharp demarcation point that distinguishes *Homo sapiens* from ancestor species like *Homo heidelbergensis* or sibling species like Neanderthals and Denisovans. Theologically, there might be a specific point in time when humanity began to be image bearers of God. Theologically, there might be a specific time when humans became sinners. Theologically, there might be reasons to reserve the word "human" for individuals who are "in the image of God." The next chapter discusses some challenges of determining when that might have begun. But from fossils and genetic data, we see that *Homo sapiens*, like nearly all species, arrived through a process of gradual changes in a large population over an extended period of time, with no specific point designating the beginning of our species.

Early Humans Were Social and Learned and Faced Increasingly Complex Choices

Simpler animals with simpler nervous systems have simpler needs. Each such species thrives in a particular environment where its instinctual and predictable behaviors meet its particular needs.

More complex animals have more complex ranges of behaviors. Their behaviors start with instinct but are shaped by what they learn from watching their parents or other animals. They can thrive in a wider range of environments. They make choices, adapting their strategy for hunting or finding shelter depending on the terrain, weather, time of day, proximity of danger, and whether they are alone, part of a group, or caring for offspring.

Most intelligent mammals live in social groups. Children learn by watching not only their parents but the entire group. The survival and the reproductive success of each individual depend on the group. Each must keep track of not only their immediate survival needs (food, shelter, etc.) but also their social status in the group and their relationships with other group members (hostile, indifferent, or friendly). Each makes choices prioritizing not only short-term versus long-term survival needs but also their own immediate desires versus their long-term relationships with others. For example, if there are several tasty food morsels within arm's reach and other group members are watching, an individual might have to consider, "Should I immediately gobble up all the morsels, or should I share them?"

As our hominin ancestors became increasingly intelligent, their social groups became increasingly important. As their social groups became larger and more complex, this complexity probably gave advantages to more intelligent individuals. At some point, our ancestors developed so many novel tools, communication skills, and social practices (all requiring a great deal of teaching and learning) that they changed their "environment." Each generation inherited both genes and cultural practices from their ancestors, and both were important for survival and reproduction. Genes and culture coevolved as neurological, social, and cultural complexity increased. Changes in culture altered genetic selection for individuals living in that culture, giving greater reproductive success to certain gene combinations. As the genetics of the population changed over generations, this in turn enabled new cultural innovations.

The Importance of Culture in Gene-Culture Coevolution

To illustrate the importance of the culture side of gene-culture coevolution, consider several important skills that children learn.

The language you speak was learned from interaction with caregivers over the first years of your life. More than that, the very consonants and vowels you can distinguish were wired into your brain early in your development. Adult speakers of one language have difficulty distinguishing similar but distinct vowels or consonants in another language when those vowels or consonants are not distinguished in their native language. Studies have shown that young babies can distinguish similar but distinct vowels and consonants from other languages, but children's brains after several years become specialized for distinguishing the vowels and consonants of their caregivers' languages.

Consider the physical skills you learned as a child—walking, running, visually tracking, pointing, throwing, catching, and so forth. These also were wired into your brain through practice and interaction with caregivers over the first several years of your life.

Consider other basic survival skills you have—how to make certain tools, knowing what things are good for food and how to obtain them, and so on. These also were wired into your brain through decades of interaction with teachers and through practice.

Consider facial recognition skills. Babies learn to recognize specific faces by interacting with people. Over time, our brains become wired to recognize people by their distinct combinations of particular sets of facial features. This becomes automatic and unconscious to the point that when, as adults, we meet people from cultural or racial groups that have common distinguishing facial features different from those of the people we grew up around, we need to make a greater conscious effort to learn to distinguish their faces.[16]

Consider your ability to sympathize and empathize with the suffering of other people. Proper development of these skills in children depends on interaction with people and teaching from caregivers. When young children are raised in socially deprived settings and are not taught these things, they are much more likely to become adults who are deficient in these abilities.

Consider your ability to make selfish or altruistic choices. When you are twenty years old, the choices you make depend on your history. That history started with your genetics and prenatal environment. It was heavily shaped by your parents, teachers, caregivers, and friends. It was also shaped by the choices you yourself made as you grew up. Every time you made a choice, you shaped your own developing brain. Your choices in turn affected the way your parents, teachers, caregivers, and friends interacted with you, which in turn affected your brain even more.

Consider stories. Children are eager to hear stories; many adults are eager to tell stories. The stories we tell children are, for the most part, chosen to help them learn the behaviors and values we want them to learn.

Our ancestors lived in groups and cooperated in order to survive and flourish. As gene-culture coevolution became increasingly important, childhood lasted longer. This allowed children more time to learn survival skills and social skills, and it allowed children more time to learn how to make choices among the sometimes-competing desires for their own immediate welfare and their social relationships.

Early Humans Had Dispositions toward Both "Nasty" and "Nice" Behaviors

Evolution helps us understand some animal behaviors. Consider this: When hungry rats or mice are placed in a new environment with food available, why do some species usually eat first and then explore, while other species usually

16. There are numerous studies of this effect. Two examples: Jessica L. Marcon, Christian A. Meissner, Michael Frueh, Kyle J. Susa, and Otto H. MacLin, "Perceptual Identification and the Cross-Race Effect," *Visual Cognition* 18, no. 5 (October 2009): 767–79; Kathleen L. Hourihan, Aaron S. Benjamin, and Xiping Liu, "A Cross-Race Effect in Metamemory: Predictions of Face Recognition Are More Accurate for Members of Our Own Race," *Journal of Applied Research in Memory and Cognition* 1, no. 3 (September 2012): 158–62.

explore first and then eat? Or why are some bird species mostly monogamous while other bird species are not?[17] The theory of evolution predicts that, other things being equal, a species' most common behavioral dispositions ought to be "adaptive." Individuals that display the most common behavioral dispositions of a species ought, on average, to produce more offspring than individuals with different behavioral dispositions.[18]

Evolutionary psychology extends the evolutionary study of animal behaviors to human behaviors. For example, the observation that humans enjoy eating sweet foods seems well suited to an evolutionary explanation. Natural foods with high sugar content typically are also highly nutritious, so it makes sense that animals and humans would evolve brain circuitry that makes eating sweet foods pleasurable. Similar hypotheses could be made about the common human predisposition to eat in groups rather than alone.

Evolutionary psychology becomes particularly relevant to theology when it makes hypotheses about moral behavior. Theology asks whether a behavior is morally right or wrong. Evolutionary psychology asks a different question: whether or not behaviors are *adaptive*. Consider, for example, feelings of guilt. Lions, we presume, feel no guilt when they kill to eat. An evolutionary argument could be made that feelings of guilt would be maladaptive in lions. Lions who felt guilt over killing gazelles would likely not hunt as effectively and would therefore leave fewer offspring. Humans, however, do feel guilt, at least when it comes to harming other humans. Feelings of guilt when harming another human are so common that we say that humans who do not feel such guilt are abnormal.

Many mammals live in social groups (e.g., prairie dogs, wolves, elephants, horses, dolphins, and especially primates). Archaeological evidence suggests that our ancestors lived in social groups over the past several million years. By observing other animals, especially primates, we can learn about what sorts of social behaviors are adaptive for them and might have been adaptive for our ancestors.

It is often said that evolution rewards "nasty" behavior. Sometimes it does. If an animal routinely steals food from weaker group members, or attacks rivals in order to win desirable mates, or kills members of a rival social group

17. J. Cartwright, *Evolution and Human Behavior* (Cambridge: MIT Press, 2000); N. B. Davis, *Dunnock Behavior and Social Evolution* (Oxford: Oxford University Press, 1992); and J. R. Krebs and N. B. Davies, eds., *Behavioral Ecology* (Oxford: Blackwell Scientific, 1991).

18. Adaptive explanations should consider complicating factors such as the possibility that a species' current environment might be different from its environments in the past, or that some behaviors might be maladaptive but necessary by-products of other adaptive behaviors, or that some behavioral dispositions might be neither adaptive nor maladaptive.

(as chimpanzees sometimes do), such actions might increase that animal's reproductive success.

But "nice" behaviors can also be adaptive. The most obvious example is parental care for their young. Another example, called "kin selection,"[19] is exhibited when an animal does something that is risky to itself but that helps a large number of its relatives, such as when a prairie dog gives a warning call when it spots a predator. Yet another well-studied example, called "reciprocal altruism,"[20] is exhibited when an animal does something that has a small cost for itself but is very beneficial for another and then can expect to receive similar help in return in the future.

Parental care, kin selection, and reciprocal altruism are well studied in animals. Humans, however, have altruistic feelings and behaviors that go beyond kin and reciprocity. Humans are often altruistic toward strangers they will never meet again. Evolutionary psychology provides several hypotheses for how this greater degree of altruism in humans might be adaptive. One hypothesis is that individuals who routinely behave altruistically develop a reputation that makes their entire social group more likely to help them in the future. Another hypothesis is that groups full of altruists who routinely help one another tend to do much better, on average, than groups full of selfish individuals.[21]

Predispositions toward "nasty" and "nice" behaviors don't just come from combinations of genes. Genes don't directly produce behavior. Genes regulate proteins. Proteins influence cell growth and signaling. Cell growth and signaling affect how the brain is wired. Certain brain circuits need to exist for humans to behave altruistically, but those brain circuits do more tasks than simply promote altruism. If altruism does have a genetic basis, it is undoubtedly the result of many genes working in combination to produce the sorts of brain circuits that promote many kinds of actions, not just altruistic acts.

Moreover, gene expression is affected by the environment. Genes "for" altruism work properly only in the context of social training. Chimpanzees raised in isolation, for example, have difficulty adapting to life in a social group. Similarly, human children raised without normal social and moral training can develop moral pathologies that last into adulthood.

19. W. D. Hamilton, "The Genetical Evolution of Social Behavior," *Journal of Theoretical Biology* 7 (1964): 1–16.

20. R. L. Trivers, "The Evolution of Reciprocal Altruism," *Quarterly Review of Biology* 46 (1971): 35–39.

21. This is an active area of research in sociobiology and evolutionary psychology. For a collection of essays on this topic, many of them written from Christian perspectives, see Philip Clayton and Jeffrey Schloss, eds., *Evolution and Ethics: Human Morality in Biological and Religious Perspective* (Grand Rapids: Eerdmans, 2004).

This brings us back to gene-culture coevolution. Each individual's genes affect how their brain develops. Brain development affects their behaviors. Human behaviors collectively shape society. But influence also runs in the other direction. Society forms the environment that shapes the brain development of children and that influences the behaviors of children and adults. Cultures can punish or reward individuals who routinely do different sorts of "nasty" or "nice" behaviors. This can affect individuals' reproductive success and therefore what sorts of genes are more likely to get passed on to the next generation.

Human social groups and human levels of cooperation are far more complex than those of any animals. Animals communicate with one another, but human communication is vastly more complex. Animals are sometimes "nice" toward one another, but humans do much more than this. Humans develop moral codes to regulate and improve behavior and transmit these codes through actions and words between individuals, between groups both near and distant, and between generations.[22]

There is much we still don't know about the behaviors of our hominin ancestors, but some things seem reasonably certain. They lived in social groups. These social groups required cooperation for survival but also allowed some in-group competition. They were attentive to the actions and plans of other group members. To a limited extent, they remembered how other individuals treated one another. To a limited extent, they could predict how others might respond to their actions. They had dispositions pushing them toward both "nasty" and "nice" behaviors.

This doesn't answer the theological question of when sin entered the world. "Nice" behavior isn't necessarily the same thing as obeying God's moral law. "Nasty" behavior isn't necessarily the same thing as sin. Addressing those theological questions will require more discussion in later chapters.

Humans Cooperate by Necessity

Our ancestors worked in groups to hunt and forage for food, stay safe from predators, and learn the skills and toolmaking necessary for survival. An individual, or a single family of parents and children, could survive for only a

---

22. To learn more, see Jeffrey P. Schloss, "Darwinian Explanations of Morality: Accounting for the Normal but Not the Normative," in *Understanding Moral Sentiments: Darwinian Perspectives?*, ed. Hilary Putnam, Susan Neiman, and Jeffrey P. Schloss (Piscataway, NJ: Transaction Publishers, 2014), 81–121, http://www.isthmussociety.org/Documents/schloss_reading.pdf.

short while without the support of a larger group—and even then only thanks to skills they had learned over a lifetime within a social group. Dependence on social groups has been true of our ancestors going back millions of years to *Ardipithecus* and probably earlier.

That God used evolution to create us means that we, by necessity, are social creatures who are interdependent. That does not automatically make humans nice to one another. Living in social groups gave our ancestors opportunities to be both "nasty" and "nice" to one another and to observe and understand some of the consequences of their choices.

The Mental, Social, and Linguistic Development of Humanity Was Probably Gradual

We would like to know exactly how advanced our ancestors were—mentally, socially, and linguistically—at every point in the past. The scientific data, however, are open to a range of interpretations. We do have some clues from the behavior of the most intelligent and social animals and from the tools and other artifacts our ancestors left behind.

Some great apes, dolphins, and elephants possess a kind of self-awareness—a conscious awareness of themselves as individuals, a sense of "me." One classic test of self-awareness is the "mirror test." Some animals, when confronted with their reflection, do not behave as if they are seeing another animal; they instead behave in a way that implies that they understand they are looking at a reflection of themselves. So it is likely that our ancestors had some sort of self-awareness long before *Homo sapiens* was a species.

Some chimpanzees have learned sign language gestures for dozens of words, taught them to others,[23] and figured out how to combine them in new ways to communicate new ideas. Some elephants can recognize other individual elephants after being separated for decades. Some dolphins have "names" for one another and respond when called by name. So it is likely that our ancestors had similar abilities, at some level, already millions of years ago.

At around 100,000 years ago, our ancestors were still living in small family-tribal groups of a few dozen individuals, hunting, gathering, and fishing. By that time, they were exhibiting some behaviors that indicate communication and cooperation well beyond that of chimpanzees or any other currently living nonhuman species—behaviors such as making decorative shell beads and

---

23. For example, see R. Allen Gardner, Beatrix T. Gardner, and Thomas E. Van Cantfort, eds., *Teaching Sign Language to Chimpanzees* (New York: SUNY Press, 1989), 281–82.

transporting and probably trading not just decorations but also raw materials over distances of hundreds of miles.

Compared to a single human life span, genetic changes in a species are slow. A genetic mutation in one individual can take many generations to spread through a population. Cultural changes, by contrast, are typically much more rapid. Cultural innovations such as new tools, new techniques, new words, and new ideas can spread from one group to many groups in a single human lifetime.

Homo sapiens about 100,000 years ago would be so similar to modern humans, anatomically and genetically, that they would be difficult to distinguish. But how similar to us were they cognitively, linguistically, and morally? We don't know. An individual's personality, linguistic abilities, social abilities, and even morality are strongly affected by the family and culture in which they were raised. Two individuals, genetically very similar, could grow into very different people if raised in very different families and cultures. We don't know how intellectually, culturally, linguistically, and behaviorally advanced our ancestors were 200,000 years ago, or even 50,000 years ago. The scientific data are consistent with a range of views.

The term "modern human behavior" is not precisely defined. It is usually applied to a collection of behaviors that include most of the following: figurative art including cave paintings and figurines, use of pigment and jewelry for self-ornamentation, burial of dead (with artifacts), transport of resources and trade over long distances, cooperative labor, stone hearths, tools of bone materials, composite tools, fishing and fowling, stone blade technology, long-term planning, and a heavy reliance on social learning. One hypothesis is that once culture reaches a certain level of complexity, individuals who grow up in that culture develop greater cognitive and neurological complexity, which in turn tends to promote greater cultural complexity and innovation. (Smart cultures raise smart individuals, and vice versa.) Significant changes could accumulate in just a few centuries. So it is possible that a typical *Homo sapiens* adult who lived, say, 60,000 years ago would have been extremely similar genetically to a typical *Homo sapiens* adult who lived 30,000 years ago, but those living 30,000 years ago would have been, on average, much more advanced socially, cognitively, and linguistically. (It's worth noting that even if this hypothesis is correct, the spread of these cultural, technological, and cognitive changes to all *Homo sapiens* across multiple continents would have taken many thousands of years.)

Researchers point out that examples of all the behaviors listed as "modern" in the previous paragraph emerged gradually with anatomically modern body shapes. By 100,000 years ago, many of the items on that list were emerging in Africa and being carried to other places. As each migrating population took slightly different technology with them and interacted with different indigenous populations along the way (e.g., Neanderthals and Denisovans), each continent experienced a slightly different development of culture and technology. For example, humans who ended up in Australia used a boomerang, while those who went to Europe made composite tools, but all humans made stone points. The data are therefore also consistent with the hypothesis that a typical *Homo sapiens* adult who lived 60,000 years ago and one who lived 30,000 years ago would have been very similar to each other cognitively and linguistically (although the latter typically would have had access to a more complex tool kit).[24]

Some Human Capabilities Developed Far Beyond Those of Animals

Some social animals communicate with one another, learn from one another, cooperate with one another, and enforce prosocial behavior within the group, but humans do these things to a vastly greater degree than any other animals. The tools of science cannot measure what makes humans unique spiritually. But the tools of science can measure behaviors and abilities that set humans apart from all other animals today. This is a dynamic field of study today, so it's helpful to quote from several biologists and philosophers who have recently written on the topic.

Philosopher Michael Murray writes regarding teaching, learning, and cultural complexity:

> While animals display some forms of culture (beavers crafting tools/products in the form of dams) and social learning (bees that signal other bees on where to find food), human cumulative culture is different in three critical respects. First, the quantity and variety of cultural products and knowledge that we have and transmit to subsequent generations is massively larger. Second, and relatedly, our ability to copy or learn from others spans a much wider repertoire (including every cognitive and motor activity over which we have volitional control). And third, we are far more committed to the practices that make the accumulation and transmission of culture possible.[25]

24. For an accessible introduction to this discussion, with links to research literature discussing the competing hypotheses, see "Behavioral Modernity," Wikipedia, updated September 6, 2020, https://en.wikipedia.org/wiki/Behavioral_modernity#Great_leap_forward.

25. Michael J. Murray, "Death, Reverse Engineering the *Imago Dei*" (paper presented at the Dabar Conference, Reclaiming Theological Anthropology in an Age of Science, Trinity Evangelical Divinity School, Chicago, IL, June 13–16, 2018).

Philosopher Daniel Dennett writes about our ability to construct meaning:

> Our ability to devote our lives to something we deem more important than our own personal welfare—or our own biological imperative to have offspring—is one of the things that set us aside from the rest of the animal world. A mother bear will bravely defend a food patch, and ferociously protect her cub, or even her empty den, but probably more people have died in the valiant attempt to protect sacred places and texts than in the attempt to protect food stores or their own children and homes. Like other animals, we have built-in desires to reproduce and to do pretty much whatever it takes to achieve this goal, but we also have creeds, and the ability to transcend our genetic imperatives. This fact does make us different, but it is itself a biological fact, visible to natural science, and something that requires an explanation from natural science.[26]

And biologist Jeffrey Schloss writes regarding the types and amount of co-operation among humans:

> Human beings are the most intensively and extensively cooperative creatures on earth. Our division of labor, cooperation with unrelated individuals, and social interactions across large groups have been described as representing a "huge anomaly in the animal world." But setting aside the debated question of just how much difference in degree is required to constitute a difference in kind, there is no disagreement that "human cooperation exceeds that of all other species with regard to scale and range." In terms of intensiveness, we invest in long-term dyadic or small-group relationships—not just collaborations but "friendships"— that are based on neither kinship nor strict reciprocity. Indeed, the distinguishing, wonderful, and somewhat mystifying mark of being friends is that we do not vigilantly keep tabs on payback. . . . Importantly, friends constitute a "we" not merely in virtue of being attentive to each other's needs, but also through a shared gaze beyond those needs. A distinctive quality of human friendships is that they are often convened around mutual commitments that ostensibly have little directly to do with the material success, much less the evident reproductive interests, of the individuals. We jointly pursue and encourage one another in moral ends. And we may also cultivate non-moral goods: common interests in music, literature, an area of scientific inquiry, even a style of surfing. . . . The intensiveness of friendships with those we know is complemented by the extensiveness of cooperation with those we don't know. We cooperate with people we are not related to and have never met—on the basis of reputation, and even across large populations in the absence of reputational familiarity.[27]

---

26. Daniel Dennett, *Breaking the Spell: Religion as a Natural Phenomenon* (New York: Penguin, 2006), 4.

27. Jeffrey Schloss, "Shared Yearnings for a Greater Good," *Minding Nature* 10 (2017): 14–22.

God might have given humans these abilities gradually, through gene-culture coevolution, but we have these abilities to a degree that uniquely sets us apart from all other species.

Early Humans Had Dispositions toward Religious Beliefs

Nearly all human cultures throughout history have had religious practices and beliefs about the supernatural. Christian theologians over the centuries have said that God created us to desire a relationship with him. As St. Augustine put it, "For Thou hast formed us for Thyself, and our hearts are restless till they find rest in Thee."[28] John Calvin wrote, "That there exists in the human minds and indeed by natural instinct, some sense of Deity [*sensus divinitatis*], we hold to be beyond dispute, since God himself, to prevent any man from pretending ignorance, has endued all men with some idea of his Godhead."[29]

This provides a satisfactory (for Christians) answer to the question of *why* all humans have a desire and capacity for beliefs about the supernatural, but it leaves open the question of *how* God created this in us. If God used evolutionary processes to create humans, they might provide part of the answer.

In recent years, this has been a research topic in the fields of cognitive science and evolutionary psychology. Some hypotheses suggest that religiousness might be adaptive—that is, societies that have the right sorts of religious beliefs and practices, and individuals with genes that tend to fit in well with such societies, tend to do well. Religious beliefs and practices can promote cooperation and discourage cheating.

Other hypotheses suggest that the human predisposition to believe in supernatural persons is not itself adaptive but is a by-product of other cognitive systems that are adaptive. For example, children grow up seeing human-made tools and discerning their design and purpose—probably an adaptive ability— and perhaps extend this to seeing design and purpose behind features of the natural world. For another example, children grow up seeing humans and animals as agents with minds who do things to achieve goals, and perhaps they extend this to seeing events in the natural world as being caused by supernatural agents who also have minds and goals.

These hypotheses are tentative. Scientists need to make advances in genetics, developmental biology, neuroscience, and other fields before we will know whether, and to what extent, each of those mechanisms contributed to

28. Augustine, *Confessions* 1.1, https://www.ccel.org/ccel/schaff/npnf101.vi.I_1.I.html.
29. John Calvin, *Institutes of the Christian Religion* 1.3.1 (Beveridge trans.), https://www.ccel.org/ccel/calvin/institutes.

human evolution.[30] For the purposes of this book, it's enough to note that there are several plausible hypotheses for how God—using mechanisms of evolution—could have created humanity with a predisposition to see design and purpose in the natural world and to seek explanations in the supernatural.

This does not mean, however, that we humans naturally develop correct theologies about the supernatural purely from our evolved mental predispositions and our interactions with the natural world. As human history shows, in the absence of special revelation from God, humans tend to fill in the picture with pantheons of gods, nature spirits, ancestral spirits, and so forth. God created us with a desire and a capacity to look beyond the natural world, but we still need God's special revelation in order to develop a reliable system of beliefs and practices.[31]

Science and the Scenarios

In the introduction, we saw four general types of scenarios that attempt to answer the questions "Who were Adam and Eve?" and "When did sin begin?"

30. For an excellent summary of this field of research, see Justin L. Barrett, "Contemporary Trends in the Science of Religion: Adaptationist and Byproduct Theories and Their Implications" (paper presented at the American Scientific Affiliation Annual Meeting, July 24, 2016), http://www2.asa3.org/movies/ASA2016Barrett.mp4, with further resources available at http://network.asa3.org/page/2016Audio/2016-Annual-Meeting-Audio.htm. Several books on this topic exploring various hypotheses include Justin L. Barrett, *Born Believers: The Science of Children's Religious Belief* (New York: Simon & Schuster, 2012); Jesse Bering, *The Belief Instinct: The Psychology of Souls, Destiny, and the Meaning of Life* (New York: Norton, 2012); Scott Atran, *In Gods We Trust: The Evolutionary Landscape of Religion* (Oxford: Oxford University Press, 2004); Pascal Boyer, *Religion Explained: The Evolutionary Origins of Religious Thought* (New York: Basic Books, 2001); Robert N. McCauley, *Why Religion Is Natural and Science Is Not* (Oxford: Oxford University Press, 2011); and Ara Norenzayan, *Big Gods: How Religion Transformed Cooperation and Conflict* (Princeton: Princeton University Press, 2013).

31. There is an interesting analogy with the development of science. As babies encounter the world, their brains appear to be hardwired to develop, within the first few months of life, certain naïve beliefs about how the natural world works—for example, that unsupported objects should fall or that an object must be contacted by another object in order to suddenly change its movement. When babies over a certain age are shown situations that seem to violate these beliefs, they react with apparent surprise and attention. From the formal standpoint of physics, these naïve beliefs are not correct. One important goal in first-year college physics courses is helping students unlearn some of their naïve beliefs about the physics of motion so that they can learn the correct laws of motion. But learning the correct laws wouldn't be possible if the students didn't already have the capacities formed from their naïve beliefs. So when it comes to both science and religion, it appears that God used evolutionary processes to create humans with mental predispositions and capacities to hold true beliefs about nature and the supernatural. These predispositions might at first prompt us to quickly develop naïve and false beliefs. But those capacities are necessary placeholders so that true beliefs can be formed through careful instruction, reflection, and encounters with revelation.

(1) Adam and Eve as particular historical individuals acting as representatives of humanity; (2) Adam and Eve as particular historical individuals; sin spread through culture or genealogy; (3) Adam and Eve as a highly compressed history referring to many individuals over a long period of time who received special revelation; and (4) Adam and Eve as symbolic figures referring to many individuals over a long period of time, all who became ready to be held accountable and chose sin.

All four are easily compatible with the scientific data summarized in this chapter. All four can easily affirm the kinds of divine action discussed in chapter 2. Distinguishing their pros and cons will rely on the theological considerations discussed in the rest of this book.

5

The Soul, the *Imago Dei*, and Special Divine Action

SCIENCE CAN TELL US a great deal about the evolution of human bodies and genes. It can even tell us some things about the evolution of human intelligence, linguistic ability, empathy, moral dispositions, and religious dispositions.

What about the soul? What about humans being created "in the image of God"? What about divine special revelation? Might God have miraculously transformed some or all living humans at some point in history? For these questions, we turn to theology. Science gives some useful bits of information, but for the rest of this book, we draw primarily on the writings of biblical scholars and theologians.

At Some Time, God Began to Give Special Revelation to Our Ancestors

God created humans with certain natural abilities—including reason, empathy, and conscience—that help us understand how our actions help or harm others. And God created us with a disposition toward religious beliefs. These are part of God's "general revelation" to all of humanity. But these get us only so far. We also need God's "special revelation"—knowledge about God and spiritual matters through God's supernatural activity. God can communicate in many ways, including through audible words, visible signs, visions, the words and actions of inspired humans, and the inner testimony of the Holy Spirit.

We don't know exactly when or how God first gave special revelation to our ancestors. If God began doing this long enough ago, it could be another way God shaped our creation as a species. Recall gene-culture coevolution, discussed in the previous chapter. Special revelation to one or more individuals in a tribe could affect their culture. Culture could affect language, food sharing, toolmaking, family structure, grudge holding, forgiveness, teaching, learning, artwork, moral practices, religious beliefs, and many other things. Tribal culture shaped the behaviors of children and adults—even shaped children's brain development. This in turn could affect what genes were more likely to get passed on to the next generation.

If we relied on only general revelation (e.g., reason, empathy, conscience, and dispositions toward religious beliefs), we might tend toward polytheism, believing that the world is controlled by many gods and nature spirits who should be manipulated or appeased through ritual. Through special revelation, we learn that there is one Creator God who governs everything and whose overriding concern is that we love God and love one another. If we relied on only general revelation, we might think that loving our neighbors and hating our enemies is good enough. Through special revelation, we learn that God expects us to love our enemies. If we relied on only general revelation, we might think that God will reward us if we simply do more good than evil in our lives. Through special revelation, we learn that any evil on our part makes us unfit for God's presence and that none of us can be sufficiently righteous by our own effort.

At some point, God began specially revealing to our ancestors truths about how they should relate to him and to one another. Our ancestors could use their God-given freedom either to obey or to disobey. Because special revelation carries with it such significant potential for human rebellion, it's worth reviewing the four general scenario types for harmonizing the doctrine of original sin and human evolution that were described at the end of the introduction.

1. Adam and Eve as particular historical individuals acting as representatives of humanity.
2. Adam and Eve as particular historical individuals; sin spread through culture or genealogy.

3. Adam and Eve as a highly compressed history referring to many individuals over a long period of time who received special revelation.

4. Adam and Eve as symbolic figures referring to many individuals over a long period of time, all who became ready to be held accountable and chose sin.

When did special revelation begin? In the first two scenarios, God's first special revelation might have been to Adam and Eve. Alternatively, God might have given special revelation to our ancestors prior to Adam and Eve in order to push gene-culture coevolution in certain directions; however, the special revelation given to Adam and Eve was the first instance of special revelation that carried with it the possibility of sin. In the third and fourth scenarios, special revelation might have occurred quite far back in history, as far back as when any of our ancestors were ready to receive it.

Some Philosophical Theories about the Body, Mind, and Soul

Science can tell us a lot about the evolution of our ancestors' bodies, and something about their behavior. But it can't tell us about the status of their souls. For this, we need insights from theology and philosophy. Humans have theorized about the relationship between body, mind, and soul—in both religious and nonreligious contexts—for centuries.

"Substance dualism" has been a common belief throughout human history, famously taught by philosophers such as Plato (c. 427–347 BC) and Descartes (1590–1650). According to this view, our physical bodies and our nonphysical souls are made of fundamentally different substances, which are joined together in a living person. The body without the soul is dead. The soul can exist without the body. In ancient times, the soul was often thought to be responsible for all mental abilities such as reason, intelligence, memory, decision-making, and consciousness; seldom was much distinction made between soul and mind. Modern versions of substance dualism acknowledge the brain's role in these abilities but assert that the soul is necessary for the brain to properly perform these functions and, in particular, that the soul is necessary for consciousness.

Aristotle (384–322 BC) used his metaphysics of matter and form to hypothesize a "matter-and-form dualism" relationship between body and soul. The body is material and the soul immaterial, but they should not be thought of as two different entities. Matter is an ingredient. The soul organizes and empowers the body, endowing it with its essential human characteristics.

The body is made of matter. The soul is the "form" of the body—that is, the body's function and organization. Aristotle used the analogy of an axe. An axe is made of metal and wood. The axe's purpose is to chop. What makes it an axe is its ability to chop. Its ability to chop is not separable from the matter of which it is made. If it loses its ability to chop, it is no longer an axe, just something made of metal and wood. Likewise, the human soul is not separable from the body. The soul is, in a sense, the total of all the abilities of the person to do various things. Aristotle thought that all living things have souls. Plants have "nutritive" souls; they are capable of self-nourishment, growth, decay, and reproduction. Animals have "nutritive" and "sensitive" souls, also capable of perception and movement. Humans have "nutritive," "sensitive," and "rational" souls, also capable of thought and reason.

In nonreligious discussions, the terms "mind" and "soul" are not always distinguished. Ancient Greek philosophers and those who followed them tended to use the term "soul." They coupled that term with the hypothesis (in substance dualism) that the soul has the ability to have mental functions, or the hypothesis (in matter-and-form dualism) that the soul is what gives the body the capacity to have mental functions. In nonreligious discussions, modern scholars often prefer to use the term "mind" rather than "soul," partly so that their discussions about how the body and mind relate to each other can remain neutral on the question of what happens after death.

Through the centuries, philosophers of various religious views have also proposed versions of mind-body (or soul-body) "monism." Monism hypothesizes that our bodies—in particular, the functioning of our brains—give rise to all our mental abilities. A common (albeit simplified) saying in modern versions of monism is "The mind is what the brain does." Neuroscience is learning how our brains work. Scientists are discovering the neural activity going on in our brains when we see and hear, when we store and retrieve memories, when we experience emotions, and when we make decisions. Neuroscience is even making some discoveries about the neural activity involved in conscious experience.[1] In modern times, this has fueled greater interest in monism. If monism is correct, then there is no need to hypothesize that something extra gives our brains these abilities.

---

1. The ability of a material brain to give rise to the immaterial experience of consciousness is sometimes called the "hard problem." Philosopher David Chalmers is often credited with popularizing this term. See David Chalmers, "Facing Up to the Problem of Consciousness," *Journal of Consciousness Studies* 2, no. 3 (1995): 200–219. The apparent difficulty of ever solving this problem pushes some scholars to prefer dualism over monism. But other scholars, especially many scientists who are impressed by the ongoing progress in understanding how the brain works, favor monism.

Christian Theology, Divine Action, and Theories about the Soul

When we Christians talk about "souls," we typically include our mental aspects—our personalities and memories, our abilities to be conscious, to feel, to think. But we mean more than that. We also mean our spiritual selves—our ability to know, love, worship, and respond to God in obedience or disobedience.[2]

Scripture does not teach that the final state of existence for humans is as disembodied souls in heaven. Scripture teaches the *resurrection of the body* and the creation of a new heaven and new earth.[3] Therefore, several theories about the soul are compatible with Christian theology.

Not all versions of substance dualism are compatible with Christian theology,[4] but some are. Many Christian theologians from the early church to modern times have assumed some version of substance dualism. Most taught that God specially creates each new soul and unites it to a newly developing body after conception. A few theologians, such as Origen (184–254), have speculated that souls preexist bodies. On this view, souls are not coeternal with God, but they are created by God prior to conception, possibly prior to the creation of the material world, and are united with bodies after conception. Some theologians, such as Tertullian (c. 155–240) and Augustine (354–430), argued for traducianism, in which the soul of each new person is naturally produced from the souls of their parents, just as their body is

2. Some Christian traditions talk about humans as "tripartite" (three-part beings): body/mind/soul or body/soul/spirit. The second part is the immaterial but "natural" aspect of us that includes our personality, will, and consciousness. The third is our spiritual aspect, the means by which we worship and connect with God. This way of thinking has some theological value. But for this book, I will follow the majority of the broad Christian tradition and use the term "soul" to refer to all of our immaterial aspects—both mental and spiritual.

3. Many New Testament passages teach about the resurrection. Only a few passages talk about our state of existence after our deaths and before the resurrection, sometimes called the "intermediate state." Theologians offer a number of theories regarding the intermediate state, but those theories go beyond the needs of this book. For our purposes, it is enough to say the following: Our existence now, here on earth, depends on God's will and continual sustaining power. Our existence as resurrected persons in the new creation will also presumably depend on God's will and continual sustaining power. So also, our existence in the intermediate state, whatever that is, will depend on God's will and continual sustaining power. This is true about the intermediate state whether one favors substance dualism, matter-and-form dualism, monism, or some other theory of the soul.

4. In the ancient Greek and Roman world, some believed that the immaterial (including the soul) was inherently good and that the material (including the body) was inherently evil. Christian theology rejected this notion because God created both the immaterial and the material world, including our bodies. Some ancient philosophers believed that souls are inherently eternal and preexisted from all eternity, and some (like Plato) believed that the souls of the dead could be reincarnated into new bodies. Christian theology rejected those ideas as incompatible with Scripture.

naturally produced from the bodies of their parents.[5] In all these views, the souls of those who die are held in existence by God's sustaining power, to be united with new bodies at the resurrection.

Not all versions of matter-and-form dualism are compatible with Christian theology, but some are. Thomas Aquinas (1225–74) synthesized Aristotle's metaphysics with Christian theology. Ever since, some theologians have favored Aquinas's version of matter-and-form dualism to explain the relationship of body and soul. In matter-and-form dualism, the soul is more dependent on the body than it is in substance dualism, yet it is still the case that after death, souls are held in existence by God's sustaining power, to be united with new bodies at the resurrection.

Not all versions of monism are compatible with Christian theology,[6] but some are. A growing number of Christian scholars have written books and articles in recent decades about ways to synthesize versions of monism with Christian theology.[7] Our bodies, especially the functioning of our brains, give rise to our mental abilities, including our capacity to have personal relationships with other humans and with God. But our spiritual lives also depend on God supernaturally establishing a relationship with us, revealing himself to us, and making promises to us. Our mental, social, and relational abilities might be "natural" results of our bodies and brains functioning as they should, but our personal relationship with God (and any hope for life after death) also relies on "supernatural" action from God. Because our mental and spiritual capacities are so dependent on our bodies, disembodied souls can exist after death only through God's miraculous sustaining activity.[8] At the resurrection, we will be embodied in new bodies that are properly suited to the new creation.

5. One argument sometimes made by supporters of traducianism is the following: If all humans are sinful from birth, and if God specially creates each new human soul, then God is in effect creating sinful souls. If, however, the soul of each child is naturally produced by the parents, then children are sinful from birth simply because sinful parents produce sinful children.

6. Some atheists who are monists simply say, "Souls don't exist." Others might say something functionally equivalent, such as, "When the body dies, the brain dies. When the brain dies, that mind stops existing forever." Christian monists reject these atheistic versions of monism.

7. For example, see Nancey Murphy, *Bodies and Souls, or Spirited Bodies?*, Current Issues in Theology 3 (New York: Cambridge University Press, 2006); Kevin J. Corcoran, *Rethinking Human Nature: A Christian Materialist Alternative to the Soul* (Grand Rapids: Baker Academic, 2006); Warren S. Brown, Nancey C. Murphy, and H. Newton Malony, eds., *Whatever Happened to the Soul? Scientific and Theological Portraits of Human Nature* (Minneapolis: Fortress, 1997); and Joel B. Green, *Body, Soul, and Human Life*, Studies in Theological Interpretation: The Nature of Humanity in the Bible (Grand Rapids: Baker Academic, 2008).

8. Among Christians who are monists, there isn't consensus on whether disembodied souls are sustained by God in some sort of conscious intermediate state or whether souls "sleep" without consciousness and are preserved within God's being until the resurrection.

Theological opinions vary on whether animals also have souls. Some versions of substance dualism claim that only humans have souls. Other versions of substance dualism, as well as matter-and-form dualism, claim that animals do have souls that enable their mental capacities but that animal souls are different from human souls. Monism claims that animal bodies and brains give rise to animal mental capacities and that those mental capacities end with the death of animals' bodies. Scripture tells us very little regarding whether animals have a relationship with God that can survive death and whether any particular animals will be resurrected in the new creation.

In all three theories of the soul, some sort of special divine action is required for humans to have souls—although the exact type of divine action is different. Monists would say that God could have created our human mental abilities through evolutionary processes; however, God's supernatural activity was required for God to reveal himself to humans and establish a relationship with them. Those adhering to substance dualism, and most versions of matter-and-form dualism, would say that God performed some sort of miracle to create the first human souls. Adherents of most versions of dualism would say that God miraculously creates every human soul, although those who favor traducianism would say that God miraculously created the first human souls but that every subsequent soul is naturally generated by the parents. In light of the scientific evidence for human evolution, modern dualists who believe that animals have souls might believe that God did not miraculously create the first human souls *de novo* but miraculously transformed the souls of the first true humans, and that this miraculous transformation was necessary for our unique mental and spiritual abilities.

When Were Our Ancestors First Ensouled?

There are several possible answers to the question "When were our ancestors first ensouled?" In all theories of the soul, part of what is meant by our "souls" is our mental aspects—our personalities and memories, our abilities to be conscious, to feel, and to think. God developed those abilities in our ancestors through his sustaining of and concurring with natural processes over a long evolutionary history. It is also possible (not required by theology, but not ruled out by scientific data) that God performed some miraculous acts of transformation in our ancestors along the way to increase their mental and social abilities. But the development of our mental and social abilities, by itself, is not enough to be called "ensoulment."

By "ensoulment," we also mean our spiritual selves—our abilities to know, love, worship, and respond to God. In all theories of the soul, these abilities depend on God supernaturally establishing a relationship with us, revealing himself to us, and making promises to us. Under monist theories, when God first began to do these things among our ancestors, that was the time they were first "ensouled." Under dualist theories, when God first began to do these things among our ancestors, as part of that act, God also miraculously created the first human souls to unite with their bodies.

Did God ensoul the entire population of our ancestors at the same time, or only a fraction of the population? That question is discussed later in this chapter and in chapter 9, along with some theological pros and cons of different answers.

Different Theological Theories about the "Image of God"

Scripture introduces the idea of the "image of God" in Genesis 1:

> Then God said, "Let us make mankind in our image, in our likeness, so that they may rule over the fish in the sea and the birds in the sky, over the livestock and all the wild animals, and over all the creatures that move along the ground."
>
> > So God created mankind in his own image,
> >   in the image of God he created them;
> >   male and female he created them.
>
> God blessed them and said to them, "Be fruitful and increase in number; fill the earth and subdue it. Rule over the fish in the sea and the birds in the sky and over every living creature that moves on the ground." (vv. 26–28)

When the original audience heard these words, they presumably understood fairly well what the author meant by the "image of God." As centuries passed, cultures and languages changed. Already in the first few centuries of the Christian church, in a culture dominated by Greek language and ideas, there was some disagreement about what that phrase meant. Greek philosophy often assumed body-soul dualism, with body and soul having different functions. This was not an Old Testament way of thinking, as David J. A. Clines explains:

> Man according to the Old Testament is a psychosomatic unity; it is therefore the corporeal animated man that is the image of God. The body cannot be

left out of the meaning of the image; man is a totality, and his "solid flesh" is as much the image of God as his spiritual capacity, creativeness or personality, since none of these "higher" aspects of the human being can exist in isolation from the body. The body is not a mere dwelling-place for the soul, nor is it the prison-house of the soul. In so far as man is a body and a bodiless man is not man, the body is the image of God; for man is the image of God. Man is the flesh-and-blood image of the invisible God.[9]

Early Christian theologians, however, often used Greek philosophical ideas about the body and soul in their theological reasoning. Many assumed a version of substance dualism like Plato's, although Aristotle's teachings were also influential. Stanley Grenz summarizes this influence:

Crucial in providing a background for the Christian conception of the *imago dei* as constituted by reason was the famous ancient definition of the human person as "the rational animal," a definition that follows the Aristotelian structure of defining things *per genus proximum et differentiam* [a definition made by its closest genus and specific differences] and thereby delineates the aspect of human nature that sets humans apart from the creatures that shared the kingdom "animal." So influential was this approach that the church fathers in both East and West took for granted that the human person was a rational animal.[10]

Most affirmed that the image of God is primarily in the soul, although the whole human (soul and body in unity) images God in this life. Reason and will are primary among the soul's abilities that enable us to image God.

The image of God was thus identified with human abilities that differentiate us from animals. Abilities typically cited are humanity's (1) mental abilities, (2) moral characteristics, and (3) capacity for spiritual holiness reflecting God's holiness. The first two were often thought to be natural abilities of humanity, while the third referred to a state of original righteousness that required supernatural gifts from God.

Irenaeus, Tertullian, and a few others made a distinction between the "image" and the "likeness" of God. Tatha Wiley describes this: "Irenaeus differentiated between two terms found in Genesis 1:26, 'image of God' and 'likeness to God.' He thought *the image of God* referred to human rational

---

9. David J. A. Clines, "Image of God in Man," *Tyndale Bulletin* 19 (1968): 86–87, https://archive.org/stream/pdfy-SLVx2c60Fa59pgFJ/The%20Image%20Of%20God%20In%20Man_djvu.txt.

10. Stanley J. Grenz, *The Social God and the Relational Self: A Trinitarian Theology of the Imago Dei* (Louisville: Westminster John Knox, 2001), 143–44.

moral nature, that is reason and freedom. Adam did not lose the image of God by his sin. *Likeness to God* referred to Adam's spiritual similarity to God. It was this spiritual similarity, Irenaeus argued, that Adam lost by his sin."[11]

Most early theologians, however, combined "image" and "likeness" into a single concept. For some, the image of God had to do specifically with the creaturely abilities that separate us from animals. For others, the image included original righteousness. Clines gives several examples: "For Ambrose, the soul was the image; for Athanasius, rationality in light of the Logos doctrine; for Augustine, under the influence of Trinitarian dogma, the image is to be seen as the triune faculties of the soul, *memoria, intelectus, amor.*"[12]

Martin Luther, in contrast to most earlier theologians, thought that the image of God referred only to original righteousness and that the loss of original righteousness was the loss of the image. But John Calvin, like most earlier theologians, thought that the image referred both to human abilities that exceed those of animals (damaged but not lost in the fall) and to the state of original righteousness (lost in the fall). Calvin wrote,

> Hence, although the soul is not the man, there is no absurdity in holding that he is called the image of God in respect of the soul; though I retain the principle which I lately laid down, that the image of God extends to everything in which the nature of man surpasses that of all other species of animals. Accordingly, by this term is denoted the integrity with which Adam was endued when his intellect was clear, his affections subordinated to reason, all his senses duly regulated, and when he truly ascribed all his excellence to the admirable gifts of his Maker. And though the primary seat of the divine image was in the mind and the heart, or in the soul and its powers, there was no part even of the body in which some rays of glory did not shine.[13]

In recent centuries, some theologians have argued that the image of God refers not to human abilities but to the personal relationship God forms with us and our response to God. Clines summarizes Karl Barth on the image of God: "As bearer of the image, man is partner of God Himself, capable of dealings with Him and of close relationship with Him. He is a being whom God addresses as Thou and makes answerable as I. Thus the image describes the I-Thou relationship between man and God."[14]

11. Tatha Wiley, *Original Sin: Origins, Developments, Contemporary Meanings* (New York: Paulist Press, 2002), 40.

12. Clines, "Image of God in Man," 54–55.

13. John Calvin, *Institutes of the Christian Religion* 1.15.3 (Beveridge trans.), https://www .ccel.org/ccel/calvin/institutes.

14. Clines, "Image of God in Man," 60.

Grenz, in *The Social God and the Relational Self*, summarizes the thinking of several theologians this way: "The relational understanding of the *imago dei* moves the focus from noun to verb. This approach presupposes that a relationship exists between Creator and creature and views the image as what occurs as a consequence of the relationship—namely, the creature 'images' the Creator."[15]

More recently, scholars of the ancient Near East have discovered that the "image" of a king or of a god had specific meanings in those cultures. Kings sometimes put statues of themselves in a conquered land to show their dominion over it. These images of the kings were meant to imply their connection to the land as its ruler, despite their physical absence.

In some cultures surrounding Israel, the king (and only the king) was called the image of the god, indicating that the king was ruling by divine ordination and that the god was ruling through the king. Genesis 1 changes this cultural picture significantly by declaring that all humans (not just kings) are created in the image of God, but it retains the idea of God's rule being exercised through his image bearers.

New scholarship on the ancient Near East in recent decades has led many biblical scholars to conclude that this concept—God's rule over the world exercised through humanity—is central to understanding the image of God in Genesis in its original cultural-historical context.[16] Richard Middleton summarizes:

> There is at present a virtual consensus among Old Testament scholars concerning the meaning of the *imago Dei* in Genesis. This virtual consensus is based, in the first place, on careful literary and rhetorical analysis of Genesis 1:1–2:3 as a textual unit. Such analysis notes the predominantly "royal" flavour of the text, and does not depend only on the close linking of image with the mandate to rule and subdue the earth and its creatures in verses 26 and 28 (typically royal functions). Beyond this royal mandate, the God in whose image and likeness humans are created is depicted as sovereign over the cosmos, ruling by royal decree. . . . These and other rhetorical clues, when taken together with the wealth of comparative studies of Israel and the ancient Near East, have

---

15. Grenz, *Social God*, 162.

16. For example, see J. Richard Middleton, *The Liberating Image: The* Imago Dei *in Genesis* (Grand Rapids: Brazos, 2005); Catherine L. McDowell, *The Image of God in the Garden of Eden: The Creation of Humankind in Genesis 2:5–3:24 in Light of the Mīs Pî Pīt Pî and Wpt-r Rituals of Mesopotamia and Ancient Egypt* (Winona Lake, IN: Eisenbrauns, 2015); Ryan S. Peterson, *The* Imago Dei *as Human Identity: A Theological Interpretation* (Winona Lake, IN: Eisenbrauns, 2016); John F. Kilner, *Dignity and Destiny: Humanity in the Image of God* (Grand Rapids: Eerdmans, 2015); and Marc Cortez, *Theological Anthropology: A Guide for the Perplexed* (New York: Bloomsbury, 2010).

led to an interpretation which sees the image of God as *the royal function or office of human beings as God's representatives and agents in the world, given authorized power to share in God's rule over the earth's resources and creatures.*[17]

The Image of God, Evolution, Divine Action, and Adam and Eve

In summary, there are four common theological theories about what the image of God is:

1. Our mental, social, and moral capabilities, especially the ones that distinguish humans from animals
2. A pre-fallen state of original righteousness
3. The personal relationship between God and humans
4. Our commission to be God's representatives to and stewards of the rest of creation

These theories are not exclusive. For example, collectively as human beings, our ability to have a personal relationship with God (3) and our commission to be God's representatives and stewards (4) depend on God first having given humanity certain mental, social, and moral capabilities (1). God gives humanity as a whole mental, social, and moral capabilities, enabling humanity as a whole to be God's stewards of creation. God also establishes a personal relationship with each individual; therefore each individual, regardless of functional disabilities or aberrations, is an image bearer of God.

God could have given humanity its mental, social, and moral capabilities simply through his governance of natural evolutionary processes. As noted in the previous chapter, it's possible that God augmented those natural processes with acts of special revelation, influencing gene-culture coevolution to shape humanity's development. It's also possible that God augmented those processes with acts of miraculous transformation. Whatever means God used, our status as God's image bearers is not based on how we received our abilities but on the fact that they are a gift from God.

At some point in human history, God established personal relationships with human beings and declared them to be his image bearers. God did this uniquely with human beings, not with any animal species with whom we might share common ancestry. This aspect of being God's image bearers

---

17. J. Richard Middleton, "The Liberating Image? Interpreting the *Imago Dei* in Context," *Christian Scholars Review* 24, no. 1 (1994): 11–12.

relies on special revelation from God to us. This supernatural act of God is independent of how God gave us our mental, social, and moral abilities.

All four types of scenarios for the entrance of sin into the world considered in this book (summarized at the end of the introduction) include God governing natural evolutionary processes, and all four include God giving special revelation to humans. Therefore, all four types of scenarios are easily compatible with the first, third, and fourth understandings of the image of God in the list above.

Some (not all) theories about the image of God also include the idea that Adam and Eve lived for a while in a state of original righteousness. (These theories fall under the second understanding in the list above.) The end of this chapter and chapter 9 discuss some pros and cons of this idea.

Did God endow the entire population of our ancestors with the image of God at the same time, or only a fraction of the population? This question is discussed in the next section and again in chapter 9.

God Might Have Miraculously Transformed Our Ancestors' Physicality

In the Old Testament, entire centuries pass with God achieving his will purely by working through human beings and human events—that is, without any record of God performing obvious miracles. But there were a few special times, especially during the lives of Moses and Elijah, when God performed multiple miraculous signs and acts of deliverance. It is reasonable to wonder if God did something similar when creating humans. God achieved his will in creating humans over millions of years using means that we describe scientifically as natural evolutionary mechanisms. But might God also have performed one or more miraculous acts of transformation at a few special occasions along the way?

For the most part, that question requires theological analysis, although science can contribute some useful data. Christians have proposed various possible miraculous acts:

1. *Biological and neurological transformation.* At one particular point in time, God might have miraculously transformed some or all of our ancestors, changing them biologically, and especially neurologically, so they had new mental and spiritual capabilities. They were the first true humans in a *theological* sense, God's image bearers.[18]

18. Whether or not these transformed individuals were also a new species in the *biological* sense (see chap. 4) is not the important question here. The important question is *how* God gave

2. *Genetic transformation.* Starting at one particular generation, God might have miraculously changed the genomes of some or all individuals at their conception so that, as they grew, they developed mental and spiritual capabilities that their parents did not have. This was the first generation of true humans in a theological sense.[19]

3. *Intensive educational transformation.* At some point in time, God might have transformed some or all of our ancestors through educational processes, awakening in them new mental and spiritual capabilities and a much greater degree of self-consciousness.[20] This made them the first true humans in a theological sense. Perhaps genetically and neurologically they were ready for such a transformation, but they had not developed a culture that enabled it. God miraculously enabled the transformation by interacting with them intensively as a teacher might. They, in turn, passed the new mental and spiritual capabilities to future generations through education, pushing gene-culture coevolution in a new direction.

4. *Ensoulment.* Assuming some version of body-soul dualism is true, at one particular point in time, God might have endowed some or all of our ancestors with human souls, thereby giving them new mental and spiritual capabilities.[21]

5. De novo *creation.* God might have performed a miracle at some point to create the first human population miraculously, without common ancestry with other primates, but did so in a way that made their genomes consistent with the predictions of common ancestry.

6. *Starting from just a single pair.* God might have created humanity miraculously, starting with just a single pair of individuals sometime in

---

our ancestors certain mental and spiritual capabilities that made them distinct *theologically* from preceding generations and whether God's means included miraculous transformation.

19. For example, see Andrew C. J. Alexander, "Human Origins and Genetics," *Clergy Review* 49 (1964): 344–53.

20. We could imagine this as similar to the "awakening" experience described by Helen Keller when Anne Sullivan taught her to associate finger movements with concepts and things in the world. See Helen Keller, *The World I Live In* (New York: New York Review Books, 2003), chap. 11.

21. Examples include Kenneth W. Kemp, "Science, Theology, and Monogenesis," *American Catholic Philosophical Quarterly* 85, no. 2 (2011): 217–36; Gregg Davidson, *When Faith and Science Collide* (Oxford, MS: Malius Press, 2009), 58–65; and Gregg Davidson, "Genetics, the Nephilim, and the Historicity of Adam," *Perspectives on Science and Christian Faith* 67, no. 1 (2015): 24–34, http://www.asa3.org/ASA/PSCF/2015/PSCF3–15Davidson.pdf. (Note that in some versions of substance dualism and all versions of matter-and-form dualism, endowing a not-yet-fully-human creature with a human soul not only endows or transforms the soul but also transforms the creature's body into a fully human body, because of the unity and interdependence of body and soul.)

the last few hundred thousand years, or even more recently, and then also miraculously increased the genetic diversity of their offspring in just such a way as to make their genomes appear consistent with what we would expect if our ancestral population was never less than several thousand individuals.

We could hypothesize God doing any one of these miraculous acts, or several together. If God did any of these, God established new relationships with our ancestors at the time of these miracles. These humans were the first image bearers of God with human souls,[22] and these new relationships had new expectations, new blessings, and new promises.

Again, Avoiding the Theological Problem of False Apparent History

Proposals 5 and 6 on the above list cannot be disproved by science, but they face the serious theological problem, discussed in chapter 2, of God creating in a way that writes a false apparent history into the genomes of every human being.

The first four proposals do not necessarily share this problem. Whether or not they share it depends on how radical the hypothesized miraculous change was. For example, if the hypothesized miraculous changes to our ancestors' genomes (proposal 2) were radical enough, we would expect to see evidence of it today in the human genome, in unique changes to human genes that defy scientific explanation. As scientists today compare the human genome to that of other primates, they do see changes unique to humans. But most scientists believe these changes are well within the range of changes that could have happened through ordinary evolutionary processes.

Similarly, if the hypothesized miraculous changes to our ancestors' mental, social, and moral abilities (proposals 1, 3, and possibly 4) were radical enough, we might expect to see archaeological evidence of a sudden advancement in our ancestors' technological abilities or social living concentrated at one particular time. If God applied these miraculous changes to all humans, we would likely see this sudden advancement appear more or less simultaneously all across the globe, wherever our ancestors were living. Alternatively, if the hypothesized miraculous changes happened to just two, or to a few, individuals, and were radical enough, we might expect to see archaeological evidence of a sudden advancement of several types of technology and social living happening at once in one location and spreading from there. Current

22. Regardless of whether you choose a monist or a dualist theory of the soul.

archaeological evidence doesn't support either of these hypotheses. Evidence of innovation is spread out in the archaeological record, indicating that significant advancements were spread out in time. And various innovations are found for the first time in many places around the globe. In archaeology, it is not unusual for a first known example of a particular technology in human history to be supplanted by a new discovery of a precursor example, a bit older, at a location far away. Therefore, most scientists believe that the technological and social changes among our ancestors happened relatively slowly, spread out geographically wherever our ancestors were living, well within what could be expected through ordinary gene-culture coevolution.

So the scientific data are open to a range of interpretations, and theology is open to a range of possibilities on this point. Science and theology tell us that God could have created humanity's unique physical, mental, and spiritual abilities without performing any of the proposed miraculous transformations. God could have achieved humanity's creation by sustaining and concurring with ordinary evolutionary processes and by establishing a special relationship with us and making us aware of that relationship through special revelation.

But God also might have performed some miracles during humanity's creation that were highly significant at the time but left no obvious evidence still detectable today. God might have transformed some or all of our ancestors in ways that were significant—if we had been able to witness those miracles when they were performed, we would have seen a dramatic change in our ancestors—but not so radical as to leave scientifically detectable evidence into the present. With that proviso, the first four proposed miracles on the list could avoid the theological objection of false apparent history. For that reason, chapter 9 will consider other theological arguments for and against them.

God Might Have Spiritually Empowered Our Ancestors with Supernatural Gifts

Our natural human abilities include reason, moral dispositions, and religious inclinations. The idea that God also endowed the first humans with certain *supernatural* gifts—given so that they (unlike us today) could live in true righteousness and holiness—goes far back in church history, from the church fathers, through medieval times, and into the present in some Christian traditions. Included here are three representative examples (quoting the scholarship of Fredrick Tennant and Tatha Wiley).

The Fall is conceived by Athanasius [297–373] as a lapse of mankind to the "natural state." In other words, the Fall is represented as consisting in the loss of what more modern theology has called supernatural endowments. From the first transgression onwards, mankind have been reduced to the condition of nature above which they were originally raised by the ψυχὴ λογική [rational soul], which, though in some of its aspects regarded as a natural endowment, is nevertheless rather a superadded gift of grace.[23]

Augustine [354–430] argued that in Adam's original state he had the ability *not to sin (posse non peccare)*. He also possessed certain gifts in this prelapsarian state. These gifts were over and beyond what human nature as nature requires. Among these gifts were immortality, integrity, and knowledge. By sin, Adam lost these gifts. Consequently, Adam's descendants are born without them.[24]

In Anselm's [1033–1109] conception of created nature, Adam was also oriented toward union with God by possession of the supernatural gift of *blessedness* or *beatitude*. The gifts of justice and blessedness assisted human nature toward its intended transcendent end, but as *supernatural gifts* they were not essential to nature. They could be taken away without destroying human nature. . . . Anselm argued that Adam lost the supernatural gift of *justitia* by his disobedience of God's command.[25]

Although theologians wrote about these supernatural gifts in different ways, a common theme was that these supernatural gifts enabled Adam and Eve to be in a state of original righteousness. Adam and Eve were not merely in a state of moral innocence but in a state of actual moral righteousness, spiritually reflecting God's holiness, able to obey all of God's moral law and not sin. (Some writers, such as Augustine, went beyond this and suggested that their supernatural gifts included exemption from suffering, sickness, and the debility of old age, as well as infused knowledge and intellectual powers far beyond those of any human since.) These supernatural gifts were lost when Adam and Eve sinned.

Athanasius, Augustine, and Anselm assumed that Adam and Eve were created miraculously. We now have good evidence that God created humans using evolutionary processes and that our ancestors evolved to have a mixture of "nasty" and "nice" behavioral dispositions. Our ancestors, by their own *natural* abilities, would not have been able to be completely holy or obey all of

23. Frederick Robert Tennant, *The Sources of the Doctrines of the Fall and Original Sin* (Cambridge: Cambridge University Press, 1903), 311–12.
24. Wiley, *Original Sin*, 62–63.
25. Wiley, *Original Sin*, 79–81.

God's moral law. Does this mean we must give up the idea that any of our ancestors were ever actually in a state of original righteousness? Not necessarily.

Consider the first two types of scenarios, in which Adam and Eve are particular historical individuals. In these scenarios, when God specially selected Adam and Eve out of a larger population and revealed himself to them, God also could have given them supernatural gifts. We might imagine this as a superabundant empowering by the Holy Spirit, enabling them for a time to be truly righteous and holy, able not to sin. They could have lived for a time in a state of true original righteousness, as theologians throughout the centuries have pictured. Even in the other two types of scenarios, in which Adam and Eve are thought of as literary or symbolic figures referring to many individuals over a long history, it is conceivable that God could have given the gift to *some* of our ancestors for a time. But further discussion of this idea is reserved for chapter 9.

6

Adam and Eve
in Scripture

SOME PARTS OF SCRIPTURE are historical; some parts are allegorical and nonhistorical; some parts are based on history but include many figurative elements. Some parts don't fit neatly into any of those categories. What is the best way to understand the Adam and Eve story in Genesis 2–3?

The introduction of this book presented four general types of scenarios for interpreting Genesis 2–3 and the entrance of sin into the world. In the first two types, the Adam and Eve of Genesis 2–3 are thought to be particular historical individuals. In the other two types, they are thought to be literary and symbolic figures referring to the experiences of many individuals.

This chapter focuses on the Old and New Testament texts that mention Adam and Eve. Numerous biblical scholars have written about these texts in the last few decades; this chapter summarizes arguments made by roughly half a dozen of them. All of these authors use historical scholarship that illuminates the cultural, linguistic, and historical contexts of the texts. All of them acknowledge the scientific evidence for human evolution. All of them affirm the divine inspiration and authority of Scripture. Yet they come to a spectrum of conclusions regarding whether or not Adam and Eve should be thought of as particular historical figures.

Genesis 2–3 (Text)

Although literal-historical interpretations of Genesis 2–3 were common in church history, the church has long recognized that certain elements suggest symbolism at work: a talking serpent, a tree that gives immortality, a tree that gives knowledge of good and evil. Even the names of the principal characters are suggestive. John Walton writes this regarding the names:

> Understanding the varied use of the term *adam* is essential to sorting out the early chapters of Genesis. But before we even get to that issue, there are two important observations to make. The first is that the word *adam* is a Hebrew word meaning "human." Regarding this observation, the fact that it is Hebrew indicates that the category designation ("human") is imposed by those who spoke Hebrew. Adam and Eve would not have called each other these names because whatever they spoke, it was not Hebrew. Hebrew does not exist as a language until somewhere in the middle of the second millennium B.C. That means that these names are not just a matter of historical reporting, as if their names just happened to be Adam and Eve like someone else's name is Bill or Mary. Although I believe that Adam and Eve are historical personages—real people in a real past—these cannot be their historical names. The names are Hebrew, and there is no Hebrew at the point in time when Adam and Eve lived. If these are not *historical* names, then they must be *assigned* names, intended by the Hebrew-speaking users to convey a particular meaning. Such a deduction leads us to the second observation. In English, if we read that someone's name is "Human" and his partner's name is "Life," we quickly develop an impression of what is being communicated (as, for example, in *Pilgrim's Progress*, where characters are named Christian, Faithful, and Hopeful). These characters, by virtue of their *assigned* names, are larger than the historical characters to whom they refer. They represent something beyond themselves.[1]

This Hebrew wordplay on *adam* has been noted by many scholars.[2] Walton also argues that the statements in Genesis 2 about how Adam and Eve were

---

1. John H. Walton, *The Lost World of Adam and Eve* (Downers Grove, IL: InterVarsity, 2015), 58–59.

2. For example, J. Richard Middleton writes, "Let us start with the name *Adam*. It is significant that this name (like many other names in the early chapters of Genesis) is clearly symbolic. Adam (*'ādām*) means 'human.' Indeed, Adam becomes a proper name only in Genesis 4 and 5; prior to that he is *hā'ādām* (the human). So we seem to be justified in viewing him both as the first human and archetypally as everyman or everyone. We should also note that the word for the first human (*'ādām*) functions as part of a Hebrew pun or word play throughout Genesis 2 and 3, where it sounds like (or resonates aurally with) the word for soil or ground (*'ădāmâ*)." J. Richard Middleton, "Reading Genesis 3 Attentive to Evolution," in *Evolution and the Fall*, ed. William T. Cavanaugh and James K. A. Smith (Grand Rapids: Eerdmans, 2017), 73.

formed—"dust" and "rib"—should be understood as referring to *all* humans rather than uniquely to two individuals. Genesis 2:7 is often translated as saying that God formed Adam "from the dust of the ground," but Walton notes that the preposition "from" is not in the original Hebrew text or the Septuagint.[3] Several biblical passages point to all humans, like Adam, as being "dust" (e.g., Ps. 103:14: "For he knows how we are formed; he remembers that we are dust"). Throughout Scripture, being "dust" is a reference to mortality. When we die, to dust we return. Likewise, several biblical passages point to all creatures, like Adam, receiving the "breath of life" from God (Gen. 7:22; Job 27:3; 32:8; 33:4; 34:14–15; Isa. 42:5). When we look at how the words used to describe the formation of Eve are used elsewhere in the Hebrew Scriptures, they imply not that Adam was in a surgical sleep and had a single rib removed but that Adam entered a visionary state (*tardemah*; Gen. 15:12; Job 4:13; Dan. 8:18) in which God took one entire side of Adam to make Eve. This is immediately followed by a statement about the relationship of all men and women in marriage—becoming one flesh—again suggesting that this passage is meant to teach about Adam and Eve as archetypes of all humans rather than a historical lesson about just two particular individuals.

Genesis 2–3 (Cultural Context)

Archaeologists have discovered several ancient Near Eastern texts with parallels to Genesis 2–11, including the Sumerian King List, the Atrahasis epic, Enuma Elish, Eridu Genesis (the Sumerian creation account), the myth of Adapa, the Sumerian myth of Enki and Ninhursag, and the Epic of Gilgamesh. Scholars have compiled lists of similar themes and motifs between Genesis 2–3 and these other texts, including but not limited to a garden paradise (Enki, Gilgamesh); streams of water that enable agriculture by irrigation (Atrahasis, Enki); humans created from the ground to cultivate the land (Atrahasis, Enki, Gilgamesh); a name that means "man/human" (Adapa); the institution of marriage (Atrahasis); a command about eating and not eating (Adapa); an immortality-granting plant and a serpent (Gilgamesh); humans losing immortality (Atrahasis, Adapa, Gilgamesh); and nakedness as a symbol of primitive life (Gilgamesh).[4]

3. Robert C. Bishop, Larry L. Funck, Raymond J. Lewis, Stephen O. Moshier, and John H. Walton, *Understanding Scientific Theories of Origins: Cosmology, Geology, and Biology in Christian Perspective* (Downers Grove, IL: InterVarsity, 2018), 548–51.

4. Taken from C. John Collins, *Did Adam and Eve Really Exist? Who They Were and Why You Should Care* (Wheaton: Crossway, 2011), 140–41; Peter Enns, *The Evolution of Adam: What the Bible Does and Doesn't Say about Human Origins* (Grand Rapids: Brazos, 2012),

The similarities between Genesis 2–3 and this other literature provide historical, cultural, and religious context. Genesis 2–3 is a type of literature known in the ancient Near Eastern culture. These other cultures' stories shared symbolic elements and motifs. Within their cultures, they answered listeners' questions about humanity's place in the cosmic hierarchy, the purpose of marriage and agriculture, and why humans were mortal. Because Genesis 2–3 shares many of these elements, its theological *differences* with those other stories are striking. In Genesis, there is only one God. Creation is good, finite, and not in any opposition to God. The sun and moon are not deities but objects made by God to serve a function in creation. God created humanity because it pleased him to do so, not out of any need on God's part. Humanity as a whole is made in God's image, and human work has God-ordained dignity.

Denis Lamoureaux writes, "Though Genesis 2 includes a number of ancient Near Eastern motifs, it delivers Messages of Faith that are radically different from pagan beliefs. The LORD is in a personal relationship with humankind. In fact, He cares about the man and woman. This relationship features obedience to a Holy God and accountability before Him. Humans have the freedom not to observe His commands, but there are serious consequences if they disregard them."[5]

The rich symbolism in Genesis 2–3 and its similarities to other ancient Near Eastern literature lead some scholars to conclude that it's best not to understand this passage as literal and historical. Peter Enns, in *The Evolution of Adam*, summarizes:

> Our growing knowledge of the cultures, religions, and worldviews of the ancient world in which the Israelites lived, thought, wrote, and worshiped has significantly reoriented our expectation of what Genesis is prepared to deliver. To observe the similarities between the creation and flood stories [of Genesis] and the literature of the ancient Near East, and to insist that all of those other writings are clearly ahistorical while Genesis is somehow presenting history— this is not a strong position of faith, but rather a weak one, where Scripture must conform to one's expectations. Genesis cries out to be read as something other than a historical description of events. Resistance to this conclusion rests at least in part on the faulty theological premise that Israel's Scripture, to be truly the Word of God, must be fundamentally different from the kind of lit-

---

39–55; Daniel C. Harlow, "After Adam: Reading Genesis in an Age of Evolutionary Science," *Perspectives on Science and Christian Faith* 62, no. 3 (2010): 182–84; and Denis O. Lamoureux, *Evolutionary Creation: A Christian Approach to Evolution* (Eugene, OR: Wipf & Stock, 2008), 200–221.

5. Lamoureux, *Evolutionary Creation*, 201.

erature other ancient Near Eastern cultures produced—and that any similarities between them are merely superficial or incidental and can be safely set to
the side. Surely (it is thought) God would not tolerate such nonsense, but give
Israel "correct" information. But to insist that, in order to convey truth, Israel's
Scripture must be isolated from the world in which it was written is a violation
of basic interpretive practice.[6]

Daniel Harlow likewise writes:

> Herein lies the crucial point for determining by literary means whether early
> Genesis is story or history: no one today takes *Gilgamesh*, *Atrahasis*, or *Adapa*
> as historical writings; therefore, since early Genesis shares the same literary
> genre as these older works—and even borrows details from them—it should not
> be taken as historical either. . . . What we have in Genesis is not propositional
> revelation, but narrative theology. Like the parables of Jesus, though, the stories
> in early Genesis are no less divinely inspired for being stories.[7]

C. John Collins, in *Did Adam and Eve Really Exist?*, agrees that the author
of Genesis 2–3 used symbolic language common to ancient Near Eastern
literature. However, Collins also argues that other aspects of the text indicate
that the original author believed he was talking about real people and actual
historical events. The rhetorical and literary techniques of Genesis 2–3 were
intended to shape the readers' attitudes toward those historical events.[8]

> (1) "Historical" in this sense is not the same as "prose," and certainly does not
> imply that our account has no figurative or imaginative elements; (2) "histori-
> cal" is not the same as "complete in detail" or "free from ideological bias,"
> neither of which is possible or desirable anyhow; (3) "historical" is not neces-
> sarily the same as "told in exact chronological sequence" unless the text claims
> that for itself. . . . The conclusion to which this discussion leads us is this: If
> as seems likely to me, the Mesopotamian origin and flood stories provide the
> context against which Genesis 1–11 are to be set, they also provide us with
> clues on how to read this kind of literature. These stories include divine action,
> symbolism, and imaginative elements; the purpose of the stories is to lay the
> foundation for a worldview, without being taken in a "literalistic" fashion. We
> should nevertheless see the story as having what we might call an "historical
> core," though we must be careful in discerning what that is. Genesis aims to
> tell the story.[9]

6. Enns, *Evolution of Adam*, 57–58.
7. Harlow, "After Adam," 184.
8. Collins, *Did Adam and Eve Really Exist?*, 16.
9. Collins, *Did Adam and Eve Really Exist?*, 34–35.

Likewise, Walton, from textual analysis of Genesis 1–5, argues that the term *adam* is used in different ways in different passages. In some (e.g., Gen. 1:26–27; 2:5; 3:22), the text is talking about human beings as a species. In some (e.g., Gen. 2:7, 18, 21, 22, 23), *adam* is an archetype, and what is being said—such as being "dust"—is true of both a particular individual and all humans. In some (e.g., Gen. 2:8, 15, 16, 19, 25; 3:8, 9, 20, 24), *adam* is a specific individual serving as a human representative. In a few cases in later chapters (e.g., Gen. 5:1, 3–5), *adam* is used as a substitute for a personal name of that individual.[10] Walton concludes from this analysis that while these chapters do not simply give straightforward biographical information about an individual named Adam, there are textual reasons to conclude that the original author believed that Adam and Eve referred to real people in a real past.

Genealogies

Genesis 4–5 provides two genealogies that include Adam. In our modern culture, we expect genealogies to be historically accurate regarding the number of individuals, their names, and the years listed. Historians have discovered that people of the ancient Near East had somewhat different expectations for genealogies.

Genealogies of that culture sometimes left out individuals in order to make the number of generations from one event to another come out to a symbolically important number. The number of years that a person lived or a king reigned also appear to have been chosen in part for symbolic significance. Of the twenty numbers given in the genealogy from Adam to Noah (age at son's birth and years lived after son's birth for ten individuals), fifteen numbers are multiples of five, and the other five are multiples of five plus the number seven.[11]

The Sumerian King List tells of reigns of kings lasting hundreds or even tens of thousands of years, with numbers typically divisible by one hundred or ten. The Sumerian King List stretches back from individuals who probably were real historical kings (at the end of the list) to individuals and ages that are obviously mythological (at the beginning of the list). It is possible that the compiler of the list thought that the individuals at the beginning of the list were mythical (perhaps included at the beginning of the list for cultural, political, and religious reasons, as a recognized literary convention). It is also possible that the compiler of the King List thought these were real historical

10. Walton, *Lost World of Adam and Eve*, 58–62, 101.
11. Denis O. Lamoureux has a useful table illustrating this. See figure 6-5 in *Evolutionary Creation*, 211.

individuals. Egyptologist Kenneth Kitchen writes, "The ancient Near East did not historicize myth (i.e., read it as imaginary 'history'). In fact, exactly the reverse is true—there was, rather, a trend to 'mythologize' history, to celebrate actual historical events and people in mythological terms. . . . The ancients (Near Eastern and Hebrew alike) knew that propaganda based on real events was far more effective than that based on sheer invention."[12]

Genealogies of the ancient Near East were not entirely like modern genealogies. Their primary purpose was not to convey exact historical accuracy regarding every individual and every number. It nevertheless seems likely (though not certain) that the original authors of the Genesis 4–5 genealogies, as they wrote them down to be passed along, were treating Adam as a historical person.[13]

Genesis 4–11

Genesis 4–5, when read in a strictly literal-historical fashion, seems to tell of the invention of music, agriculture, and the forging of bronze and iron tools within a few generations after Adam and Eve. However, archaeology indicates that iron smelting did not become widely practiced until well after 1500 BC,[14] while bronze toolmaking happened by 3200 BC. Agriculture had its beginning at least 12,000 years ago.[15] The earliest musical instruments found so far are dated as much as 40,000 years ago. Genesis 4–5 seems to be telling a highly stylized and compressed history. It concentrates into a single story, in a small geographical region, events that took place over several continents and tens of thousands of years.

Genesis 11 tells the story of the Tower of Babel. When read in a strictly literal-historical fashion, it implies that all humans had a single language and culture in a single geographical location in the ancient Near East at some point in the past (presumably, a few generations after Noah) and that all the languages and cultures of the earth spread out from there. But historians and linguists today can trace the long history of the development of languages

12. Kenneth A. Kitchen, *On the Reliability of the Old Testament* (Grand Rapids: Eerdmans, 2003), 262, 300, quoted in Collins, *Did Adam and Eve Really Exist?*, 32.

13. Walton, *Lost World of Adam and Eve*, 102.

14. There are a few artifacts dated earlier. One frequently cited example is a dagger blade found in a tomb dated about 2500 BC. See Richard Cowen, "The Age of Iron" (chapter 5 in a series of essays on Geology, History, and People prepared for a course at the University of California at Davis, April 1999), https://web.archive.org/web/20100314155922/http://mygeology page.ucdavis.edu/cowen/~GEL115/115CH5.html.

15. One source for information on the early history of agriculture is Peter S. Bellwood, *First Farmers: The Origins of Agricultural Societies* (Hoboken, NJ: Wiley-Blackwell, 2004).

over many continents, many cultures, and many millennia. Genesis 11, like Genesis 4–5, seems to be telling a highly stylized and compressed history. For theological purposes, it concentrates into a single story events and trends that actually took place over several continents and millennia. However, that concentration does not invalidate the truth of its message; rather, it communicates the message in the way God intended.[16]

Genesis 6–9 tells the story of a global flood. (In fact, there is textual evidence that Genesis 6–9 edits and knits together two original stories into a single story.)[17] When read in a strictly literal-historical fashion, it implies that the entire world was flooded and that only eight humans and only two animals out of each of many species survived. However, geologists have known since the eighteenth century that geological evidence from around the world is not consistent with a global flood. Biologists of the twentieth and twenty-first centuries have found evidence in the genetic diversity of many species, including humans, that their populations never dropped down to just one or a few pairs.

The flood account of Genesis 6–9 (like the flood stories of other neighboring cultures) refers to the ancient Near Eastern cosmological picture of primeval waters below the (flat) earth and waters above the sky held back by a firmament. The flood of Genesis 6–9 is not just about a lot of ordinary rain. The "springs of the great deep burst forth" and the "floodgates of the heavens were opened" (Gen. 7:11). To the original audience, this would not have been merely poetic language but a reference to physical structures that they really believed were there. Read as literal history, the flood of Genesis 6–9 is an unmaking of days 2 and 3 of Genesis 1—an unmaking of the ordering of creation—followed by a reestablishment of the order.[18]

Archaeologists have found other texts from the ancient Near East that help biblical scholars understand this text. The Atrahasis epic, Eridu Genesis (the Sumerian creation account), and the Epic of Gilgamesh include stories of a global flood, with many similarities to Genesis 6–9.[19] Of course, the theology

16. One theological message of Genesis 11 seems to be that God's hand is in the dispersing of people across the earth, including the human creation of many languages and many cultures. Also, God's hand is against proud cultures like Babylon, famous for building towers like the one in Genesis 11.

17. Lamoureux, *Evolutionary Creation*, 217–20, lays this out in a helpful, readable fashion. For a different textual analysis, see Joshua A. Berman, *Inconsistency in the Torah: Ancient Literary Convention and the Limits of Source Criticism* (Oxford: Oxford University Press, 2017).

18. Tremper Longman III and John H. Walton, *The Lost World of the Flood: Mythology, Theology, and the Deluge Debate* (Downers Grove, IL: InterVarsity, 2018).

19. Denis O. Lamoureux has a useful table illustrating this. See figure 6-7 in *Evolutionary Creation*, 221.

of Genesis 6–9 is radically different from that of the Mesopotamian flood stories. In those flood stories, the gods had created humans to provide food for them (in the form of animal sacrifices), and humans depended on the gods to maintain an orderly world so that agriculture and civilization were possible. When the gods became annoyed with humans[20] and decided to wipe them out with a global flood, disaster for both gods and humans was nearly the result.

Genesis 6–9 presents a very different theological picture. God does not depend on humans; however, God is grieved by human sin. No doubt the ancient Israelites wondered, "Why doesn't God forcibly wipe out all evil people and start over with just the righteous?" Genesis 6–9—a story with judgment in the middle and God's grace at the beginning and the end—is an inspired answer to that question. This fits the pattern of Adam and Eve and Cain and Abel in earlier chapters. God judges and punishes sin, but God does not utterly destroy the sinners, and in the end, God extends grace.[21]

The cultures surrounding Israel had their own creation and flood stories. Israel needed creation and flood stories. God gave them the stories they needed. They are not the stories we would expect in our modern culture (that is, historically and scientifically accurate accounts). God accommodated his Scripture to the limitations and needs of the original audience, using the literary conventions with which they were familiar, to teach them the truths they needed to hear.

The Historicity of Adam and Eve in Light of Genesis 1 and 4–11

Genesis 1 and 4–11 give us insights into the historicity of Genesis 2–3, but they don't settle the question.

In favor of the view that the Adam and Eve of Genesis 2–3 refer to particular historical individuals, one could argue as follows: In the ancient Near East, there were many actual local floods. There were many actual towers built. One possible interpretation of Genesis 6–9 is that it (and possibly the other flood stories as well) was based on one particular local flood whose details are now lost to history. The inspired authors of Genesis 6–9, using literary conventions that were common in the ancient Near East, rewrote the story of that local flood to give it global significance. The story became a way to convey

---

20. The reason the gods were annoyed with humans could be translated as humans making too much noise, complaining too much about their hard work, hubris, and irreverent or wicked behavior. See Longman and Walton, *Lost World of the Flood*, 67.

21. Longman and Walton, *Lost World of the Flood*, 101–6.

theological truths that God wanted to communicate to everyone. Likewise, it is possible that Genesis 11 was based on the construction of one particular tower whose details are now lost to history. The inspired author rewrote the story to give it global significance, so that the story would become a way to convey global theological truths. Likewise, although the genealogies of Genesis use themes and motifs similar to those of other ancient Near Eastern genealogics, including symbolism regarding numbers and the names of individuals, textual analysis implies that the authors thought of the individuals listed as real, historical persons who lived in the real past. Therefore, although the text of Genesis 2–3 also includes many symbolic elements, it seems likely that it has a historical core referring to real, particular individuals.

In favor of the view that the Adam and Eve of Genesis 2–3 are literary and symbolic figures—figures intended to teach about the experiences of many individuals—one could argue as follows: Several times in Genesis 1 and 4–11, events that were spread out over long periods of time are described in a theologically rich story set in one particular place and time.

1. God created the sun and moon and stars and all the structures of the universe, the earth's atmosphere and oceans and dry land, and all life forms on the earth using processes that spanned billions of years. Genesis 1 compresses this into a few days in an inspired text that responds to the idolatrous beliefs in the creation stories of surrounding cultures. Moreover, Genesis 1 refers to physical structures that don't exist (the firmament, waters above and below) but were thought at the time to exist.

2. The development of music, agriculture, and bronze and iron tools spanned tens of thousands of years of human history and several continents. Genesis 4 compresses this into the space of a few generations after Adam and Eve and attributes the development of such things to named individuals.

3. The historical core of Genesis 11 might not be the construction of any one particular tower but the general practice of building towers. The separation of humanity into distinct cultures, language groups, and geographic regions spanned tens of thousands of years of human history and several continents. Genesis 11 compresses this into a story of a single event invested with theological significance.

4. The historical core of Genesis 6–9 might not be one particular local flood but many local floods in the ancient Near East. There never was a global flood that nearly undid creation and destroyed all but a tiny fraction of people and animals. But the cultures of the ancient Near

East developed several global flood stories involving their pantheons of gods. God inspired Genesis 6–9 to teach a very different theology than the theology of other cultures' flood stories—a story of human sin, divine judgment, and divine grace.

All of these could be examples of what John Calvin called God's accommodation. God taught the original audience what they needed to learn in a way they could understand, using literary styles with which they were familiar. If so, then it is consistent to interpret Adam and Eve in Genesis 2–3 as literary, theological, and symbolic figures who tell truths about many human beings but are not particular historical individuals.

Adam and Eve in Second Temple Period Writings

Several Jewish texts from the intertestamental period and the first century AD (including what is called the "Second Temple period") refer to Adam (and sometimes Eve). These include Tobit, the Life of Adam and Eve, 4 Ezra, 2 Baruch, Biblical Antiquities of Pseudo-Philo, Sirach (Ecclesiasticus), the Wisdom of Solomon, the works of Philo of Alexandria, Jubilees, and Josephus's *Jewish Antiquities*. These texts help us understand the cultural, historical, and theological traditions regarding Adam and Eve at the time of the New Testament and therefore help us understand Paul's references to Adam in his letters.

The writers of these texts reference Adam to make a variety of theological arguments, each wrestling with their own particular concerns.[22] Scot McKnight, in *Adam and the Genome*, summarizes the work of Felipe de Jesús Legarreta-Castillo in grouping these texts into three thematic categories (italics added by McKnight):

> The *Hellenistic* authors "interpret the story of the creation of Adam and the
> fall incorporating Hellenistic traditions and thoughts to preserve Judaism or

22. Some surveys of this literature include Felipe de Jesús Legarreta-Castillo, *The Figure of Adam in Romans 5 and 1 Corinthians 15: The New Creation and Its Ethical and Social Reconfiguration* (Minneapolis: Augsburg Fortress, 2014); John R. Levison, *Portraits of Adam in Early Judaism: From Sirach to 2 Baruch*, Journal for the Study of the Pseudepigrapha Supplement Series 1 (Sheffield: JSOT Press, 1988); John J. Collins, "Before the Fall: The Earliest Interpretations of Adam and Eve," in *The Idea of Biblical Interpretation: Essays in Honor of James L. Kugel*, ed. Hindy Najman and Judith H. Newman, Supplements to the Journal of the Study of Judaism 83 (Leiden: Brill, 2004); John R. Levison, "Adam and Eve," in *The Eerdmans Dictionary of Early Judaism*, ed. J. J. Collins and Daniel C. Harlow (Grand Rapids: Eerdmans, 2010), 300–302; and Gary A. Anderson, *The Genesis of Perfection: Adam and Eve in Jewish and Christian Imagination* (Louisville: Westminster John Knox, 2001).

accommodate it to their larger historical and cultural milieu. They portray Adam as *paradigm of humankind and the ancestor of Israel who faces the dilemma of freedom and its implications.*"

The *"rewritten" Bible* texts "freely follow the biblical narrative in order to find the place and function of Israel in the world. These interpretations include apocalyptic and wisdom features that express hope in a future reward on the condition that one keep God's commandments contained in the Law. In these interpretations Adam's sin is characterized as disobedience to God's commandment and functions as *the prototype of the historical transgressions of Israel and the nations that brought into the world all sorts of misfortunes for humankind*, especially untimely death. The story of the Fall also explains the misfortunes of Israel, typically the destruction of the temple and Jerusalem. In this context, the righteous are exhorted to adhere to the Law in order to attain the promised restoration in the eschaton."

The *apocalyptic* texts "emphasize the story of the fall over the story of the creation of humankind to explain the hardships and the destruction of Jerusalem and its temple. It is interpreted as *an example and an effect of the protoplasts' disobedience to God's commandment on their descendants as well as their own unfaithfulness to the covenant.* In these interpretations, heavenly beings typically reveal the destruction of the wicked—Israel's enemies or sinners—and the salvation of the righteous in the eschaton. The destruction of this world anticipates the coming of a new creation."[23]

While these writers use Adam and Eve to make different theological points, there are some commonalities. In general, these Jewish writers appear to have interpreted the Adam of Genesis 2–3 as a historical person (although there is some debate on that point),[24] the first human being, and the first sinner. They also interpreted Adam as an archetype for all humans in general and/or Israel in particular.

The fact that Adam and Eve are used in multiple ways in order to make multiple points might help us understand why these texts make statements that, at first glance, seem to contradict one another regarding who is to blame for sin. For example, the Syriac Apocalypse of Baruch (2 Baruch) says on the

23. Scot McKnight and Dennis Venema, *Adam and the Genome* (Grand Rapids: Brazos, 2017), 149–50. The texts Sirach/Ecclesiasticus and Wisdom of Solomon and the writer Philo of Alexandria belong to the Hellenistic tradition referred to by McKnight and Legarreta-Castillo. Jubilees, Biblical Antiquities, the Life of Adam and Eve (also called Apocalypse of Moses), and certain works by Josephus belong to the rewritten-Bible tradition. To the apocalyptic texts belong 4 Ezra and 2 Baruch.

24. See, for example, Tremper Longman III, *Confronting Old Testament Controversies: Pressing Questions about Evolution, Sexuality, History, and Violence* (Grand Rapids: Baker Books, 2019), 68–69; and James D. G. Dunn, *Romans 1–8*, Word Biblical Commentary 38A (Dallas: Word, 1988), 289.

one hand, "When Adam sinned a death was decreed against those who were to be born" (23:4) and "What did you [Adam] do to all who were born after you?" (48:42). But it also says, "Adam is, therefore, not the cause, except only for himself, but each of us has become our own Adam" (54:19) and "Although Adam sinned first and has brought death upon all who were not in his own time, yet each of them who has been born from him has prepared for himself the coming torments" (54:15).[25]

Joel B. Green summarizes commonalities among these Second Temple period writings this way:

> Although Israel's scriptures [the Old Testament] are themselves bereft of theological reflection on the ongoing significance of Adam and Eve's disobedience in the Garden, a few Jewish texts from the Second Temple period do work with Genesis 3 as they tell something of the story of sin. These texts agree in two important respects: (1) Adam (or Eve's) disobedience results in their own mortality and in the mortality of all who would come after them, and (2) human beings remain responsible for their own actions. . . . In short, when sin's origins are discussed, Jewish writers of the Second Temple period refer to human choice even as they speak of Adam's (or Adam and Eve's) influence. Sin is not compulsory, even if its ubiquity might suggest its inevitability.[26]

These interpretations of Adam and Eve were part of the cultural and religious background when the apostle Paul and the church fathers wrote.

Paul's Beliefs about the Historicity of Adam

Luke refers to Adam in his genealogy of Jesus (Luke 3:38) and possibly (though not by name) in Paul's speech at the Areopagus in Athens (Acts 17:26). But the primary texts of interest from Paul's Letters are 1 Corinthians 15:20–22, 42–49 and Romans 5:12–21.

25. For additional insights on this topic, see William D. Davies, *Paul and Rabbinic Judaism: Some Rabbinic Elements in Pauline Theology*, 4th ed. (Philadelphia: Fortress, 1980), 17–35; and Alexander John Maclagan Wedderburn, "The Theological Structure of Romans V. 12," *New Testament Studies* 19, no. 3 (1973): 339–54.

26. Joel B. Green, "'Adam, What Have You Done?' New Testament Voices on the Origins of Sin," in *Evolution and the Fall*, ed. William T. Cavanaugh and James K. A. Smith (Grand Rapids: Eerdmans, 2017), 105. Green adds a footnote: "See the similar conclusion in Thomas H. Tobin, *Paul's Rhetoric in Its Contexts: The Argument of Romans* (Peabody, MA: Hendrickson, 2004), p. 171–74 (especially p. 172); Peter C. Bouteneff, *Beginnings: Ancient Christian Readings of the Biblical Creation Narratives* (Grand Rapids: Baker, 2008), p. 9–26 (especially p. 26); John E. Toews, *The Story of Original Sin* (Eugene, OR: Pickwick, 2013), p. 37."

But Christ has indeed been raised from the dead, the firstfruits of those who have fallen asleep. For since death came through a man, the resurrection of the dead comes also through a man. For as in Adam all die, so in Christ all will be made alive. . . .

So will it be with the resurrection of the dead. The body that is sown is perishable, it is raised imperishable; it is sown in dishonor, it is raised in glory; it is sown in weakness, it is raised in power; it is sown a natural body, it is raised a spiritual body.

If there is a natural body, there is also a spiritual body. So it is written: "The first man Adam became a living being"; the last Adam, a life-giving spirit. The spiritual did not come first, but the natural, and after that the spiritual. The first man was of the dust of the earth; the second man is of heaven. As was the earthly man, so are those who are of the earth; and as is the heavenly man, so also are those who are of heaven. And just as we have borne the image of the earthly man, so shall we bear the image of the heavenly man. (1 Cor. 15:20–22, 42–49)

Therefore, just as sin entered the world through one man, and death through sin, and in this way death came to all people, because all sinned—

To be sure, sin was in the world before the law was given, but sin is not charged against anyone's account where there is no law. Nevertheless, death reigned from the time of Adam to the time of Moses, even over those who did not sin by breaking a command, as did Adam, who is a pattern of the one to come.

But the gift is not like the trespass. For if the many died by the trespass of the one man, how much more did God's grace and the gift that came by the grace of the one man, Jesus Christ, overflow to the many! Nor can the gift of God be compared with the result of one man's sin: The judgment followed one sin and brought condemnation, but the gift followed many trespasses and brought justification. For if, by the trespass of the one man, death reigned through that one man, how much more will those who receive God's abundant provision of grace and of the gift of righteousness reign in life through the one man, Jesus Christ!

Consequently, just as one trespass resulted in condemnation for all people, so also one righteous act resulted in justification and life for all people. For just as through the disobedience of the one man the many were made sinners, so also through the obedience of the one man the many will be made righteous.

The law was brought in so that the trespass might increase. But where sin increased, grace increased all the more, so that, just as sin reigned in death, so also grace might reign through righteousness to bring eternal life through Jesus Christ our Lord. (Rom. 5:12–21)

Paul certainly believed that Christ was a real, historical individual; so it seems likely from these passages that Paul believed that Adam was a real, historical individual. Of course, it is possible for a teacher like Paul to juxtapose a mythic figure with an actual historical person for teaching purposes. For example, a historian might juxtapose two figures in this way: "The early American use of trees can be encapsulated in two individuals: Paul Bunyan and Johnny Appleseed. Paul Bunyan exemplifies those who chop down forests to use the wood. Johnny Appleseed exemplifies those who plant selected trees in selected areas for their usefulness to humans." Paul Bunyan is a mythic figure who epitomizes and represents no single individual but many real lumberjacks who went into the forests to chop down trees and bring the wood back to towns and cities for human use. Johnny Appleseed is a nickname for a real historical person named John Chapman. Readers who grew up in American grade schools would probably understand what the historian was doing with those two names. Readers who grew up in different cultures, and especially people who might read that quotation hundreds of years from now, might mistakenly believe that this historian thought that both Paul Bunyan and Johnny Appleseed were literal-historical figures.

James D. G. Dunn and Tremper Longman III have argued that Paul might well have done something similar—purposefully drawing analogies between a literary figure from the theological tradition (Adam) and an actual historical figure (Christ).[27]

Textual analysis of Paul's Letters (especially Paul's repeated use of the term "one man"), along with Paul's cultural context of Second Temple–era Jewish writings, leads many other scholars to conclude that Paul really did believe that Adam was a historical figure. If so, then Paul probably also believed that this Adam was the sole male progenitor of all humans. And like other Second Temple era writers, Paul probably also saw Adam not only as a historical figure

---

27. Longman, *Confronting Old Testament Controversies.* Dunn, *Romans 1–8*, 289, cites examples of literature written in Paul's era:

> In particular, it would not be true to say that Paul's theological point here depends on Adam being a "historical" individual or on his disobedience being a historical event as such. Such an implication does not necessarily follow from the fact that a parallel is drawn with Christ's single act: an act in mythic history can be paralleled to an act in living history without the point of comparison being lost. So long as the story of Adam as the initiator of the sad tale of human failure was well known, which we may assume (the brevity of Paul's presentation presupposes such knowledge), such a comparison was meaningful. Nor should modern interpretation encourage patronizing generalizations about the primitive mind naturally understanding the Adam stories as literally historical. It is sufficiently clear, for example, from Plutarch's account of the ways in which the Osiris myth was understood at this period that such tales told about the dawn of human history could be and were treated with a considerable degree of sophistication with the literal meaning largely discounted.

but also as an archetype for Israel's history (Adam and Eve were in paradise; they disobeyed God's command; they were expelled).

Unlike other Second Temple–era writers, Paul used Adam as a way to bring gentiles into the story of the Jewish Messiah. Before his conversion, Paul had believed that the Messiah was for the nation of Israel—that the Messiah would free Israel from its political oppressors and restore Israel to a relationship with God through obedience to the law of Moses. That changed with Paul's dramatic encounter with the risen Christ on the road to Damascus, followed by years of obediently preaching the gospel to gentiles. Paul needed to explain this inclusive gospel. He needed to explain that the life and death and resurrection of the Jewish Messiah were not just for the nation of Israel. They were for all nations. They were not only about freedom from political oppression or even obedience to the law of Moses. Rather, they were about reconciliation to God, overcoming the estrangement that resulted from the sins of all human beings. Paul makes this argument in Romans 1–3 without any direct reference to Adam, writing about how the gentiles are sinners even though they do not have the law of Moses and how they can be reconciled to God through Christ rather than through the law. In Romans 5, Paul uses Adam as another way to bring gentiles into the story of the Messiah.

Paul's Use of Adam to Teach about Christ

It would not be surprising if Paul believed that Adam was a historical figure. But Paul did not write about Adam's disobedience for its own sake; he used it to make a theological argument about Christ. Let's consider these issues separately.

Does the mere fact that Paul's writings—inspired by the Holy Spirit— reflect a *belief* that Adam was a historical figure, the first man, the first (male) sinner, and the sole male progenitor of all humans require Christians today to believe the same things? As we have learned from church history and the principle of accommodation, the answer is no. Ancient inspired writers of Scripture believed that the earth was fixed and that there were waters above the sky and beneath the earth. Scripture references those ancient beliefs, but Scripture does not teach those things. Ancient inspired writers of Scripture believed that humans thought with their hearts and intestines. Scripture references those ancient beliefs, but Scripture does not teach those things.

But Paul didn't merely reference those beliefs about Adam; he used them to teach a core doctrine: the universal need for God's grace to overcome sin and death and the sufficiency of Christ's life, death, resurrection, and reign to achieve this. Does the fact that Paul used those beliefs about Adam to teach a core doctrine require Christians today to believe the same things about Adam? As we have learned from church history and the principle of accommodation, the answer is "Not necessarily." George Murphy writes regarding this:

> The fact that Judaism of the time, and Paul himself, thought of Adam as a historical figure doesn't mean that we must understand Adam that way. . . . Outdated information about the physical world in Genesis should be seen as a result of the Holy Spirit accommodating inspiration to the state of human knowledge in the cultures of the biblical writers. That was not just a matter of authors using elementary language to describe things that their contemporaries didn't understand. There is no reason to think that the writer of Genesis 1 knew about the big bang but chose to speak in terms of ancient near eastern cosmology. We can understand Paul's references to Adam as a historical individual as similar accommodation. Paul's purpose in Romans 5:12–21 is to state the importance of Christ for the human problems of sin and death, not to give information about the early history of humanity.
>
> On the other hand, the claim that Adam is not a historical individual in the modern sense does not mean that Paul is talking only about the existential situation of all people, or that the origin of sin is not in view in the text. In verse 12, he speaks of sin coming into the world, not as something simply given in creation. The spread of death is due to the fact that "all have sinned." Yet there is some difference between the sin of "all" and the primordial sin, for Paul refers to "those whose sins were not like the transgression of Adam" (5:14). The first sin had causal efficacy: "By the one man's disobedience the many were made sinners" (5:19).[28]

Paul's core teachings about Christ in 1 Corinthians 15 and Romans 5—the universal need for God's grace to overcome sin and death and the sufficiency of Christ's life, death, resurrection, and reign to achieve this—are taught in many other places in Scripture (e.g., Rom. 1–3 and many other passages that don't mention Adam). This truth about Christ's redeeming work *does not depend* on what we decide about the historicity of Adam.

But we are asking the question in the opposite direction. Does the authoritative teaching about Christ's redeeming work in 1 Corinthians 15 and Romans 5 *imply* anything about the historicity of Adam? We can focus the question further. How deeply are Paul's beliefs about a historical individual, whom he calls Adam, incorporated into the *logic* of Paul's theological

28. George L. Murphy, *Models of Atonement: Speaking about Salvation in a Scientific World* (Minneapolis: University Lutheran Press, 2013), 59.

teaching? Again, different passages from the New Testament allow for different arguments to be made.

In favor of a less historical reading of Adam, here are two other examples in which New Testament authors used a literal interpretation of a portion of Genesis 1–11 to teach a core theological doctrine:

> The authors of Philippians 2:10 and Revelation 5:3, 13 didn't just believe in an ancient, three-tiered picture of the universe (the heavens, the earth, and under the earth); they used that belief to teach the theological doctrine of the universal rule of the risen Christ. However, the theological doctrine of Christ's universal rule is taught in many other ways in many other places in Scripture. Its truth does not imply that we must also believe in a three-tiered picture of creation.
>
> The author or authors of 1 Peter 3:20 and 2 Peter 3:5–6 didn't just believe that the world was formed out of water and by water and that it was destroyed by a global flood, leaving only eight survivors; they used that belief to teach the theological doctrine of the surety of God's coming final judgment. However, the theological doctrine of God's coming final judgment is taught in many other ways in many other places in Scripture. Its truth does not imply that we must also believe there was a global flood that killed all but eight people.

These examples further support the conclusion that the Holy Spirit uses the principle of accommodation in inspiring Scripture.

In favor of a more historical reading of Adam, note a prominent example in Paul's writing in which his theological teaching is unquestionably tied to a historical event—the resurrection of Jesus. This is an event that the church throughout the ages has affirmed must, in fact, have historically happened in order for its theology to make sense.

> As shown in many passages, but especially in 1 Corinthians 15:12–19, Paul not only believed that Jesus's resurrection from the dead and ascension to reign in heaven were historical facts; he used those historical facts to teach the core doctrine of the coming resurrection of all. Moreover, Paul forcefully insists that the historical fact of Jesus's resurrection must be true in order for us to sensibly believe in the coming resurrection of all. It is true that the coming resurrection is taught in many other places in the New Testament, but in almost every case, that theological doctrine is tied to Jesus's historical resurrection. Every New Testament author

thought that this core doctrine and this historical fact of Jesus's resurrection were inseparable.

Most (not all) of the scholars cited in this chapter agree that Paul thought Adam was a historical individual. They generally agree that Paul used a literal interpretation of Genesis 2–3 to make a theological point about Christ. They disagree on whether Paul's use of Adam is best seen as an argument in favor of us, today, also believing that Adam was a historical figure (similar to Paul's teaching in 1 Cor. 15 about the resurrection) or whether Paul's use of Adam is best seen as another example of the principle of accommodation (similar to beliefs about the three-tiered universe in Phil. 2 and the universal flood in 1 and 2 Peter).

Arguments from Six Scholars

I quote here at length six scholars whose writings I have been summarizing. Each scholar considers arguments made from the Old and New Testaments. The first three believe that Adam and Eve are best seen as literary and symbolic figures referring to an entire population of our ancestors. The second three believe that Adam and Eve are best seen as particular historical individuals (perhaps of different names, perhaps not living in Mesopotamia, perhaps part of a larger population) who also carry theological and archetypal significance.
   According to Scot McKnight:

The Adam of Paul is the archetypal, moral Adam who is the archetype for both Israel and all humanity. . . . One could argue that Paul *began with Christ* and found opposites in Adam just as easily as one could argue that he *began with Adam* and found opposites in Christ. What matters in our context is only that Paul *uses* Adam to bolster his Christology and to magnify the accomplishments in Christ. One can explain our passage as yet one more representation of reuse of the literary Adam of Genesis for theological purposes. However one explains it, the emphasis here in Paul is the comparison of Adam with Christ. For Paul, Christ is the Second Adam just as he is the true Israelite. That is, God's design all along when he created Adam and Eve was for them to reflect God's glory and rule God's creation, but they rejected that mission; so in God's right timing he created Israel to be that Adam, but Israel too did not live up to the divine calling, and so in God's right timing he sends his Son, Jesus, to be Adam and to be Israel. Jesus, then, is seen by Paul to be the true Adam and the true Israelite who, unlike Adam and Israel, accomplishes the divine mission.[29]

29. McKnight, *Adam and the Genome*, 180–81.

According to Daniel Harlow:

> Paul's main interest is to depict Christ as a representative figure, one whose act affected not only himself but the entire human race. He brings in Adam less as a figure of history than as a type of Christ—a symbolic stand-in for fallen humanity. Paul, like Luke, no doubt regarded Adam as a historical person, but in his letters he assumes the historicity of Adam instead of asserting it, and in Romans 1–3 he can describe the problem and universality of sin at great length without any reference at all to Adam. This latter point, in particular, suggests that a historical Adam was not essential to his teaching. Paul had little reason *not* to regard Adam as a historical figure, whereas today we have *many* reasons for recognizing him as a strictly literary one. What does the apostle actually say about Adam's role in sin and death? If one examines carefully Paul's wording in Romans 5:12, his use of prepositions is revealing. He says that sin entered the world *through* (not because of) Adam, and that death spread to all *because* all sinned. Adam was the first sinner, but the responsibility for humanity's sin falls squarely on the human race as a whole, as in Romans 1:18–3:20. Moreover, Paul never claims or even implies that human nature underwent a fundamental change with Adam's sin. For Paul, then, Adam's act *affected* the human race but did not infect it; he attributes to Adam less a causal role in the sin of all humanity than a temporal and representative one.[30]

According to Peter Enns:

> Paul's reading of the Adam story was conditioned by his experience of the risen Christ. As Paul does so often in his use of the Old Testament in general, he interprets it in such a way as to highlight the work of Christ and the equality of Jew and gentile. The death and resurrection of the Son of God was a surprise ending to Israel's story. No one familiar with the Old Testament messianic hope was prepared for a crucified—and risen!—messiah. This jarring climax to Israel's story, according to Paul, served to relativize Israel's story; faithful Torah obedience was no longer the necessary preparation to usher in the messianic age (understood as Jewish political and religious freedom). Torah was actually part of the problem; it merely exacerbated and made plain a much deeper truth about the human condition—that we are broken and alienated people, in need of rescue (Rom. 5:20). The solution that God gave in the death and resurrection of Christ served not only to show the depth of God's love for his creation but also revealed—for the first time clearly—the extent to which that creation was in need of deliverance (Rom. 8:19–23). Paul, as a first-century Jew, bore witness to God's act in Christ in the only way that he could have been expected to do so, through ancient idioms and categories known to him and his religious tradition

---

30. Harlow, "After Adam," 190.

for century upon century. One can believe that Paul is correct theologically and historically about the problem of sin and death and the solution that God provides in Christ without also needing to believe that his assumptions about human origins are accurate. The need for a savior does not require a historical Adam. A proper view of inspiration will embrace the fact that God speaks by means of the cultural idiom of the authors—whether it be the author of Genesis in describing origins or how Paul would later come to understand Genesis. Both reflect the setting and limitations of the cultural moment.[31]

According to N. T. Wright:

Just as God chose Israel from the rest of humankind for a special, strange, demanding vocation, so perhaps what Genesis is telling us is that *God chose one pair from the rest of early hominids for a special, strange, demanding vocation.* This pair (call them Adam and Eve if you like) were to be the representatives of the whole human race, the ones in whom God's purposes to make the whole world a place of delight and joy and order, eventually colonizing the whole creation, were to be taken forward. God the Creator put into their hands the fragile task of being his image-bearers. If they failed, they would bring the whole purpose for the wider creation, including all those other nonchosen hominids, down with them. They were supposed to be the life-bringers, and if they failed in their task, the death that was already endemic in the world as it was would engulf them as well.[32]

According to C. John Collins:

When Paul in [1 Cor. 15:]21 refers to "a man," he is referring to a single human being, as verse 22 clarifies: Adam is the human being by whom came death, while Christ is the human being by whom the resurrection of the dead has come. Then in verse 22 Paul uses one of his characteristic formulae, "in Adam" and "in Christ." To explain these expressions, I shall cut a long story short and simply say that in my judgment, to be "in A" means to be a member of the people for which A serves as the covenantal representative. This membership sets up a kind of solidarity, where what happens to the representative affects all members of the group, and vice-versa. . . . This person A is an individual who serves a public role as a representative, and there is no evidence that one can be covenantally "in" someone who had no historical existence. . . . Indeed, Paul's argument is historical and narratival: one person did something to cause the

31. Enns, *Evolution of Adam*, 142–43.
32. N. T. Wright, "Excursus on Paul's Use of Adam," in Walton, *Lost World of Adam and Eve*, 177–78. See also N. T. Wright, *Surprised by Scripture: Engaging Contemporary Issues* (New York: HarperCollins, 2014), 37–38.

problem for those he represented, a later person did something to rescue from the problem those he represented.[33]

According to John Walton:

> When we identify Adam and Eve as historical figures, we mean that they are real people involved in real events in a real past. They are not inherently mythological or legendary, though their roles may contribute to them being treated that way in some of the reception history. Likewise, they are not fictional. At the same time, there may be some elements in their profile that are not intended to convey historical elements. I have already noted that their names are not their historical names. Likewise, if the forming accounts are archetypal, those are presenting truth about the identity of Adam and Eve rather than historical events. Despite these qualifications and caveats, I believe the textual information leads to the conclusion that Adam and Eve should be considered real people in a real past for several important reasons. . . . If we were working from the Old Testament alone, there would be a lot of flexibility concerning how we thought about the entrance and spread of sin. The New Testament, however, particularly the discussion of the impact of the work of Christ, places many more demands on our theological interpretation. The New Testament views the reality of sin and its resulting need for redemption as having entered at a single point in time (punctiliar) through a specific event in time and space. Furthermore, Paul correlates that punctiliar event with a corresponding act of redemption: the death of Christ with its resulting atonement—also a punctiliar event.[34]

Hermeneutics and Theology

The doctrine of original sin is not only (or even primarily) about whether Adam and Eve are best interpreted as historical individuals. The doctrine addresses many related questions: What damage was done to human nature? What damage was done to human relationships with God and with one another? How did sin spread from the first sinners to the rest of humanity? Why would the sin of a few affect all? What is the status of infants who have not yet committed willful sins? Is it possible, even in theory, to live a sinless life? Why did God create us in such a way that sin was even possible? Why are all humans today apparently unable to avoid sinning and therefore utterly dependent on Christ's grace? The rest of this book addresses these questions using systematic theology.

33. Collins, *Did Adam and Eve Really Exist?*, 79–81.
34. Walton, *Lost World of Adam and Eve*, 101–3.

The Doctrine of Original Sin through Church History

WHAT HAVE THEOLOGIANS throughout church history taught about the entrance of sin into the world?

The doctrine of original sin addresses many interrelated theological questions. This chapter summarizes writings from theologians throughout church history so that we can use their insights as we consider modern scenarios that include human evolution.

Saint Augustine did not invent the doctrine of original sin. Its history can be traced through Old Testament concepts of sin, through developments in the intertestamental period, and into New Testament writings. The previous chapter looked at Old and New Testament passages that refer to Adam and Eve. This chapter traces the history of the doctrine of original sin starting with church fathers of the second century AD, giving special attention to Augustine because of his great influence.

Augustine did not simply deduce his version of the doctrine from Scripture. He frequently referred to Scripture, but he also used the writings of earlier church fathers. He also used several Greek philosophical theories and focused on particular theological controversies of his time.

In the centuries after Augustine, theologians explored alternative versions of the doctrine. Numerous books analyze this history. This chapter only summarizes some of the highlights, paying special attention to how theologians of the past answered the following questions: What was the state of our ancestors just prior to their first sin? What was the nature of the first sin? In what way did sin damage them? How was that damage transmitted to later generations? Why did God permit sin?

Church history gives us competing theories surrounding the doctrine of original sin. As we examine them, we will try to avoid two opposite temptations.

The first temptation is to conclude that all the competing versions of the doctrine are equally valuable—or equally non-valuable—for us today. Even if a theological point has been debated for centuries, it might still be correct for us today to consider it a settled part of the core doctrine. It is not unusual for teachings to undergo long debate before achieving the status of core doctrine. (The doctrine of the Trinity is one such example.)

The opposite temptation is to take one particular theologian's formulation of the doctrine as the canonical formulation, interpreting everything written before as mere precursors to the canonical formulation and everything written since as a degeneration away from truth. Just because a theological theory has had the approval of most theologians for many centuries does not automatically make it a settled point of core church doctrine. Sometimes the Holy Spirit prompts the church to reexamine such beliefs. (The belief that Scripture teaches that the earth is fixed in place is one historical example.)

Each theologian summarized in this chapter sought to distill truths taught in Scripture. To the extent they succeeded, their teachings derive their authority from Scripture. Each theologian addressed particular controversies of their particular age. They drew on the linguistic and philosophical resources of their particular cultures to express their ideas. Reviewing this history lets us use the collective insights of past generations to help us today.

Church Fathers prior to St. Augustine

Frederick R. Tennant, in *The Sources of the Doctrines of the Fall and Original Sin*, notes that the Apostolic Fathers of the late first and early second century sometimes discuss the universality of sin, but none of the Apostolic Fathers discuss whether Adam's sin influenced his descendants. Tennant adds:

> It is when we come to Justin Martyr's [c. 100–165] writings that we first need to weigh the question whether or not an approach towards the doctrine of Original Sin is to be detected. Justin speaks strongly of the universality of sin, and of our need of grace, and he alludes to an evil inclination which is in the

nature of every man. These things, however, are not deduced from, or connected with, the Fall. When that event is mentioned, Justin would seem to represent it merely as the beginning of sin rather than as the cause of sinfulness, and he does not appear to derive from it any hereditary taint or imputation of guilt.[1]

Tatha Wiley, in *Original Sin*, notes that Justin Martyr's writings on this topic are similar to those of other church fathers of that era. "Like other Christian thinkers, Justin acknowledged the sinful condition of humankind. Also like them, he was not concerned with developing an explicit principle explaining what he took as fact, the universality of sin. The regularity of personal sins seemed reason enough for Justin. People sin. This is what separates them from God."[2]

Tennant summarizes the writings of other church fathers prior to Irenaeus (Tatian, c. 120–c. 180; Theophilus of Antioch, c. 120–c. 184; Athenagoras of Athens, c. 130–c. 190) this way:

> It will have been seen, from what has been said of the Greek Apologists, that they had not advanced very far towards the later ecclesiastical doctrine of Original Sin. They differ in their conceptions of the unfallen state of man, and are very indefinite in their estimation of the consequences for the race of the Fall of its first parents. They do not seem to have thoughts of such a thing as a tainted nature having been thereby imparted to mankind; man's psychological condition, his freedom of will and other moral capacities, are not represented as having suffered change; nor are his natural desires and appetites conceived as in any way sinful in themselves: sin is in the will alone. The sinfulness of Adam's posterity is due to the following of Adam's example in becoming subject to the dominion of evil spirits. Its universality is not associated with the unity and solidarity of the race.[3]

The writings of Irenaeus (c. 130–202) contain a more developed theory of original sin. Opposing the teachings of the Gnostics, who made God the source of both good and evil, Irenaeus appealed to Genesis and the writings of St. Paul to point to Adam and Eve's disobedience as an explanation for humanity's sinful tendencies. But Irenaeus's theology is different from Augustine's in several ways. In particular, Irenaeus pictures Adam and Eve in the garden of Eden as children—immature beings not yet ready for all

---

1. Frederick Robert Tennant, *The Sources of the Doctrines of the Fall and Original Sin* (Cambridge: Cambridge University Press, 1903), 275–76.

2. Tatha Wiley, *Original Sin: Origins, Developments, Contemporary Meanings* (New York: Paulist Press, 2002), 42.

3. Tennant, *Sources of the Doctrines of the Fall and Original Sin*, 282.

the gifts God had planned for them. They were supposed to develop into moral maturity, but they were lured into disobedience. John Hick describes Irenaeus's views this way:

> There is thus to be found in Irenaeus the outline of an approach to the problem of evil which stands in important respects in contrast to the Augustinian type of theodicy. Instead of the doctrine that man was created finitely perfect and then incomprehensibly destroyed his own perfection and plunged into sin and misery, Irenaeus suggests that man was created as an imperfect, immature creature who was to undergo moral development and growth and finally be brought to the perfection intended for him by his Maker. Instead of the Fall of Adam being presented, as in the Augustinian tradition, as an utterly malignant and catastrophic event, completely disrupting God's plan, Irenaeus pictures it as something that occurred in the childhood of the race, an understandable lapse due to weakness and immaturity rather than an adult crime full of malice and pregnant with perpetual guilt.[4]

Scholars writing since Hick helped clarify what Irenaeus meant by Adam and Eve being created immature and "imperfect." Gerald Hiestand writes:

> According to Irenaeus, it is only through "long periods" of development that human beings become what God has all along intended. "His [God's] wisdom [is shown] in his having made created things parts of one harmonious and consistent whole; and those things which, through his super-eminent kindness, receive growth and a long period of existence, do reflect the glory of the uncreated One, of that God who bestows what is good ungrudgingly." This process of development is not a necessity due to the fall, but is a necessary corollary of the fact that creation (including human beings) is mutable and finite. Not even God could have created perfect (i.e., complete, finished) creatures—for creatures are, by definition, mutable, and thus inevitably fall short of the glory of God.[5]

While there are some differences between Irenaeus's views and the later views of Augustine, they have several points in common. Hiestand notes, "Irenaeus, just as much as Augustine, views human corruption and death as resulting from sin. Adam and Eve, while not created perfectly complete (such as we find in Augustine) were nonetheless created full of goodness,

---

4. John Hick, *Evil and the God of Love*, rev. ed. (New York: Harper & Row, 1977), 214–15.
5. Gerald Hiestand, "The Irenaeus Option: How Irenaeus Does (and Does Not) Reduce the Tension between Christian Theology and Evolutionary Science," *Bulletin of Ecclesial Theology* 6, no. 2 (Fall 2019): 40–41.

and without corruption or sin. Irenaeus' idea that humanity was created as infantile was not meant to suggest any sense of corruptibility in humanity."[6]

After Irenaeus, theologians continued to debate to what extent the guilt of Adam's sin was passed to later generations, in what ways human nature was damaged by Adam's sin, to what extent all of humanity is united in Adam's sin, and to what extent humans after Adam could avoid sinning. Wiley notes, "To oppose Gnostic determinism, Clement of Alexandria [c. 150–c. 215] and others emphasized human freedom, self-determination, and moral responsibility. They argued that God could not very well demand human obedience to moral precepts if human beings did not have the capacity to obey such commands. While personal acts of wrongdoing 'stain the soul' and weaken human nature, temptation could be resisted."[7]

In some cases, church fathers revised some of their views during their lifetime. Origen (c. 184–c. 254), in his earlier writings in *De Principiis*, declared the fall story of Genesis to be allegorical and its meaning to be mystical; the sinfulness of human nature comes from the damage done by each individual's sin, not by Adam's sin. But Origen's later writings, such as his *Commentary on the Epistle to the Romans*, teach a theology of original sin much closer to that developed by Augustine.[8]

Athanasius (297–373) believed that human beings were created mortal and corruptible in their "natural state." Prior to temptation, Adam and Eve were given supernatural gifts—namely, the unique creaturely privilege of bearing the image of God, which gave them moral righteousness and access to immortality—elevating them above this natural state. By sinning, Adam and Eve damaged the image of God within them and slid into the inevitable decay inherent to all mortal creatures. Tennant writes:

> The Fall is conceived by Athanasius as a lapse of mankind to the "natural state." In other words, the Fall is represented as consisting in the loss of what more modern theology has called supernatural endowments. . . . In this state of nature, into which Adam fell, all subsequent generations have been born. But this universal fall does not seem to be ascribed definitely to the one great

---

6. Hiestand, "Irenaeus Option," 45. For other recent scholarship on Irenaeus, see Matthew Steenberg, "Children in Paradise: Adam and Even as 'Infants' in Irenaeus of Lyons," *Journal of Early Christian Studies* 12, no. 1 (2004): 1–22; and Andrew M. McCoy, "The Irenaean Approach to Original Sin through Christ's Redemption," in *Finding Ourselves after Darwin: Conversations on the Image of God, Original Sin, and the Problem of Evil*, ed. Stanley P. Rosenberg, Michael Burdett, Michael Lloyd, and Benno van den Toren (Grand Rapids: Baker Academic, 2018), 160–72.

7. Wiley, *Original Sin*, 40.

8. Tennant, *Sources of the Doctrines of the Fall and Original Sin*, 296–301.

sin of Adam, so that all the race sinned in him or with him, or were constituted sinners in consequence of his transgression and independently of their own actual sins. On the contrary, Athanasius regards the fallen state of the race as a whole as having been brought about gradually.[9]

Tennant goes on to note about Athanasius, "In other writings of this Father, however, we meet with expressions which bespeak a nearer approach to the later doctrine of Original Sin. . . . He certainly held that Christ's sacrifice was offered 'that He might make all men upright and free from the old transgression.'"[10]

In Tertullian (c. 155–c. 240) we find a theology of original sin very close to that of Augustine. Unlike Origen, Tertullian believed in "traducianism": the idea that each new human soul, like each new human body, is produced by the union of the parents. The soul does not enter the body after conception; it is produced with the body. Tennant writes, "Inasmuch as the soul of the child was regarded by Tertullian as derived from the soul of its father, like a shoot from the parent stock of a tree, it followed that he must look upon every human soul as ultimately a branch of Adam's soul. And inasmuch as the soul inherits from its parents their spiritual characteristics and qualities, those of Adam must have been transmitted to all his descendants." Thus, according to Tertullian, Adam's corrupted nature, his mortality, and his punishment for his sin are passed on to all his descendants.[11]

Ian McFarland summarizes the writings of theologians prior to Augustine this way:

> In summary, the basic theological framework common to Christian theologians reading the Genesis narrative in the pre-Augustinian period included two very general convictions: first, that Adam's disobedience represented the historic occasion for the entrance of sin and death into the world, and, second, that the effects of this primordial sin on subsequent generations of human beings can only be overcome through the redemptive work of Christ. As noted in the preceding paragraphs, this move seems to have been motivated chiefly by resistance to Gnostic Christian and pagan philosophical schemes that traced evil to God or matter. At the same time, opposition to the perceived fatalism of these same schemes caused theologians to place great stress on human beings' capacity to avoid sin. This deep-seated belief in human freedom stood in implicit tension with the determinism of the Adamic theory of the fall, with the result that

---

9. Tennant, *Sources of the Doctrines of the Fall and Original Sin*, 311–12.
10. Tennant, *Sources of the Doctrines of the Fall and Original Sin*, 311–12. He here quotes Athanasius, *On the Incarnation of the Word* 20.
11. Tennant, *Sources of the Doctrines of the Fall and Original Sin*, 331–35.

Christians' answers for the following three questions remained in considerable flux throughout the pre-Augustinian period: (1) The degree to which the Paradise story was to be interpreted literally; (2) whether the sin described there directly implicates later generations of human beings; and (3) the effect of that sin on the freedom of post-Adamic humanity.[12]

St. Augustine

Saint Augustine (354–430) developed his theology of original sin amid the theological controversies of his time, in particular his disagreements with Pelagius (360–418). Pelagius emphasized God's gift of a moral nature in human beings, which made it possible for humans to know and do what is right. According to Pelagius, we have the grace we need to obey God insofar as we have the law, reason, and free will; each person is responsible for the sin they commit. Pelagius believed that Adam's sin harms us only when we follow Adam's example.

One of Augustine's driving concerns was "soteriology": the doctrine of salvation. Jesus is humanity's sole Savior. In Augustine's view, all humans are fallen, and all inevitably sin; therefore, all need Christ. Pelagius was concerned that Augustine's view took away too much human responsibility for sin.[13] Augustine, in turn, was concerned that Pelagius's view implied that humans could earn their own justification apart from Christ by avoiding sin. Augustine insisted that every human, even infants (who, Augustine agreed, had not yet willfully sinned), required Christ's atonement.

The need for even infants to be saved from sin led to Augustine's second driving concern, "theodicy": how a good and sovereign God can permit evil. God is wholly good and wholly sovereign. God created humans. Why, then, are all humans today incapable of not sinning? The blame for this must lie with our first parents, not with God. This reasoning led Augustine to some particular hermeneutical and metaphysical choices in developing his version of the doctrine of original sin. According to his perspective: (1) Genesis 2–3 should be interpreted in a much more literal-historical fashion than Genesis 1; (2) humans were created sinless, in a state of grace, able to avoid sinning; (3) humans were nevertheless able to sin because they were created *ex nihilo* (out of nothing) rather than out of divine substance; (4) the sin of

---

12. Ian A. McFarland, *In Adam's Fall: A Meditation on the Christian Doctrine of Original Sin* (Oxford: Wiley-Blackwell, 2010), 32.

13. Wiley writes, "For his part, Pelagius just took the existence of human freedom as evidence that human nature can do either good or evil. If nature does not have the potential to avoid wrongdoing, Pelagius argued, how may a person be held morally responsible?" *Original Sin*, 68.

Adam and Eve damaged their human nature and lost for them some divine gifts, and as a result of this loss, they fell into bondage to sin and were no longer able not to sin; (5) new human souls are naturally generated from the parents during reproduction; (6) the damage to human nature from sin is passed from parents to children; (7) in addition, the guilt of sin is passed from parents to children; (8) and although God foreknew that Adam and Eve would choose to sin and bring about all these consequences, God nevertheless created them and permitted their sin because of greater goods that this would enable.

Augustine's views on a literal reading of Genesis changed over time. In his early writings, such as *On Genesis against the Manicheans* (388–89), Augustine took a basically allegorical approach to Genesis 2–3. In his *Confessions* (397–98), he continued to advocate hermeneutical flexibility. But as his theology of original sin developed in *The Literal Meaning of Genesis* (401–16), he wrote that Genesis 2–3 should be understood as simply telling things that happened and that paradise should be understood literally rather than figuratively.[14]

Manichaeism, as both a philosophy and a religion, was a rival to Christianity in Augustine's time. Manichaeism taught that both good and evil are eternal. Opposing Manichaeism, Augustine and other church fathers maintained that Scripture teaches that only God is eternal and that God is wholly good. For this reason, God would not have created Adam sinful. Adam must have had the ability to avoid sin. This ability not to sin came both from Adam's good created nature and from supernatural gifts given to him.[15]

Unlike Irenaeus, who believed that Adam and Eve were initially immature and in need of moral development, Augustine thought that Adam and Eve were not only mature but also, thanks to their uncorrupted created nature and supernatural gifts, superhuman in several ways. Augustine was not alone in thinking of Adam's prelapsarian (pre-fall) state this way. Other theologians before and after him similarly concluded that God, in his goodness, must

---

14. Augustine, *The Literal Meaning of Genesis* 8.2, 4, ed. John E. Rotelle (Hyde Park, NY: New City, 2002), 346–47.

15. Wiley writes, "In the state of original blessedness, Augustine argued, Adam had the capacity to choose and do what is good. Because God is the ultimate good, the choice of any good is the choice of God. Because Adam was also created with freedom, however, his choice of the good was not necessary. Augustine argued that in Adam's original state he had the ability *not to sin* (*posse non peccare*). He also possessed certain gifts in this prelapsarian state. These gifts were over and beyond what human nature as nature requires. Among these gifts were immortality, integrity, and knowledge. By sin, Adam lost these gifts. Consequently, Adam's descendants are born without them." *Original Sin*, 62–63.

have created the first humans not only in a state of moral righteousness but also with superior mental and physical powers, including perpetual youth, freedom from all sickness, and mental abilities far above the most brilliant thinkers ever since.[16]

How, then, was it possible for Adam to sin? Augustine tied the possibility of sin to the doctrine of creation *ex nihilo*. Augustine reasoned that God did not create this world out of divine substance, because if he had, there could not have been sin. Nor did God create this world out of some other eternally existing substance, because only God is eternal. God created this world out of nothing. In some way, being created *ex nihilo* gave Adam and Eve the freedom to reject their unity with God and choose sin.

Why did Adam choose sin? Augustine thought that the first sin was the sin of pride. In *The City of God*, he writes,

> For "pride is the beginning of sin." And what is pride but the craving for undue exaltation? And this is undue exaltation, when the soul abandons Him to whom it ought to cleave as its end, and becomes a kind of end to itself. This happens when it becomes its own satisfaction. And it does so when it falls away from that unchangeable good which ought to satisfy it more than itself. This falling away is spontaneous; for if the will had remained stead-fast in the love of that higher and changeless good by which it was illumined to intelligence and kindled into love, it would not have turned away to find satisfaction in itself.[17]

---

16. N. P. Williams, *The Ideas of the Fall and of Original Sin: A Historical and Critical Study* (London: Longmans, Green, 1927), 361–62, writes:

> So we find, according to Augustine, that Adam in Paradise was exempted from all physical evils, and endowed with immortal youth and health which could not be touched by the taint of sickness or the creeping debility of old age. The gift of immortality lay within his reach; the taste of the Tree of Life would have enabled him to transcend physical limitations, to refine and transubstantiate his earthly nature into pure spirit, so that it would have passed painlessly from this life to the fuller life of Heaven, without the gloomy passage through the grave and gate of death. His intellect was endowed with an "infused knowledge" which, we are told, made his mental powers as far superior to those of the most brilliant modern philosophers as the flight of birds surpasses in swiftness the sluggish movements of the tortoise. . . . His will, moreover, was confirmed in good-ness by an implanted rectitude, an interior spirituality, a settled bias and determination towards virtue, which was the equivalent of that steadfast character which the greatest saints have acquired through a lifetime of struggle. Yet Adam in Paradise knew no struggle: his character of perfect holiness was presented to him as it were ready-made by his Creator. He had no temptations with which to contend; all he had to do was to keep out of the way of temptation, and to preserve the "original justice" with which God had endowed him.

17. Augustine, *The City of God* 14.13, http://www.ccel.org/ccel/schaff/npnf102.iv.XIV.13 .html.

Augustine distinguished the eventual state of humans redeemed, glorified, and no longer able to sin (*non posse peccare*) from the prelapsarian state of Adam and Eve as able to sin but also able not to sin (*posse non peccare*). Sin damaged their created nature and caused them to lose supernatural gifts, resulting in their being in a state in which they were no longer able not to sin (*non posse non peccare*).

Why should the sin of our first parents in paradise affect all their offspring? On this point, Augustine argued for the unity of all humanity in Adam, using both biblical theology and Greek metaphysics. The theological theme of unity—unity with God and unity with one another—is important throughout Augustine's writings. In *The City of God*, Augustine appeals to Genesis 2 specifically to argue for the unity of all of humanity.[18]

Augustine also used Greek metaphysical ideas available to him. Augustine had available at least four theories on the origins of each human soul. One theory is that while each new human body is generated by its parents, God specially creates each new human soul with each conception (creationism). A second theory is that God created all human souls at once prior to the creation described in Genesis 1 and that one of these souls is joined to a human body with each conception. Augustine rejected these two theories in part because they would mean that God created souls that already suffered the stain of sin. A third theory is that human souls existed in eternity prior to creation and that one of them is joined to a body with each new conception (eternalism). Augustine rejected this because he believed that only God is eternal. A fourth theory is that both the body and the soul of each new human come from the parents by natural generation (traducianism). Augustine chose this theory as fitting well with his theology. When Adam sinned, his human nature became damaged. He naturally passed this damage on to all his offspring.

Adam's sin caused both damage to human nature and a loss of supernatural gifts. As a result, humans are no longer able not to sin. The word typically associated with this view is "concupiscence," which comes from the Latin word *concupiscentia*, referring to longing or yearning. In Augustine, this term came to mean desire that is disordered—that is, desire turned away from God, its proper focus. The existence of desire is not the problem. The problem is that humans come to desire created things in and of themselves rather than in their proper ordering and relationship to God. Disordered desire is part of the fallen human condition and cannot be fully washed away by baptism.

---

18. Augustine, *The City of God* 12.21, http://www.ccel.org/ccel/schaff/npnf102.iv.XII.21 .html.

The Holy Spirit works through both supernatural and natural means, in those who follow Christ, to regenerate their nature.

Augustine believed that each human is born not only with the damage caused by Adam's sin but also with the guilt of Adam's sin. Even infants, who have not yet willfully sinned, require Christ's atonement. Augustine supported this teaching in several of his writings by reference to Romans 5:12.[19] Augustine used a Latin translation of Romans that is often translated into English as "By one man sin entered into the world, and death by sin, and so death passed upon all men by him in whom all sinned." It is reasonable to assume that Augustine believed on the basis of this text that all humans were "in" Adam when Adam sinned and therefore share in the guilt of Adam, "*in whom* all sinned." Modern scholars point out that this is not the best translation of the original Greek. A more common modern translation of Romans 5:12 from the Greek is "Therefore, just as sin entered the world through one man, and death through sin, and in this way death came to all people, *because* all sinned." Modern translations, therefore, seem to provide less support for Augustine's teachings on inherited guilt than the translation with which Augustine was working.

However, Augustine did not derive his belief in inherited guilt solely from that passage. He also pointed to the church's practice of infant baptism. Augustine reasoned that infants have not yet committed willful sins, so infant baptism must remove the inherited guilt (but not all the inherited damage) of original sin. Augustine's metaphysical belief in traducianism (in which the souls of offspring are, in some sense, "in" their ancestors) also supported his belief in inherited guilt, as did his theological emphasis on the unity of all people (drawn from many biblical texts). Because of the way in which God created humanity, all humans are united with one another naturally by their descent from Adam and Eve.[20]

Did God foreknow Adam's sin and its dire consequences? If so, why did God permit it? Augustine concluded that God did indeed foreknow that Adam would sin; however, God also foresaw that many would be forgiven

19. Augustine, *A Treatise against Two Letters of the Pelagians* 4.7, http://www.ccel.org/ccel/schaff/npnf105.xviii.vi.vii.html; Augustine, *A Treatise on the Merits and Forgiveness of Sins, and on the Baptism of Infants* 1.55, http://www.ccel.org/ccel/schaff/npnf105.x.iii.lv.html; Augustine, *A Treatise on the Grace of Christ, and on Original Sin* 2.34, http://www.ccel.org/ccel/schaff/npnf105.xv.iv.xxxiv.html; Augustine, *Sermons* 65.1, http://www.ccel.org/ccel/schaff/npnf106.vii.lxvii.html.

20. A summary of this dual inheritance of concupiscence and guilt resulting from Adam's sin can be found in Christopher M. Hays and Stephen L. Herring, "Adam and the Fall," in *Evangelical Faith and the Challenge of Historical Criticism*, ed. Christopher M. Hays and Christopher B. Ansberry (Grand Rapids: Baker Academic, 2013), 47.

and justified. And God chose to create humanity in a way that emphasizes unity:

That God Foreknew That the First Man Would Sin, and That He at the Same Time Foresaw How Large a Multitude of Godly Persons Would by His Grace Be Translated to the Fellowship of the Angels

And God was not ignorant that man would sin, and that, being himself made subject now to death, he would propagate men doomed to die, and that these mortals would run to such enormities in sin, that even the beasts devoid of rational will, and who were created in numbers from the waters and the earth, would live more securely and peaceably with their own kind than men, who had been propagated from one individual for the very purpose of commending concord. For not even lions or dragons have ever waged with their kind such wars as men have waged with one another. But God foresaw also that by His grace a people would be called to adoption, and that they, being justified by the remission of their sins, would be united by the Holy Ghost to the holy angels in eternal peace, the last enemy, death, being destroyed; and He knew that this people would derive profit from the consideration that God had caused all men to be derived from one, for the sake of showing how highly He prizes unity in a multitude.[21]

McFarland summarizes Augustine's twin concerns with soteriology and theodicy this way:

In summary, in the context of developing the dogmatic principle (derived from the confession that Jesus is humanity's sole Savior) that all human beings are sinners in need of salvation, an Augustinian theology needs to defend three claims regarding the Fall and its effects: 1) an *ontological* claim affirming the solidarity of all subsequent generations of human beings with the first human being *in* sin, 2) a *psychological* claim that postlapsarian humanity suffers from a congenital bondage of the will *to* sin, and 3) a *moral* claim that all postlapsarian human activity unaided by grace *is* sin. If the primary motivation behind the Augustinian turn in Christian reflection on the Fall is soteriological, each of these corollaries amplifies the questions of theodicy that earlier Christian theologies of the Fall were intended to help resolve. Is it just of God to ascribe Adam's sin indiscriminately to all of his descendants? Or to condemn human beings for sin that they are constitutionally unable to avoid? Or to view all deeds human beings perform by their own power as equally damnable? The theological challenges posed by these questions were already the focus of opposition to Augustine during his lifetime, and they continue to set the agenda for criticism of his doctrine of original sin.[22]

---

21. Augustine, *The City of God* 12.22, http://www.ccel.org/ccel/schaff/npnf102.iv.XII.22.html.
22. McFarland, *In Adam's Fall*, 35.

Medieval and Reformation Developments

Medieval and Reformation-era theologians generally stayed close to Augustine's version of the doctrine of original sin, with some variations.

Saint Thomas Aquinas (1225–74), like Augustine, believed that Adam and Eve prior to the fall had been given supernatural gifts that made it possible for them to avoid sinning. Aquinas called this prelapsarian state "original justice."[23] Aquinas, like Augustine, struggled to explain how these first humans, in such a state, could fall into sin. Wiley notes,

> In his theology of original sin, Thomas left unaddressed the paradox that Adam could or would sin when the gift of original justice oriented his nature wholly toward God. He raised the question in the context of his metaphysics of evil, specifically in his discussion of free will as the cause of evil. When human beings fail to attend to reason and divine law as the rule and measure to which their actions should conform, there is a "free defect" in the will, a privation or failure in being. The moral evil is in the action, but its root is in the voluntary failure of free will to conform to reason and divine law. There is no further prior cause to be sought for moral evil other than freedom. This is sin, and in the end it is inexplicable.[24]

According to Aquinas, Adam's descendants inherit through birth a fallen human nature deprived of the supernatural gift of original justice. All humans share guilt not so much because of an inherited defect but because all participate in a common human nature.[25]

Like Augustine, Aquinas addressed the question of why God would create humans who he foreknew would fall into sin. Aquinas answered first that a creation that includes both incorruptible creatures and corruptible creatures (those who sometimes do fall into sin) is better than a creation that includes only incorruptible creatures.[26] Second, Aquinas pointed to the supreme good of grace and redemption. As Hick notes:

---

23. Wiley writes, "For Thomas, original justice established internal harmony in human nature by holding 'all the soul's parts together in one.' The right order in nature is a threefold subjection: (1) the subjection of human reason to God, (2) the subjection of the moral will to reason, and (3) the subjection of the powers of the body to the powers of the soul (will and reason). . . . Because of sin, God had removed the gift of *justitia* from the soul, leaving nature to itself. Now absent was the condition necessary for moral integrity." *Original Sin*, 85.

24. Wiley, *Original Sin*, 87.

25. Rik Van Nieuwenhove and Joseph Wawrykow, *The Theology of Thomas Aquinas* (Notre Dame, IN: University of Notre Dame Press, 2010), 154–55.

26. Thomas Aquinas, *Summa Theologiae* I.48.2, https://www.newadvent.org/summa/1048.htm#article2, writes,

> The perfection of the universe requires that there should be inequality in things, so that every grade of goodness may be realized. Now, one grade of goodness is that of the

For in his treatise on the Incarnation, he says (though without elaboration) that "God allows evils to happen in order to bring a greater good therefrom," and quotes the startling and pregnant sentence of the "*O felix culpa*"; and in his treatise on Grace he exalts as the supreme activity of divine grace the saving of sinners: "The justification of the ungodly, which terminates at the eternal good of a share in the Godhead, is greater than the creation of heaven and earth, which terminates at the good of a mutable nature."[27]

Martin Luther (1483–1546) rejected the idea that humans were given supernatural gifts that were lost because of the fall. Wiley writes, "The paradigmatic sin he [Luther] saw in Adam's disobedience was the lack of faith. When Luther employed the notion of privation, he did not mean, as the scholastics did, the absence of a supernatural power of habit, but the absence of faith in God."[28] Luther, unlike Augustine and Aquinas, did not distinguish between humans inheriting a status (original sin) and humans inheriting disordered desires (concupiscence). Concupiscence is a fundamental self-centeredness and a propensity to sinful cravings. Wiley continues, "In Luther's judgment, the inner experience of disharmony, disorder, self-contradiction, and moral impotence the early church writers named 'concupiscence' is the root sin—in the sense of *original*—with which human beings [since the fall] are always afflicted. The chief manifestation of this root sin, in his view, was the last of the prohibitions of the ten commandments, coveting."[29]

John Calvin's (1509–64) views on original sin were similar to Augustine's. Calvin's theology emphasized God's sovereignty and the utter necessity of divine grace in overcoming original sin. Calvin also insisted that although God both foreknew and ordained this state of affairs, humans retain responsibility for their sins. Calvin wrote,

> We call predestination God's eternal decree, by which he determined with himself what he willed to become of each man. For all are not created in equal

---

good which cannot fail. Another grade of goodness is that of the good which can fail in goodness, and this grade is to be found in existence itself; for some things there are which cannot lose their existence as incorruptible things, while some there are which can lose it, as things corruptible. As, therefore, the perfection of the universe requires that there should be not only beings incorruptible, but also corruptible beings; so the perfection of the universe requires that there should be some which can fail in goodness, and thence it follows that sometimes they do fail.

27. Hick, *Evil and the God of Love*, 97–98. Hick cites the following from Thomas Aquinas, *Summa Theologiae* III.1.3: "'O felix culpa, quae talem ac tantum meruit habere redemptorem'— 'O fortunate crime which merited such and so great a redeemer'" (97n5).

28. Wiley, *Original Sin*, 97.

29. Wiley, *Original Sin*, 90.

condition; rather, eternal life is foreordained for some, eternal damnation for others. Therefore, as any man has been created to one or the other of these ends, we speak of him as predestined to life or to death. . . .

Since the disposition of all things is in God's hand, since the decision of salvation or of death rests in his power, he so ordains by his plan and will that among men some are born destined for certain death from the womb, who glorify his name by their own destruction. . . .

Again I ask: whence does it happen that Adam's fall irremediably involved so many peoples, together with their infant offspring, in eternal death unless because it so pleased God? . . . The decree is dreadful indeed, I confess. Yet no one can deny that God foreknew what end man was to have before he created him, and consequently foreknew because he so ordained by his decree.[30]

Hick summarizes Calvin's views on human responsibility for sin this way:

And since God Himself thus set in train the fatal sequence that has led to man's present sinful state, the question arises whether men are justly punishable for their sinfulness. Calvin supposes an objector to ask, "Why from the beginning did God predestine some to death who, since they did not yet exist, could not yet have deserved the judgment of death?" And his answer is that, although predestine to it, men sin freely, and are therefore all personally guilty and rightly condemned. "If all are drawn out of a corrupt mass, no wonder they are subject to condemnation! Let them not accuse God of injustice if they are destined by his eternal judgement to death, to which they feel—whether by will or not— that they are led by their own nature of itself." Calvin is here making use of the conception of human freedom and accountability at which he arrived in book II of the *Institutes*. We may say that, for Calvin, to have a will and to have free will are the same. Thus the sinner, whose fallen nature is such that he necessarily wills wrongly and who cannot, with his perverted nature, will rightly, remains nevertheless a free and responsible agent; for he is acting voluntarily and not from external compulsion.[31]

Throughout the medieval and Reformation periods, nearly all theologians assumed a literal-historical interpretation of Genesis 2–3, with Adam and Eve as the sole progenitors of all humans. But they offered a range of ideas about what exactly happened to human nature when sin began. Some believed that created human nature was unchanged but that humanity lost supernatural gifts that had enabled a state of original righteousness. Others believed that

30. John Calvin, *Institutes of the Christian Religion*, ed. John T. McNeill, trans. Ford Lewis Battles, Library of Christian Classics 21 (Philadelphia: Westminster, 1960), 3.21.5; 3.23.6–7.
31. Hick, *Evil and the God of Love*, 120–21.

original created human nature was in a state of righteousness without the need for supernatural gifts but that this created nature was corrupted by sin. Others believed both that the created nature was corrupted and that supernatural gifts were lost.

Likewise, they had a range of ideas about the transmission of the guilt of sin. Some thought that the guilt of sin is passed from parents to children because there is a real, ontological unity to all humans. Others thought that all humans inherit Adam's guilt because Adam was, in something analogous to a legal sense, the "federal head" of humanity. Others thought that guilt itself is not inherited but that the state of corruption (which is inherited) carries with it guilt. Others thought that only corruption is inherited and that each individual is guilty only for sins they individually commit (a view more common prior to Augustine).

What about Eve?

Until modern times, theologians writing about original sin seldom mentioned Eve. They typically wrote about "Adam's sin." For some of these theologians, we might make a charitable interpretation of their omission and assume that they simply wrote "Adam" as shorthand for "Adam and Eve," seeing both individuals as equally important but Adam as assigned a traditional "headship" role in the family. For many theologians, however, their writings imply that they did not see Adam and Eve as equally important. They really thought that it was *Adam's* sin that determined the status of all future generations.

From the early church until modern times, theologians lived in cultures that accepted many hierarchical assumptions about gender. A common belief until modern times (at least among males) was that males were superior to females physically, emotionally, rationally, and even spiritually. When theologians of premodern eras did mention Eve, often it was simply to blame Eve for Adam's sin, with Adam's sin being the theologically important sin. A few went much further than this and blamed women throughout history for most of men's actual sins.[32]

32. Wiley summarizes, "Early church theologians appealed to the story of Adam and Eve as divine revelation. In their writings, reference to Genesis 2–3 often includes specific concerns with gender. The history they found revealed was threefold: (1) woman's creation as an inferior human being, (2) woman's sin as the cause for the fall of humankind from divine friendship, and (3) male rule as a divinely willed feature of the created order." *Original Sin*, 155.

Some Post-Enlightenment Ideas

During the last three centuries, natural scientists discovered that the earth is billions of years old. Archaeological discoveries have expanded our knowledge of early human history and of ancient Near Eastern cultures and literature. In response, a number of theologians developed versions of the doctrine of original sin that do not rely on literal-historical interpretations of Genesis 1–3.[33] In some of these, Genesis 2–3 is seen as a stylized retelling of an actual historical fall from a paradisiacal state. In others, Adam and Eve are seen as symbolic figures for every human being.

Karl Barth (1886–1968), in his *Church Dogmatics*, affirmed the universal reality of sin and the need for redemption in Christ. "There can be no objection to the Latin expression *peccatum originale* if it is not given this more exact definition. It is indeed quite adequate, telling us that we are dealing with the original and radical and therefore the comprehensive and total act of man, with the imprisonment of his existence in that circle of evil being and evil activity. In this imprisonment God speaks to him and makes Himself his liberator in Jesus Christ."[34] While Barth affirmed the universal human condition of original sin, he did not see Adam as a historical figure nor the fall as occurring at a particular point in time. For Barth, Adam is a symbolic figure for every human; Adam is "everyman." In Adam, we see what we all are outside of Christ. Barth used the term "saga" to describe the genre of Genesis 2–3. "We miss the unprecedented and incomparable things which the Genesis passages tell us of the coming into being and existence of Adam if we try to read and understand it as history, relating it either favourably or unfavourably to scientific paleontology. . . . Saga in general is the form which, using intuition and imagination, has to take up historical narration at the point where events are no longer susceptible as such of historical proof."[35]

Reinhold Niebuhr (1892–1971) discussed original sin in volume 1 of *The Nature and Destiny of Man*.[36] Niebuhr, like theologians before him, wrestled with the difficulty of maintaining both that all humans inevitably sin and that individuals retain responsibility for their sins.[37] Niebuhr rejected the

33. Some leading liberal Christian theologians, such as Friedrich Schleiermacher (1768–1834) and Rudolf Bultmann (1884–1976), offered useful ideas. For this chapter, however, I summarize the writings of a few theologians with more orthodox views about the divinity of Christ and the inspiration of Scripture.

34. Karl Barth, *Church Dogmatics* IV/1, *The Doctrine of Reconciliation*, trans. G. W. Bromiley and T. F. Torrance (Edinburgh: T&T Clark, 1956), 500.

35. Barth, *Church Dogmatics* IV/1, 508.

36. Reinhold Niebuhr, *The Nature and Destiny of Man: A Christian Interpretation*, 2 vols. (Louisville: Westminster John Knox, 1996).

37. Niebuhr, *Nature and Destiny of Man*, 1:243.

interpretation of Adam as a historical figure and the fall as a historical event. Instead, he saw the story of Adam as an archetype of the way that all humans sin.[38] To understand what sinless humanity should be, we should look not to a pre-fallen individual Adam but, rather, to Christ.[39]

Frederick R. Tennant (1866–1957), in addition to studying the historical development of the doctrine of original sin, integrated insights from Darwin's theory of evolution into his version of the doctrine. Humans inherited impulses from our animal ancestors to behave in ways that, for animals, are morally neutral but that, for humans, are immoral. But humans also evolved in social groups, and each individual develops in a social environment, which promotes the development of morality and conscience.[40] Our free will and moral nature oppose our natural animal tendencies for selfishness. Achieving the ideal of true self-effacement requires divine grace.[41]

C. S. Lewis (1898–1963) accepted the scientific evidence for evolution, including human evolution, although he also frequently wrote against atheistic interpretations of evolution. In *The Problem of Pain*, he offered a scenario in which some of our ancient ancestors were, for a real time in history, in a paradisiacal and sinless state like that envisioned by Augustine in which their creaturely desires were entirely subject to their wills and their wills were subject to God. From this state they fell through an act of self-will.[42]

38. Niebuhr, *Nature and Destiny of Man*, 1:267–68.

39. Niebuhr, *Nature and Destiny of Man*, 2:76–90.

40. Frederick Robert Tennant, *The Origin and Propagation of Sin: Being the Hulsean Lectures Delivered before the University of Cambridge*, 2nd ed. (Cambridge: Cambridge University Press, 1902), 117.

41. Daniel K. Brannan, "Darwinism and Original Sin: Frederick R. Tennant's Integration of Darwinian Worldviews into Christian Thought in the Nineteenth Century," *Journal for Interdisciplinary Research on Religion and Science* 1 (2007): 193.

42. See C. S. Lewis, *The Problem of Pain* (Grand Rapids: Zondervan, 2001), 65–72:

I offer the following picture—a "myth" in the Socratic sense, a not unlikely tale. For long centuries God perfected the animal form which was to become the vehicle of humanity and the image of Himself. . . . Then, in the fullness of time, God caused to descend upon this organism, both on its psychology and physiology, a new kind of consciousness which could say "I" and "me," which could look upon itself as an object, which knew God, which could make judgements of truth, beauty, and goodness, and which was so far above time that it could perceive time flowing past. . . . The new consciousness had been made to repose on its Creator, and repose it did. However rich and varied man's experience of his fellows (or fellow) in charity and friendship and sexual love, or of the beasts, or of the surrounding world then first recognized as beautiful and awful, God came first in his love and in his thought, and that without painful effort. . . . Judged by his artefacts, or perhaps even by his language, this blessed creature was, no doubt, a savage. All that experience and practice can teach he had still to learn. . . . We do not know how many of these creatures God made, nor how long they continued in the Paradisal state. But sooner or later they fell. Someone or something whispered that they could become as

John R. W. Stott (1921–2011) likewise accepted the scientific evidence for human evolution.[43] In *Understanding the Bible*, he proposes a scenario for a historical Adam and Eve who were specially selected and transformed out of a larger population:

> But my acceptance of Adam and Eve as historical is not incompatible with my belief that several forms of pre-Adamic "hominid" may have existed for thousands of years previously. These hominids began to advance culturally. They made their cave drawings and buried their dead. It is conceivable that God created Adam out of one of them. You may call them *Homo erectus*. I think you may even call some of them *Homo sapiens*, for these are arbitrary scientific names. But Adam was the first *homo divinus*, if I may coin a phrase, the first man to whom may be given the Biblical designation "made in the image of God." Precisely what the divine likeness was, which was stamped upon him, we do not know, for Scripture nowhere tells us. But Scripture seems to suggest that it includes rational, moral, social, and spiritual faculties which make man unlike all other creatures and like God the creator, and on account of which he was given "dominion" over the lower creation.[44]

Some Recent Scholarship

During the last few decades, the fields of psychology and sociology have improved our understanding of human behavior and decision-making. Their discoveries make the question "What is the damage caused by sin?" even more complex to answer. Here are three examples.

1. The relationship between our genes and our culture is complicated. Our behavior is never simply a case of "nature versus nurture." Our genes and our culture shape each other, and they shape each of us in deeply interconnected ways.
2. The relationship between our impulses and our will is complicated; they affect each other in deeply interconnected ways. Our tendency to sin cannot simply be the failure of our will to keep our animal impulses

---

gods—that they could cease directing their lives to their Creator. . . . For the difficulty about the first sin is that it must be very heinous, or its consequences would not be so terrible, and yet it must be something which a being free from the temptations of fallen man could conceivably have committed. The turning from God to self fulfills both conditions. It is a sin possible even to Paradisal man, because the mere existence of a self—the mere fact that we call it "me"—includes from the first, the danger of self idolatry.

43. John R. W. Stott, *Understanding the Bible*, expanded ed. (New York: HarperCollins, 2011), 54–55.

44. Stott, *Understanding the Bible*, 55–56.

under control, nor can it simply be a prideful act of will to put ourselves ahead of God independent of our creaturely impulses.

3. Our relationships with one another are complicated. As individuals, each of us is profoundly dependent on others and depended on by others. To be human is to be interdependent. From before birth and throughout our lives, we are radically shaped by the actions of others and the culture around us.

In *The God of Evolution*, Denis Edwards offers one possible way to synthesize these three complexities into an understanding of original sin. Many modern scholars (although they might phrase things differently) would agree with his summary about the complex relationships between genes, culture, free choice, and sin. Edwards explains his view as follows:

Thesis 1: Human beings are a fallible symbiosis of genes and culture, who experience drives and impulses from the genetic side of their inheritance as well as from the cultural side, and these drives and impulses can be disordered and mutually opposed. This essence is *intrinsic* to being an evolutionary human but it is not sin. . . .

Thesis 2: Original sin consists of the fact that human beings have a cultural history of personal and communal sin which enters into and becomes an inner dimension of each person's situation. . . . Our existential state then is constituted by (1) our evolutionary structure as a fallible symbiosis of genes and culture, and (2) the additional fact that the history of human sin is an inner constitutive element in our own free acts. This second element twists, compounds, and distorts the complexity and fallibility that is part of our evolutionary makeup. It is only this second element that is properly associated with original sin.

Thesis 3: Original sin has an impact on the whole person. It is *not* to be associated with only the biological side of the human; nor is it to be associated only with the cultural side. It involves our free response to both our genetic inheritance and our cultural conditioning. I believe that it is a mistake to identify selfishness and sin with the biological side of the human being. I think it is also a mistake to identify unselfish behavior with the cultural side. On the one hand, our genetic inheritance carries messages that are necessary for human life, and these are to be seen, according to biblical tradition, as part of God's good creation. On the other hand, culture, and religion as part of culture, can carry not only messages of altruistic love, but also messages of systemic evil.[45]

45. Denis Edwards, *The God of Evolution: A Trinitarian Theology* (New York: Paulist Press, 1999), 65–68.

While there is near consensus among recent scholars on some points, there is still considerable disagreement on others. One particular point of disagreement is over how to answer the question "When did sin begin?" Perhaps the most extensive collection of essays proposing different answers to this question is the one on the BioLogos website.[46] Some scenarios see Adam and Eve as symbolic figures and humanity's sinful rebellion against God as happening over a long period of time. Others see Adam and Eve as real historical figures, members of a larger population, and sin entering the world in a concentrated historical event. These types of scenarios are explored in more depth in chapter 9.

46. The collection can be accessed at https://biologos.org/resources, select topic "Bible," subtopic "Adam & Eve."

What Is Sin?

"SIN" IS A SMALL WORD wrapped around a huge concept. What do we mean by it?

Sin is both action and the attitude that precedes the action. Sin is both willful disobedience and a condition that is beyond our control. Sin is both individual and communal. Sin is both rebellion against God and causing harm to God's creatures. We are aware of sin through both general and special revelation. Sin would keep us away from God eternally without God's rescue.

This chapter is primarily about how we experience sin today. The next chapter discusses what changed when sin began.

Metaphors for Sin

The fact that Scripture uses so many metaphors for sin helps us understand the magnitude of the problem.

> Sin and the guilt of sin are a burden that we bear (e.g., Exod. 28:38; Num. 5:31; 9:13; 18:1, 22; 1 Sam. 25:31; Ps. 38:4; Isa. 53:11; Ezek. 4:4; Hosea 13:16).[1] Jesus invites us, "Come to me, all you who are weary and burdened, and I will give you rest" (Matt. 11:28).

1. A frequently cited source on metaphors for sin, especially sin as a burden and a debt, is Gary A. Anderson, *Sin: A History* (New Haven: Yale University Press, 2009). Other important

Sin is a debt to be paid. Jesus used this metaphor to teach about God's forgiveness (Matt. 18:21–35; Luke 7:41–50). In Colossians, it is said that our indebtedness has been nailed to the cross (Col. 2:14).

Sin is disobeying God's spoken and written laws. Exodus, Leviticus, Numbers, and Deuteronomy are filled with laws. Joshua (1:7) urges and warns God's people upon entering the promised land to obey God's law. Numerous psalms celebrate the goodness of God's law and the importance of obedience (e.g., Pss. 19; 119). Paul (e.g., Rom. 2–5) tells us that knowledge of the law makes us aware of our sin.

Sin is moral evil that people do, even when they do not know God's spoken and written laws (e.g., Rom. 1:18–32; 2:12–16).

Sin is rebellion against God, the rightful ruler (e.g., Exod. 23:21; Lev. 16:21; Num. 17:10; Deut. 1:26; Josh. 22:16, 22; Pss. 78; 106; Prov. 17:11; Isa. 1:2).

Sin is a stain or disease that makes us spiritually unclean (e.g., Job 31:7; Ps. 51:7; Isa. 1:18; Jer. 2:22; Eph. 5:26–27; 1 Tim. 6:14).

Sin is a power that enslaves and rules over us (e.g., Rom. 6:6, 12; 8:15; Heb. 2:15).

Sin is a predator that seeks to devour us (Gen. 4:7; 1 Pet. 5:8).

Sin is turning from the path that God would have us follow (e.g., Josh. 1:7; numerous psalms and proverbs; Isa. 2:3; 3:12). Both the Hebrew term for sin (hata) and the Greek (hamartia) have meanings derived from missing the mark or going astray.

Sin is a broken relationship with God. The prophets—especially Hosea, who used the metaphor of marriage—spoke of Israel's sin in these terms.

Sin is a hardening of the heart against God, a failure to love God (e.g., Ps. 95:8; Prov. 28:14; Isa. 63:17; Heb. 3:8–15).

Sin Is Both Actions and Attitudes

Sin is not only in our actions but also in the attitudes that precede our actions. Jesus taught in the Sermon on the Mount that committing adultery is sin, but so is committing adultery in one's heart by indulging in lustful thoughts (Matt. 5:28). Murder is sin, but so is nursing anger (Matt. 5:22). Anything

---

works are Mark J. Boda, *A Severe Mercy: Sin and Its Remedy in the Old Testament* (Winona Lake, IN: Eisenbrauns, 2009); and Mark E. Biddle, *Missing the Mark: Sin and Its Consequences in Biblical Theology* (Nashville: Abingdon, 2005).

short of loving one's enemies is sin. "Be perfect, therefore, as your heavenly Father is perfect" (Matt. 5:48).

In summarizing God's laws, Jesus said, "'Love the Lord your God with all your heart and with all your soul and with all your mind' [Deut. 6:5]. This is the first and greatest commandment. And the second is like it: 'Love your neighbor as yourself' [Lev. 19:18]" (Matt. 22:37–39).

When asked about eating ritually unclean food, Jesus taught that it is not what goes into a person's mouth that makes them unclean; it is what comes out of their mouth (in other words, that which comes from their heart). "For out of the heart come evil thoughts" (Matt. 15:19).

Sin Is Both Actions We Can Control and a Condition beyond Our Control

There are times when we choose to sin or not to sin. But we also experience sin as a kind of condition or compulsion. None of us are able to choose not to sin all the time. The apostle Paul sometimes writes about sin as a power at work within us, sometimes referred to as the "flesh" or the "sinful nature." It feels like a power that works to control us; nevertheless, we remain responsible for our decisions. Paul agonizes with this conundrum: "So I find this law at work: Although I want to do good, evil is right there with me. For in my inner being I delight in God's law; but I see another law at work in me, waging war against the law of my mind and making me a prisoner of the law of sin at work within me" (Rom. 7:21–23).

Sin affects us not only on an individual level but also on a societal level. In *Not the Way It's Supposed to Be*, Cornelius Plantinga writes,

> Sin is more than the sum of what sinners do. Sin acquires the powerful and elusive form of a spirit—the spirit of an age or a company or a nation or a political movement. Sin burrows into the bowels of institutions and traditions, making a home there and taking them over. The new structure that is formed by the takeover is likely to display some combination of perversion, formlessness, or excessive rigidity. Law, for example, may be bent to end the freedoms of selected pariah groups. Whole companies may dissolve in an orgy of intertwined deceit and neglect. Whole nations may join in lockstep with brutal dictators. No traditional Christian wants to admit that the powers rob us of all freedom and accountability, that they cause us to sin. . . . Still, the powers are aptly named. As Hendrikus Berkhof says, personal goodness cannot lick them.[2]

2. Cornelius Plantinga, *Not the Way It's Supposed to Be: A Breviary of Sin* (Grand Rapids: Eerdmans, 1996), 75–76.

Sin Is Broken Fellowship with God

In Hosea 11:1–3 God says, "When Israel was a child, I loved him, and out of Egypt I called my son. But the more they were called, the more they went away from me. They sacrificed to the Baals and they burned incense to images. It was I who taught Ephraim to walk, taking them by the arms; but they did not realize it was I who healed them." In many passages, especially in the Prophets, God speaks with great love and longing toward his people, and with great disappointment and anger at their sinful breaking of fellowship with him.

Jaroslav Pelikan beautifully summarizes this aspect in his entry on sin in the *Encyclopedic Dictionary of Religion*:

> The Old Testament, with its manifold legislation about the ritual and moral conduct of the Israelite, often identifies sin with transgression of this legislation. Yet biblical religion does not make this definition of sin decisive of itself, for the law whose transgression makes an act sinful is not first of all a written code (even though it is also a code and is eventually written), but the revealed will of the creator. Breaking the law, therefore, means acting deliberately in disobedience to him and in rebellion against his intention for his creatures. . . . The deepest insight of Christian faith into the nature of sin has been recognition that sin is an act of severing, or at least of jeopardizing, the intimate relation between creator and creature. . . . Conversely, the forgiveness of sins is not merely the removal of moral guilt, but the restoration, by God himself as the injured party, of this personal relationship.[3]

Sin Is Broken *Shalom*

A proper relationship with God should naturally flower into proper relationships with one another and with all of God's creation. Plantinga describes *shalom* this way:

> The webbing together of God, humans, and all creation in justice, fulfillment, and delight is what the Hebrew prophets call *shalom*. We call it peace, but it means far more than mere peace of mind or a cease-fire between enemies. In the Bible, shalom means *universal flourishing, wholeness, and delight*—a rich state of affairs in which natural needs are satisfied and natural gifts fruitfully employed, a state of affairs that inspires joyful wonder as its Creator and Savior

3. Jaroslav Pelikan, "Sin," in *Encyclopedic Dictionary of Religion*, ed. Paul Kevin Meagher, Thomas C. O'Brien, and Consuelo Maria Aherne, 3 vols. (Washington, DC: Corpus, 1979), 3:3307–8.

opens doors and welcomes the creatures in whom he delights. Shalom, in other words, is the way things ought to be.[4]

Tragically, our broken relationship with God naturally leads to destructive relationships with other people and with God's creation.

Sin Is a Perversion of Good and a Parasite of Good

Popular culture often portrays good and evil as equal opposites—perhaps not equal in power (good usually triumphs in our stories), but equal metaphysically and ontologically (that is, equal in terms of their reality). This makes for good drama as two forces struggle for power, or as an individual struggles to decide whether to do good or evil. It's good drama, but it's bad theology.

God is eternal and self-existing. God created everything else from nothing. God is good. If evil does not come from God, and if evil does not come from some other self-existing and eternal source, where does evil come from? According to Augustine and many other theologians, evil has strength only insofar as it draws strength from good, distorting the proper ordering and purpose of good things.

We are created with desires for many good things: healthy and tasty food, pleasurable recreation, safety for ourselves and our family members, esteem from peers, the power to accomplish things, and success in our efforts. But our loves for good things must be properly ordered. Love God above all. Love our neighbors as ourselves. We sin when we make idols out of creaturely goods—seeking them as goals in and of themselves, out of proportion and out of proper relationship with other good things. Gluttons seek short-term pleasure at the expense of the long-term good of their health and the good things they could accomplish with healthy bodies. Those who are stingy with money seek safety and self-esteem at the expense of charity and the welfare of their neighbors. Bullies seek a quick path to self-esteem or the esteem of their peers by harming rather than helping others. In each of these cases, the highest good—God's will—is set aside in the pursuit of something else.

Augustine wrote about the proper ordering of loves in *The City of God*:

Now he is a man of just and holy life who forms an unprejudiced estimate of things, and keeps his affections also under strict control, so that he neither loves what he ought not to love, nor fails to love what he ought to love, nor

---

4. Plantinga, *Not the Way It's Supposed to Be*, 10.

loves that more which ought to be loved less, nor loves that equally which ought to be loved either less or more, nor loves that less or more which ought to be loved equally. No sinner is to be loved as a sinner; and every man is to be loved as a man for God's sake; but God is to be loved for His own sake. And if God is to be loved more than any man, each man ought to love God more than himself.[5]

Regarding sin as a parasite on the good, Plantinga writes, "Nothing about sin is its own; all its power, persistence, and plausibility are stolen goods. Sin is not really an entity but a spoiler of entities, not an organism but a leech on organisms. Sin does not build shalom; it vandalizes it. . . . Good is original, independent, and constructive; evil is derivative, dependent, and destructive. To be successful, evil needs what it hijacks from goodness."[6]

Sin Is Both Individual and Communal

We usually think of sin in terms of an individual's actions and attitudes. Scripture gives us good reason to think that way. King David agonized over his sins and repented of them (e.g., Ps. 51). John the Baptist and Jesus called on individuals to repent. Many of Jesus's parables point to the ultimate judging of each individual (e.g., the weeds and the wheat, Matt. 13:24–30; the net and the fish, Matt. 13:47–52; the sheep and the goats, Matt. 25:31–46).

But Scripture also speaks of communal sin (e.g., Lev. 4:13; Num. 14:40; 1 Sam. 7:6; 12:10; 1 Kings 8:33–36; Ezra 9:6–7; Neh. 1:6; Isa. 30:1; 42:24; Jer. 11:10; Ezek. 14:13, to give a very incomplete list). Presumably, some members of those communities were "more guilty" than others. But the entire community was punished or warned of punishment, and the entire community was called to confess and repent.

If we reflect on our society today, we can think of some things that merit communal repentance. I might abhor how the past generations of Americans treated Black slaves and Native Americans, but I today benefit from the wealth that flowed to some by the exploitation and death of others. I might oppose social systems of the past and the present that entrench racism and sexism, unjustly giving privilege to some at the expense of others, but I benefit from those systems today and don't do enough to change them. I might believe that our society doesn't do enough to give support and opportunity to the poor,

5. Augustine, *The City of God* 1.27, https://www.ccel.org/ccel/schaff/npnf102.v.iv.xxvii.html.
6. Plantinga, *Not the Way It's Supposed to Be*, 89.

but I am living comfortably in that system, and I don't do enough to speak for the powerless. I share some responsibility for the sins of my community.

Sin Spreads

From our everyday experience, we know some of the ways that sin spreads. In families, workplaces, schools, and even recreation, manipulative or abusive interpersonal relationships can push bystanders or even victims into becoming future victimizers. Power relationships and social conventions can reward greed, promote envy, or praise conspicuous consumption. They can crush hope and mock charity. Popular television shows, movies, and books can sometimes portray sinful behavior as normal and appropriate and portray God as irrelevant and absent.

God enables each of us to be created cocreators of our future selves, of others, and of our societies. When we do this sinfully, sin spreads from us to others, and from others back to us.

Sin Is Known by Both General Revelation and Special Revelation

In many Scriptures, human sin is a disobedient response to God's specially revealed will. In Genesis 3, eating the fruit of the tree of the knowledge of good and evil might be interpreted symbolically rather than literally. But in Genesis 3, Adam and Eve were also given a verbal command not to eat. The apostle Paul, in Romans 2:17–3:20, argues that knowledge of God's law does not make us righteous (because we cannot obey it perfectly). But knowledge of God's law does make us aware of our sin. In Romans 5:13 Paul says, "Sin was in the world before the law was given, but sin is not charged against anyone's account where there is no law."

Yet even without knowledge of an explicit command from God, humans have enough of God's general revelation to know that certain actions and attitudes are morally wrong. We have feelings of guilt, promptings of conscience, stirrings to altruism, and reasoning from experience that moral behavior creates a better life for the entire community. These also can convict us of sin. God described some of the practices of the people living in Canaan prior to Israel (and who therefore did not have the law of Moses revealed to Israel) as "detestable" (e.g., Deut. 20:18; 1 Kings 14:24; Ezra 9:1). In Romans 2:14–15 Paul writes, "Indeed, when Gentiles, who do not have the law, do by nature things required by the law, they are a law for themselves, even though they do not have the law. They show that the requirements of the law are written on their hearts, their consciences also bearing witness, and their thoughts sometimes accusing them and at other times even defending them."

"Good Enough" Isn't Good Enough

Each of us would like to believe that we are "good enough" for God's approval. We'd like to believe that, even though we aren't perfect, if we just do enough good things and avoid doing enough bad things, God has to reward us. This is a tempting and worldly way of thinking.

Both Paul (e.g., Gal. 3:10–11; 5:1–4) and James (2:8–10) teach that if we try to justify ourselves before God by obeying God's law, and break just one law, we have failed. In the Sermon on the Mount, Jesus taught that obeying the letter of God's written law isn't enough. "Be perfect, therefore, as your heavenly Father is perfect" (Matt. 5:48).

Metaphors for Atonement

To understand what sin is, it helps to better understand God's chosen means of overcoming sin. Just as Scripture gives us multiple metaphors to help us understand sin, it gives us multiple metaphors to help us understand how Christ's incarnation, life, death, resurrection, and ascension to rule overcome sin and reconcile us to God. At the center of this story is Christ crucified, "a stumbling block to Jews and foolishness to Gentiles" (1 Cor. 1:23).[7]

Perhaps the most widespread metaphor for atonement in Scripture is sacrifice. Jesus is both the High Priest and the sacrifice (Heb. 9:11–12). This calls to mind the Old Testament sin offerings (e.g., Lev. 4–6), the scapegoat (Lev. 16), and the Passover lamb (Exod. 12). The sacrifice metaphor is a central scriptural theme, but it might prompt us to think of a loving Son of God placating a wrathful Father who hates us. We must also remember that Jesus said, "Anyone who has seen me has seen the Father" (John 14:9). In Jesus's self-sacrificial love for us, we see the ultimate revelation of the Father's love for us.

Another metaphor is ransom or redemption to set us free from slavery (Matt. 20:28; Rom. 6; 1 Pet. 1:18–19). This reminds us that we could not free ourselves from sin. We needed a redeemer; and Christ did indeed pay a price.

If sin has power over us, then another metaphor is Christ's death and resurrection winning victory over that power, breaking its hold on us. The imagery

---

7. There are numerous summaries of different theories of atonement. One recent study is Peter Schmiechen, *Saving Power: Theories of Atonement and Forms of the Church* (Grand Rapids: Eerdmans, 2005).

in Scripture isn't of a military victory achieved through violence but of a victory achieved through obedience to God and self-sacrificial love.

Both the Old and the New Testament also use legal language to describe the consequences of sin, and the language of guilt and condemnation in particular. So we also have a forensic metaphor, sometimes called "penal substitution." It reminds us that our sin has consequences. In our modern human legal systems, when a person is guilty of a crime, we might let a second person pay a fine for them, but we would not allow a second person to go to prison in place of the guilty party. So how, in God's divine judgment, does the suffering of Christ overcome the guilt and condemnation of our sin? We don't know all the details. We do know that because God is holy, our sinfulness would make his presence unbearable to us. Our sin has consequences—the worst consequences imaginable: separation from God's presence, God-forsakenness. In Jesus's suffering, especially on the cross, he suffered what we should suffer. Though he was innocent, he suffered the consequences of our sin. By suffering the worst consequences of sin and passing along forgiveness in its place, Jesus somehow makes possible a restored relationship between humans and their Creator.

Sin is broken fellowship with God. Christ's atonement brings reconciliation to that relationship (Rom. 5; 2 Cor. 5:18–21). Reconciliation is more than just forgiveness of sin, although that is a necessary step. It is a restoration of the relationship to the way it ought to be.

Christ is our example. As followers of Christ, we are to be imitators of Christ (e.g., 1 Thess. 1:6). We are to participate in his sufferings (1 Cor. 10:16; Phil. 3:10). Christ has commissioned the church to advance the kingdom of God here on earth. We participate in Christ and his work by demonstrating self-sacrificial love.

Through all these metaphors for atonement taken together, we see Christ addressing the many aspects of sin. Christ's work addresses the guilt of the sinful choices we make. Christ breaks the power of sin that is beyond our control. Christ restores our relationship to God. Christ gives us the ultimate example of how to love God above all and to love our neighbors as ourselves. Christ shows us how to halt the spread of sin and the damage it causes through self-sacrificial forgiveness.

Sin and Our Evolutionary History

How do these pictures of sin relate to our evolutionary past? As noted in chapter 4, our hominin ancestors lived in social groups and learned from one another. As their intelligence grew, they faced increasingly complex choices about how to behave in order to satisfy their many biological and social needs and desires. They had dispositions toward both "nasty" and "nice" behaviors. And they had dispositions toward religious beliefs. This helps explain why sin is so multifaceted and how sin could warp our human nature in so many ways once it entered the story.

Sin is a perversion of good and a parasite of good. God created us, using evolutionary processes, with desires for many creaturely goods. Desires for food, safety, pleasure, and close relationships are not intrinsically evil. We sin when we desire and pursue them out of proportion and out of proper relationship. We sin when we harm someone in order to satisfy a desire for food or pleasure. We sin when we harm someone in order to increase our power over them or to elevate our social status. We sin when we pursue pleasure in a way that makes us unable to help others who rightly should have our help. Sin dis-orders our loves.

Sin is broken shalom; *sin spreads; sin is both individual and communal; sin is both actions we can control and a condition beyond our control.* God created us to live in families and social groups, to make relationships, to learn from one another. Because of our interdependence, our sins hurt other people and their sins hurt us. All of us together create a society in which we learn sin from one another. Each new generation inherits a society in which the effects of sin are inescapable.

Sin is known by general revelation. God created us to be able to choose. We are given the power to act in ways that serve our immediate desires at the cost of hurting others. God also created us with desires to help others. God created us with the ability to feel empathy, to feel guilt when we hurt someone, and to understand from reason and experience the consequences of hurting or neglecting others.

Sin is known by special revelation; sin is broken fellowship with God; sin is both actions and attitudes. God created us with natural dispositions toward religious beliefs. But without special revelation to teach us truth, we are prone to making idols out of all sorts of created things, and we are prone to making religious practices that serve our own desires for power and control. General revelation might prompt us to love our neighbors and hate our enemies, but special revelation makes it clear that we are supposed to love our enemies. Through God's special revelation, we learn that our destructive behavior toward other people, toward ourselves, and toward creation also breaks our fellowship with God. Through special revelation, we learn that sin is both actions and attitudes, because God desires that we have not only clean hands but also a pure heart (Ps. 24:4).

The next chapters compare the four general types of scenarios introduced at the end of the introduction for the entrance of sin into the world. The differences among the four types of scenarios become inconsequential once sin has spread to the entire population. All four can incorporate the multifaceted picture of sin presented in Scripture.

These four types of scenarios differ from one another much more significantly, however, when it comes to these questions: What did the first historical sin look like? How did sin spread from the first sinners to the rest of the population?

9

What Changed
When Sin Began?

ANIMALS DON'T SIN (we presume). Humans do. What happened, and when did it happen?

Social animals such as elephants, dolphins, and chimpanzees treat each other in "nasty" ways (which look like precursors to self-reflective immoral behavior) and "nice" ways (which look like precursors to self-reflective moral behavior). Our hominin ancestors also exhibited both nasty and nice behaviors toward one another.

For us today, when we are nasty toward one another, we are violating God's law of love. We are sinning. But sin is more than just nasty behavior toward others. Sin is also a disruption in our relationship with God. In order for actions to be considered sinful, a certain kind of God-human relationship must be in place. At some point in our ancestors' history, God must have established a new kind of relationship with them. And with that new relationship, it also became possible for them to sin.

Here again are the four general types of scenarios for harmonizing the doctrine of original sin and human evolution:

1. Adam and Eve as particular historical individuals acting as representatives of humanity
2. Adam and Eve as particular historical individuals; sin spread through culture or genealogy
3. Adam and Eve as a highly compressed history referring to many individuals over a long period of time who received special revelation
4. Adam and Eve as symbolic figures referring to many individuals over a long period of time, all who became ready to be held accountable and chose sin

A Theological Roundtable Question-and-Answer Discussion

How intellectually and morally advanced were the first humans who sinned? How did God establish a relationship with them? What changes happened to them as a result of the first sin? How did sin spread from the first sinners to the rest of humanity?

We'd like to know the answers to these questions. Genesis 2–3, Romans 5, and 1 Corinthians 15 don't give us many details, so systematic theologians have drawn on the rest of Scripture—as well as other fields of knowledge such as philosophy, psychology, sociology, and evolutionary biology—to propose answers. This is valuable work. But theologians haven't all arrived at the same answers. Chapter 7 took a historical approach, summarizing how several theologians throughout church history answered these questions. This chapter takes a question-and-answer approach.

This chapter won't directly contrast the four types of scenarios, because each of them allows multiple possible answers to the questions posed in this chapter. Think of this chapter like a roundtable discussion. Imagine that theologians of the past and present have gathered to ask tough questions. None of them are committed to one particular scenario. For each question, they propose a range of answers. For each answer, they suggest some theological strengths and express some theological concerns. This chapter cannot list every possible question, every possible answer, or every possible strength or concern. Not every strength or concern raised is equally weighty. This chapter's goal is to raise as many strengths and concerns as it can, in limited space, to aid future discussion.

The wide range of questions and answers in this chapter shows the richness of Christian theology. The wealth of the church's theological reflections accumulated over the centuries will help us today sort through the strengths and challenges of each proposed scenario.

How "Advanced" Were the First Sinners?

Until the last few decades, many theologians assumed that Adam and Eve were created as adults, not too different in abilities from human adults today except without sin. Some, like Irenaeus, theorized that Adam and Eve were initially immature—innocent of sin, but still needing to mature in intellect and moral understanding. Others, like Augustine, theorized that Adam and Eve's created nature, which was uncorrupted by sin, and their supernatural gifts made them superhuman in several ways—not only spiritually and morally but also intellectually and physically. Scripture does not explicitly teach any of these possibilities, but neither does it rule them out.

In light of the evidence that God used evolutionary processes while creating humanity, the question of how "advanced" the first sinners were is connected to *when* the first sin occurred.

If Adam and Eve refer to particular historical individuals, as in scenario types 1 and 2, when did they live? If Adam and Eve refer to many individuals over a long period of time, as in scenario types 3 and 4, when did that time period begin? Here are several possible answers.

Perhaps the first sin occurred *millions of years ago*, when our ancestors (long before they were *Homo sapiens*) were just beginning to have glimmerings of self-awareness or just beginning to have the ability to think about complex ideas and to communicate them linguistically.

Or perhaps the first sin occurred *nearly a million years ago*, when our ancestors were still classified as *Homo erectus* (or *heidelbergensis*), before the lines leading to Neanderthals and Denisovans had split off. At this stage, our ancestors had brains nearly as large as ours, on average, but not organized in quite the same way. They had crossed some thresholds of cognitive development beyond that of any animals, but they perhaps were not yet at the level of modern adult humans today.

Or perhaps the first sin occurred *approximately 150,000 years ago*, around the time of the most recent population bottleneck in *Homo sapiens*. At this point, our ancestors were almost completely modern anatomically and genetically, and they might have been nearly modern cognitively.

Or perhaps the first sin occurred *around 40,000 years ago*, when certain kinds of unambiguously modern human behavior first emerged.[1]

---

1. Some commonly suggested "modern human behaviors" include ceremonial burial of dead, creation of symbolic paintings and sculptures, musical instruments, large and complex social groups and trading networks, or some combination of these (see chap. 4).

Or perhaps the first sin occurred *around 12,000 years ago* in the region of
Mesopotamia, with the development of modern agriculture and other
Neolithic innovations.

Or perhaps the first sin occurred *closer to 6,000 years ago*, near the advent
of modern writing.

There are reasons to favor each of the above answers. First let's consider
why one might favor locating the first sin *millions of years ago*, very early
in our ancestors' history. God's will for us can be summarized as "Love God
above all; love your neighbor as yourself" (see Matt. 22:36–40). Once our
ancestors became aware of themselves as "selves" and of their neighbors as
other "selves," it became possible for them to love their neighbors as themselves. And if they had some knowledge of God through general or special
revelation, it became possible for them to love God. If that was God's will for
them, then it also became possible for them, at that time, to disobey God's
will. If it is sinful for us today to fail to love our neighbors as ourselves, then
perhaps the first sins of our ancestors were their first self-reflective failures to
love their neighbors as themselves. And to the extent that they sensed a divine
authority that they *ought to* obey, becoming aware of something like the law
of love, their disobediences could have been considered sinful.

There is a theological concern with this answer, however. Millions of years
ago, our ancestors would have been more advanced than chimpanzees today
but well below modern human levels. As discussed in chapter 4, some great
apes, dolphins, and elephants possess some self-awareness and linguistic abilities. If we assume that these animals are not capable of sin (however selfish
and destructive some of their behavior might sometimes be by human standards), then the prerequisites for sin must be beyond the self-awareness and
linguistic abilities of these animals. However, this theological concern does
not necessarily rule out the idea that the first sin occurred near the dawning
of self-awareness in our ancestors. Human babies are "selfish" in that they
focus on their needs and wants, but most would say that babies do not willfully sin. Eventually, they develop into children who do willfully sin. We don't
know exactly when this transition happens in each individual child, although
presumably God does. We believe that God has a relationship with each child,
and that relationship means something even before the child is capable of
willful sin. (Also, God has a relationship with each animal that is appropriate
to it.) So it's possible that God had a different sort of relationship with our
ancestors millions of years ago than he does with dolphins, chimpanzees, or
elephants today—even though our ancestors were barely more intelligent back

then than dolphins, chimpanzees, or elephants—because God knew what they would develop into. Thus, God would have known when our ancestors transitioned from not-yet-sinful selfishness to willful sin.

There are reasons to favor locating the first sin *nearly a million years ago*. Our ancestors then were more developed cognitively than any animals today, but they were probably not yet at the level of modern humans. Sin might have entered the world, and begun having an impact on human nature, as soon as our ancestors crossed some threshold of cognitive development. They might have been in a state similar to how Irenaeus pictured Adam and Eve—initially innocent of sin but still needing to mature in their intellect and moral understanding. Their offspring included Neanderthals and Denisovans as well as *Homo sapiens*. All of these would be considered "human"; therefore, there are no theological concerns raised by later interbreeding.

There is a theological concern with this answer, however. During the time from one million years ago to the present, our ancestors experienced significant genetic, cultural, and cognitive changes. Locating the first sin a million years ago or earlier implies that humanity's sinful *rebellion* was happening, in some sense, simultaneously with humanity's *creation* during the last million years. In contrast, theology has traditionally thought of humanity's sinful rebellion as something occurring *after* humanity was fully created. However, this theological concern does not necessarily rule out this answer. Each of us, as individuals, began to sin willfully when we were young, when we were much less developed intellectually and socially than we are as adults. Those sins shaped us to some extent as we developed into adults. By analogy, it should not surprise us if our ancestors began to sin once they reached some threshold of cognitive development, even if they were still less developed than most humans today. Once sin entered the world, it shaped humanity's further development.

There are reasons to favor locating the first sin *around 150,000 years ago*, during the most recent population bottleneck in *Homo sapiens*. These humans were almost completely modern anatomically and genetically, and they might have been nearly modern cognitively. If sin entered during the population bottleneck, its effects could have spread from the first sinners to the rest of *Homo sapiens* (assuming that sin spread culturally or genealogically) more quickly than it could have at earlier times or later times, when the population sizes were larger.

There is a theological concern with this answer, however. The last common ancestor of Neanderthals, Denisovans, and *Homo sapiens* is thought to have lived more than 500,000 years ago. However, some *Homo sapiens* interbred with Neanderthals and Denisovans only around 50,000 to 60,000 years ago.

What was the spiritual status of Neanderthals and Denisovans at that time? Were they also humans, made in God's image? And if so, were they also sinners? If Neanderthals and Denisovans are considered not human theologically, then the interbreeding raises some significant theological difficulties. However, this theological concern does not necessarily rule out this answer. If Neanderthals and Denisovans were not considered fully human, then perhaps God nevertheless allowed a small amount of interbreeding to take place, with the resulting offspring considered human. On the other hand, since interbreeding was possible, perhaps Neanderthals and Denisovans should be considered human as well. In that case, however, one of the advantages of this answer (the quick spread of sin from the first sinners to the rest of the human population) is lost.

There are reasons to favor locating the first sin *around 40,000 years ago*, when modern human behavior first emerged. Perhaps God considered it important that the first possibility of sin—the first human decisions to trust God obediently or to rebel against God—were made by individuals who had more or less fully modern linguistic, cultural, and cognitive capabilities.

There are some theological concerns with this answer, however. One theological concern is that, by this time, *Homo sapiens* had spread throughout Africa, Europe, Asia, and Australia. The transmission of sin from the first sinners to the rest of the population either would have had to happen immediately via *representation* (scenario 1) or—if sin was transmitted *culturally* or *genealogically* (scenarios 2 or 3)—would have taken many thousands of years. Each of these options is discussed later in this chapter.

A second theological concern with this answer has to do with how advanced *Homo sapiens* already were. By this time, they were making sophisticated tools (indicating advanced planning and cultures that transmitted information by teaching and learning) and artwork, including painting and carvings. Some of them buried their dead with flower petals and ornaments. It would not be surprising if they already had religious beliefs of some sort. They had those same dispositions toward nasty and nice behaviors that their earlier ancestors had and an increasingly self-reflective understanding of how their actions hurt or helped others. So just *prior* to the first sin, there would have been many fully modern *Homo sapien*s acting in both nasty and nice ways scattered across several continents. Yet according to this answer, their nasty behavior was not considered sinful. However, this theological concern does not necessarily rule out this answer. Perhaps God did not hold our ancestors responsible for their nasty behavior or consider such acts sinful until God had first given them a certain kind of *special* revelation, establishing a new kind of divine-human relationship. It's possible that the cultural, linguistic, and cognitive developments corresponding with modern human behavior—starting approximately 40,000 years ago—are also what first allowed our ancestors to understand such a special revelation.

An additional theological concern with this answer (and all previous answers) has to do with the kind of world on display in Genesis 2–11. These chapters are set in the Near East, in a culture that included agriculture, metalwork, and cities. These are things that humanity developed only within the last few thousand years. Locating the first sin 40,000 or more years ago, when our ancestors lived in small hunter-gatherer tribes, raises the question of why Genesis 2–3 and subsequent chapters are located in a cultural setting (and possibly a geographical setting) far from where the events to which they refer actually happened. However, this concern does not necessarily rule out these answers. Just as Genesis 1 is a retelling of God's creation of the world in a way that accommodated the original audience's beliefs about a flat earth and dome firmament, so Genesis 2–3 could be a retelling of the story of the entrance of sin into the world in a cultural setting familiar to the original audience—the Near East of a few thousand years ago—as part of God's accommodation to the original audience.

There are reasons to favor locating the first sin *around 12,000 to 6,000 years ago* in the region of Mesopotamia. Genesis 2–11 corresponds, in terms of cultural details, to Mesopotamian culture of that era. Perhaps it was at this time and place that God first began to speak to humanity in ways that we would call special revelation. Perhaps God waited to hold humans responsible for their actions, morally and religiously, until he had given them this special revelation.

There are some theological concerns with this answer, however. By this time, cognitively modern humans (with language, agriculture, representational art, and religious beliefs) would have existed for thousands of years already. By this time, humans had spread all over the earth, including to the Americas. So by this time, all over the globe and for thousands of years already, humans would have been able to clearly understand how their nasty and nice behaviors affected others. This answer needs to explain why such actions were not considered sinful until God gave some sort of special revelation forbidding such behaviors.

A second theological concern with this answer has to do with whether the entrance of sin had any sort of corrupting influence on human nature. If sin began only 12,000 to 6,000 years ago, although the entrance of sin into the world might have had a profound effect on how the sinners related to God, it would not have had much effect on how humans treated one another, because they already had developed complex cultures. They were already being nasty and nice to one another in many complicated ways.

However, these theological concerns do not necessarily rule out this answer. While sin does affect how we treat one another, sin is first and foremost about our relationship to God. God uses many metaphors in Scripture to describe himself in relation to humans, including king, judge, husband, shepherd, maker, and more. God might have waited until humans achieved a certain level of cultural advancement—a level at which they could understand the richness of their relationship with God by the use of such metaphors—before specially revealing his will to them and holding them accountable.

Did God Miraculously Transform Our Ancestors?

As noted in chapter 5, neither the fossil record nor human genetics shows evidence of God miraculously transforming our ancestors in the past. The evidence is consistent with God using only evolutionary processes plus special revelation. A hypothetical miraculous transformation that was too radical would run into the theological problem of false apparent history. However, the evidence is also consistent with the hypothesis that God transformed some or all of our ancestors in ways that were significant (in the sense that if we had been able to witness those miracles when they were performed, we would have seen a dramatic change in our ancestors) but not so radical as to leave evidence that is scientifically detectable for us today. This avoids the problem of false apparent history. With that proviso, the scientific data are open to several interpretations, and theology is open to a range of possibilities.

Perhaps *God chose not to perform any such miracles*. Perhaps God created humanity's physical, mental, and spiritual abilities by sustaining and concurring with ordinary natural processes, plus establishing a special relationship with us through special revelation.

Or perhaps at one particular point in time, *God miraculously transformed all of our ancestors* so that they had new mental and spiritual capabilities. God might have transformed them in one or more of the ways discussed in chapter 5: biologically, genetically, through intensive education, or through ensoulment. They were the first true humans in a theological sense, God's image bearers.

Or perhaps at one particular point in time, *God miraculously transformed some of our ancestors* (perhaps just a single pair of individuals, perhaps more) so that they had new mental and spiritual capabilities. They were the first true humans in a theological sense. As their descendants mixed with the rest of the population, these transformations spread culturally, genealogically, genetically, or by some combination of these.

Or perhaps *God created Adam and Eve miraculously* de novo *as adults*, but God created them in such a way that their offspring could blend in and interbreed with the larger population already existing at that time.

There are theological reasons to favor the idea that *God did not perform any such miracles*. This clearly avoids the theological problem of God of the gaps. As noted in chapter 4, science affirms that human mental, cultural, and linguistic abilities are far beyond those of any animals. But there are still many gaps in our scientific understanding of how those abilities developed over time among our ancestors. It is tempting to propose miracles to fill those gaps, thinking that this somehow makes God more involved in the process. But God is just as involved in processes that we can explain scientifically as he is in those we cannot. God could have created humans as his image bearers without performing any miraculous acts of physical transformation on our ancestors. God could have created their mental, cultural, and linguistic abilities through sustaining and concurring with gene-culture coevolutionary processes. And then through special revelation, God could have commissioned them to be his image bearers. We should not propose additional miraculous acts if our *only* reason for doing so is that it makes us feel that God is more involved.

There are some theological concerns with this answer. Scripture teaches that humans have a distinct status in creation and a distinct relationship with God compared to animals. If this answer is correct, there would not have been a particular point in time when our ancestors' mental and social abilities made a distinct, qualitative leap. However, this theological concern does not necessarily rule out this answer. Through acts of divine special revelation, God could have begun a distinct relationship with humanity without miraculously changing their abilities.

A second theological concern with the idea that God did not perform any such miracles comes from considering dualist versus monist theories about the soul (discussed in chapter 5). If one of the versions of body-soul dualism is correct, then there must have been a particular time in our ancestors' history when God began giving them human souls. This would have been a miraculous transformation that changed their spiritual status. However, this concern does not rule out this answer. If some version of dualism is correct, it might be the case (depending on which particular version of dualism is being considered) that this transformation changed their spiritual status without significantly changing their mental, social, and linguistic abilities.

A third theological concern with this answer comes from how Scripture describes humanity's creation. Genesis 1:26–30 describes the creation of humanity in greater detail than the creation of other animals. In Genesis 2:19–20 God gives the man a special task of naming the animals, and Genesis 1:28 teaches that God gave humans a special mandate, placing them in a position of authority and responsibility toward other creatures and the earth. Genesis 2:7 is translated, "The LORD God formed a man from the dust of the ground and breathed into his nostrils the breath of life, and the man became a living being." Even if this language is stylized and symbolic, it might suggest some kind of special divine intervention. However, this interpretive concern does not rule out this answer. We need to be cautious about what we might read into the Genesis texts. As modern readers in our modern culture, we might believe that Genesis 2:7 sounds like a supernatural miracle. But we need to understand how the original author and intended audience understood it, keeping in mind the cultural and historical context of the passage and the principle of God's accommodation. As noted in chapter 6, the preposition "from" in modern translations of 2:7 is not in the Hebrew text or the Septuagint. Moreover, passages throughout the Old Testament refer to all humans (not just Adam) being "dust," and these are references to human mortality. Applying the principle of God's accommodation to Genesis 2:7, we can read this passage as an ancient, prescientific way of teaching theological truths about human mortality and dependence on God for life.

There are theological reasons to favor the idea that at one particular point in time, *God miraculously transformed* all *of our ancestors* so that they had new mental, social, and spiritual capabilities. If this is what God did, then it is easy to pick this as the moment when human sin first became possible. In addition, the Scripture texts mentioned in the previous paragraph, while not proving that God performed a miracle, could lend support for the idea. Furthermore, if some version of body-soul dualism is correct, and if God did miraculously create or transform the first human souls at some point, this would also be a logical time for God to miraculously physically transform the first humans so that their bodies and souls were suitable for each other.

There are some theological concerns with this answer, however. First, it must take care to avoid God-of-the-gaps thinking. We should not propose additional miraculous acts simply because we feel like such acts keep God more involved. However, this theological concern does not rule out this answer. If we acknowledge that God is sovereign over all the scientifically understandable evolutionary steps that God used along the way, then proposing that God performed an additional miracle need not diminish our understanding of God's sovereignty. So if some version of body-soul monism is correct, it might be the case that while God *could* have given us our mental, cultural, and linguistic abilities through sustaining and concurring with evolutionary processes, God chose to include some miracles. It might simply have delighted God to do so. And if some version of body-soul dualism is correct, then it was necessary for God to miraculously create the first human souls, but this does not detract from the ordinary evolutionary means God used before and since.

A second theological concern with the idea that God miraculously transformed all our ancestors comes from the theological problem of God creating with the appearance of false history. As noted in early chapters, scientific evidence is consistent with gradual evolutionary changes in our ancestors' genomes over a long period of time, and with gradual increases in human mental and social capabilities. However, this theological concern does not rule out this answer. This concern is avoided if God transformed our ancestors in ways that were significant (if we had been able to witness those miracles when they were performed, we would have seen a dramatic change in our ancestors) but not so radical as to leave evidence that is scientifically detectable for us today.

A third theological concern with this answer comes from considering how God creates each new human being today. Each of us joins the psalmist in saying that God "knit me together in my mother's womb" (Ps. 139:13). However, we do not propose that God has to perform miracles to accomplish this. Since God does not need to routinely perform miracles for each human today, there does not seem to be a theological need for God to perform such miracles for the first humans. However, this theological concern does not rule out this answer. Even if there is no theological *need* for miracles, perhaps God chose to perform miracles for God's good pleasure.

A fourth theological concern with this answer comes from considering the long history of evolution leading to *Homo sapiens*. Placing the proposed act of miraculous transformation at any particular point along that time line creates some new theological difficulties, depending on where it is placed. For example, the last common ancestor between *Homo sapiens* and Neanderthals was about 500,000 years ago, yet *Homo sapiens* and Neanderthals interbred in Europe and Asia about 40,000 years ago. We could propose that God performed these miraculous transformations (corresponding to Gen. 2–3) more than 500,000 years ago. At that time, our ancestors were part of the late *Homo erectus* or *heidelbergensis* species. This would mean that half a million years of unrecorded history—and quite a bit of gene-culture coevolution—took place *after* the miraculous transformation of our early ancestors but before the rest of recorded biblical history began (just a few thousand years ago). However, this theological concern does not necessarily rule out this answer. Genesis 4–11 might be interpreted as a highly compressed and stylized history in which God is telling us about important spiritual developments but not about the actual length of the history involved in those developments.

Alternatively, we could propose that God performed these miraculous transformations approximately 200,000 years ago, when modern-looking *Homo sapiens* appeared. In that case, we face a decision regarding the status of Neanderthals and Denisovans. We could propose that they also were "human" and were transformed along with *Homo sapiens*. If so, we might wonder why they remained distinct populations for so long and subsequently died out. However, this concern does not rule out this answer. God might have simply permitted these populations to die out the way he permits groups and cultures of *Homo sapiens* to die out. Or we could propose that Neanderthals and Denisovans were "not human" and not transformed along with *Homo sapiens*. If so, we might wonder why interbreeding was permitted. However, this concern does not rule out this answer. Even if *Homo sapiens* had a different theological status than Neanderthals and Denisovans, they were close enough biologically to interbreed. So perhaps God simply allowed a small amount of interbreeding to take place and considered the resulting offspring human.

Alternatively, we could propose that God performed these miraculous transformations approximately 30,000 years ago, presumably after such interbreeding occurred. At this point, *Homo sapiens* were already spread over Africa, Europe, Asia, and Australia; they already had sophisticated tool kits, musical instruments, and figurative art. They lived in interconnected social groups, had the ability to understand that their actions could help or hurt others, and very likely had predispositions to religious beliefs, if not actual religious beliefs. The question might then be asked, given how advanced they already were, what additional changes might God have needed to make that would have required miraculous transformation? However, this concern does not rule out this answer. There might have been some particular moral or spiritual capabilities that, despite their advanced behaviors, our ancestors still lacked. God might have chosen to give these capabilities to our ancestors miraculously. This might not have resulted in the kind of changes in behavior that leave archaeological evidence, but it would have been important to God and important for our ancestors' relationships to God.

There are reasons to favor the proposal that at one particular point in time, *God miraculously transformed* some *of our ancestors* (perhaps just a single pair, perhaps more) so that they had new mental and spiritual capabilities. God established a new relationship with them, with new expectations, blessings, and promises. They were still the same biological species as the larger population, but they had a different theological status. They were the first true "humans" in the theological sense of the term, image bearers of God with human souls. Their abilities and their status were passed on to their offspring. Their offspring spread out and interbred with the larger population so that the changes God miraculously made to this first group eventually spread to the entire population culturally, genealogically, genetically, or through some combination of these.

This answer shares with the previous answer (that God miraculously transformed *all* of our ancestors at once) all the same reasons in its favor, all the same theological concerns, and all the same potential answers to those concerns. One additional reason in favor of this answer comes from its similarity to events in Scripture in which God began something new in salvation history by starting with just a few individuals. Abraham and Sarah were chosen out of their homeland to receive a new covenant with God, one that applied to them and their children. David was called out of the nation to be king of Israel, with promises made to him and his offspring. The church of the New Testament began small, with just a handful of individuals called by Jesus. God choosing and transforming a few individuals out of a larger population, rather than transforming the entire population at once, fits this pattern.

An additional theological concern with this proposal is related to how radical the proposed transformation was. On the one hand, if Adam and Eve and their offspring had drastically greater mental and spiritual abilities than the larger population, then the idea of this transformation spreading to the larger population through interbreeding becomes problematic theologically. Given how Genesis 2:23 pictures marriage from the beginning (Adam is united with one who is, in his words, "bone of my bones and flesh of my flesh"), it seems contradictory for God to plan the spread of the first humans' drastically greater mental and spiritual abilities via interbreeding with those who are distinctly other precisely in not possessing those abilities. Also, as noted in chapter 5, the archaeological evidence puts some constraints on how drastic such a transformation could have been. Archaeology does not support the hypothesis of multiple technological and social advances starting at one place and time and spreading from there. On the other hand, if the transformation of Adam and Eve and their offspring was essentially one of spiritual awareness and status—one that left their mental and social abilities essentially similar to those of the larger population—then the theological problems regarding interbreeding are removed. However, if the transformation did not significantly increase our ancestors' mental or social abilities, we then have to ask whether this was actually a *miraculous* transformation. Could the transformation have been accomplished simply via special revelation? However, these theological concerns do not rule out this answer. God might have miraculously given Adam and Eve some particular *moral or spiritual capabilities*, which the surrounding population did not yet have, that were theologically significant but did not make them radically different from the surrounding population intellectually or socially.

The idea that *God created Adam and Eve miraculously* de novo *as adults* but in such a way that their offspring could blend in and interbreed with the larger population, already existing at that time, is a variation on the previous proposal. We could hypothesize that God created them, *de novo*, different enough from the surrounding population to avoid the theological problem of false apparent history but similar enough so that their offspring could blend in and interbreed with the larger population.[2] If this proposal were correct, human genomes today would not show evidence of a *de novo* creation of Adam and Eve simply because the overwhelming majority of DNA in our genomes today would have come from the surrounding population.

This proposal shares with the previous proposal (that God miraculously transformed *some* of our ancestors) all the same reasons in its favor, all the same theological concerns, and all the same answers to those concerns. An additional theological concern with this proposal has to do with the fact that humans are fundamentally interdependent. So much of who we are as adults was shaped by our caregivers as we grew up: the language we speak, our physical skills, our survival and toolmaking skills, our facial recognition skills, our ability to empathize and sympathize with others, our ability to understand the difference between selfish or altruistic moral choices, and so forth. Our bodies, our brains, and our decision-making are deeply shaped by our upbringing, especially by our families and friends. This would have

2. It's challenging to imagine how this might be. There are many ways that your body retains evidence of your personal history as you grew from zygote to fetus to infant to child to adult. You have a belly button. Your teeth have wear patterns from what you've eaten. Your skin has scars. The lenses of your eyes have accumulated ultraviolet damage. You might have healed bone fractures. You are a genetic chimera. Popular scientific literature sometimes says that every cell in your body has the same DNA, but that's not quite true. Almost every time a cell divides, there are a few mutations. So already when you were at the two-cell, four-cell, and eight-cell stage, each cell was slightly different genetically from the others. The patterns of mutations in each cell in your body record some information about your fetal development. Your immune system has molecules that retain information about diseases you have fought in the past. The bacteria in your gut that help you digest food are affected by food you've eaten in the past and people who live near you. Your bone and tooth chemistry contain information about the environments in which you lived, ate, and drank over the past several years. If Adam and Eve were created *de novo*, their bodies presumably would have been functional, but they would *not* have needed to be created in a way that implied a similar richly detailed developmental history from zygote to fetus to infant to child to adult.

been true of all the biological humans in the larger population prior to the *de novo* creation of Adam and Eve. It would have been true of Adam and Eve's offspring, as future generations interbred with the larger population. But it would not have been true of Adam and Eve. Their bodies and brains would have been however God created them *de novo*. In what sense, then, are they representatives of the rest of humanity? However, this theological concern does not rule out this answer. We could hypothesize that God created them, *de novo*, with social and moral decision-making abilities that were similar enough to those of the surrounding population that Adam and Eve could, in some important sense, act as representatives of the surrounding population but different enough that God thought it was important to create them *de novo*.

Is General Revelation Sufficient? Is Special Revelation Necessary?

Because of God's special revelation, we know that we sin. As discussed in chapter 8, general revelation—including our conscience, reason, and empathy—also tells us that we fail to live up to God's moral standard, "Love your neighbor as yourself" (Matt. 22:39).

What sort of revelation did the first sinners have when they first sinned? Here are two possible answers.

Perhaps *general revelation is sufficient*. We don't need an explicit command from God to know that assault and theft are harmful acts. Our empathy tells us that we have hurt another. Our conscience makes us feel guilt. Our reason tells us that everyone is better off when we love one another. In addition, we have a natural disposition toward religious beliefs and a natural sense that our relationships with one another and our relationship with the divine are interconnected. Nonverbal promptings from the Holy Spirit, strengthening these gifts, could also be considered part of God's general revelation to humanity. At some point in history, our ancestors crossed a threshold of intellectual, social, and spiritual development where they, like us today, understood these things deeply enough. General revelation was enough so that their selfish and hurtful acts toward one another began to be considered sinful—not merely harmful to others but also a disruption of their relationship with God.

Or perhaps *special revelation is necessary*. Sin involves disobedience to God's revealed will. Our ancestors might have had empathy, reason, and pangs of conscience when they hurt one another, but perhaps it was not counted as sin until God *said* that it was sinful. At some point in history, God specially revealed his will to some of our ancestors. This special revelation might have been verbal or nonverbal, but it was clearly understandable. Our ancestors chose disobedience to God's unambiguously revealed will.

There are reasons to favor the answer that *general revelation is sufficient.* As discussed in chapter 8, in the Old Testament various peoples who did not have God's law were nevertheless condemned for doing things detestable to God. The New Testament church came to realize that gentiles could be saved by faith in Jesus Christ apart from the law, and moreover, gentiles needed salvation through faith in Christ even though they had never had the law of Moses. In Romans 2:14–15 Paul writes, "Indeed, when Gentiles, who do not have the law, do by nature things required by the law, they are a law for themselves, even though they do not have the law. They show that the requirements of the law are written on their hearts, their consciences also bearing witness, and their thoughts sometimes accusing them and at other times even defending them."

There are some theological concerns with saying that general revelation is sufficient. The strength and reliability of conscience, reason, and empathy vary from person to person. Their development relies on growing up in the right sorts of social settings. However, this theological concern does not necessarily rule out this answer. God knows (even if we do not) just how responsible and accountable each individual is.

A second theological concern has to do with the definition of sin. Sin is not merely doing nasty things to one another. Sin disrupts the God-human relationship. It could be argued that some form of special revelation is important for establishing such relationships. However, this theological concern does not necessarily rule out this answer. Humans who lived after God's law was specially revealed to the Israelites but in cultures with no contact with biblical Scriptures still had some responsibility to God and to one another for their actions. Their harmful actions toward one another were, we believe, still considered by God to be sinful.

A third theological concern with saying that general revelation is sufficient is that it would seem to make humanity's fall into sin, in some sense, almost inevitable. Our ancestors all had dispositions toward both nasty and nice behaviors. None of them could be expected to perfectly obey God's standard of "love your neighbor as yourself" (unless God had empowered them with supernatural gifts). However, this theological concern does not necessarily rule out this answer. The question of whether humanity's fall into sin was, in any sense, inevitable is discussed at greater length in the next chapter.

There are reasons to favor the answer that *special revelation is necessary*. Perhaps God gave our ancestors the gifts of conscience, reason, and empathy but did not hold them spiritually accountable until God had also given them a more direct, clearer special revelation regarding how they ought to behave. In Romans 5:13 Paul writes, "To be sure, sin was in the world before the law was given, but sin is not charged against anyone's account where there is no law."

There are some theological concerns, however, with saying that special revelation is necessary. This answer seems to require some version of the "divine command theory" of sin—according to which actions are not sinful unless and until God gives special commands against such actions. For humans today, when our conscience tells us not to steal or bully or gossip, and we do it anyway, we are sinning. General revelation makes us accountable to God even without knowledge of any explicit commandments. Once our ancestors had crossed a threshold of cognitive and spiritual development so that they had the same level of general revelation that we have today, why would they also need an explicit command from God in order to be held accountable? However, this theological concern does not necessarily rule out this answer. Perhaps God chose to not hold our ancestors who lacked special revelation accountable for sin until special revelation had time to shape their cultures.[3] Their cultures, eventually shaped by special revelation, in turn shaped each new generation of people until eventually they reached the point where we are today, where general revelation makes us accountable to God even without knowledge of any explicit commandments.

A second theological concern with saying that special revelation is necessary is that it raises the question of the spiritual status and eternal destiny of our ancestors immediately prior to that first special revelation. They had conscience, reason, and empathy. They were sometimes nasty and sometimes nice to one another. If they were not held accountable for sin because they did not have special revelation, what was their status in terms of the resurrection of the dead and the final judgment? However, this theological concern does not necessarily rule out this answer. It is possible for Christians simply to say, "Scripture doesn't answer that question. God is the judge, so we leave the matter to God's justice and grace."

A third theological concern with this answer is that it raises the question of whether our human tendency to sin was, in any significant way, shaped

---

3. John H. Walton has written about this possibility in *The Lost World of Adam and Eve* (Downers Grove, IL: InterVarsity, 2015), 154–55.

by the first sin. As discussed in chapter 7, church tradition for centuries has taught that the first sins of our ancestors affected them and their offspring, making all humans since then prone to sin. Today we all have desires to steal, bully, and gossip, and we sometimes succumb to these desires. We should not do these things, but we do them in part because our human nature is affected by sin. But our ancestors, prior to God's first special revelation, also had desires to steal, bully, and gossip, and they sometimes succumbed to those desires. If God's special revelation was necessary in order for such actions to be considered sinful, then did human nature actually change when sin entered the world? Did God's special revelation simply change how such actions were classified—suddenly classifying them as "sinful"—without actually changing human nature? However, this theological concern does not necessarily rule out this answer. Perhaps at first God did not hold our ancestors accountable for sin unless some special revelation made the situation very clear to them. Their failure to obey God and the knowledge that they had sinned shaped their minds and their cultures. Disobedience to God became a habit of mind, reinforced by culture. Their cultures shaped each new generation. So after many generations, we are in a situation different from that of our distant ancestors; it is now true to say that our minds and cultures are deeply shaped by sin.

Original Innocence or Original Righteousness?

We all sin. We don't know exactly when each child has grown enough to be considered responsible for willfully sinning. But we do know—both from Scripture and from our everyday experience—that no one can avoid sinning.

What about the very first humans who sinned? What was their state just before they sinned? Here are four possible answers. (Most of these answers could work with any of the four types of scenarios for Adam and Eve.)

Perhaps the first humans who sinned were, for a time, in a state of *original righteousness*. God's law was "written on their hearts." They were fully morally aware and mature, able to fulfill God's law and remain holy, but they were not compelled to do so.

Or perhaps they were, for a time, in a state of *moral innocence*. They were not yet able to fulfill (and perhaps not even understand) all of God's moral law. But they had more limited responsibilities to God and to one another that they could understand and obey. God held them responsible only for what they were able to do at that time. They were supposed to grow in understanding and responsibility over time, through obedience and maturation, until eventually they or their descendants could understand and obey all of God's moral law as it applies to us today.

Or perhaps they were in a state of *moral neutrality*. Animals today do nasty and nice things to one another, but we do not consider their actions sinful or righteous. We might call that moral neutrality. Long enough ago, things must have been the same with our ancestors. Perhaps none of our ancestors, after growing beyond a state of moral neutrality, ever lived for any significant length of time in a state of moral innocence. Perhaps from the earliest moments when our ancestors first began to understand what it meant to be responsible to God and morally responsible to one another, they began to sin and began to be held accountable.

Or perhaps they were in a state of *legal innocence*. Perhaps God allowed our ancestors to advance quite far, mentally and culturally, before specially revealing his law to them and holding them accountable. They might have had empathy. Their consciences might have bothered them when they were nasty to one another, and their reason might have told them how much better things would be if everyone was nice. But they were not held spiritually accountable until God's clear revelation told them about this accountability.

There are reasons to favor the answer that the first humans who sinned were, for a time, in a state of *original righteousness*. This was the view of Augustine and many theologians throughout church history. Genesis 2–3 by itself does not explicitly say this. These theologians made a reasonable deduction based on several other things that Scripture does clearly teach: God is good and holy; God created humans "in his own image" (Gen. 1:27); after creating humans, God declared creation to be "very good" (Gen. 1:31); God does not tempt people to sin (James 1:13).

There are, however, some theological concerns with the idea that the first humans who sinned were in a state of original righteousness. Throughout most of church history, most theologians believed that Adam and Eve were created miraculously and *de novo*. Some theologians believed that, while Adam and Eve did enjoy some supernatural gifts such as close fellowship with God, they were *in their created nature* in a state of original righteousness. Their sin corrupted their created nature, and they passed this corrupted nature on to their offspring. Other theologians believed that Adam and Eve were in a state of original righteousness because God gave them, in addition to their created nature, supernatural gifts. Their sin caused these supernatural gifts to be withdrawn.

Because God used evolutionary processes to create humans, we can now be reasonably certain that our ancestors evolved with a mixture of nasty and nice behavioral dispositions. Because of their genes, their brain wiring, their psychology, and their cultures, they would have had strong inclinations toward selfish behaviors. In order for some of them to have been in a state of full original righteousness, even for a limited time, they would have needed the aid of some remarkable supernatural gifts—what we today might call a superabundant empowering by the Holy Spirit.

Perhaps God did this. Perhaps God specially selected a few of our ancestors who were ready, specially revealed himself to them, and gave them such a supernatural empowering. They were to live for a time in a state of original righteousness and close communion with God. Perhaps if they had done this long enough without sinning, the possibility of their choosing to sin would have become more and more distant. Perhaps eventually, through continued obedience, original righteousness would have become permanent for them and their descendants. And perhaps if the first few humans had held on to these gifts long enough, these gifts would have spread to all humanity.

One theological concern with this idea is that it requires a significant amount of theological speculation, both about how these individuals were empowered by God and about what would have happened if they had not sinned. Genesis 2–3 does not explicitly say that Adam and Eve were in a state of original righteousness. It does not talk about supernatural gifts enabling them to avoid sinning. It does not say how long Adam and Eve were supposed to avoid temptation before the possibility of sinning would have faded away (if ever). It does not say that if only they had avoided sinning, they and all of their descendants would have eventually become human beings who would have lived perpetually without sinning. So this answer reads into Genesis 2–3 several speculations on points that the text itself does not mention. However, this theological concern does not necessarily rule out this answer. We are supposed to read every passage of Scripture in the light of every other passage of Scripture. If it is plausible for theologians such as Augustine, Aquinas, and Calvin to infer, based on other passages of Scripture, that the first humans lived for a while in a state of original righteousness, then we need not be concerned that Genesis 2–3 doesn't mention this. No single passage of Scripture answers every question that we might want answered. Scripture, taken as a whole, tells us what we need to know.

A second theological concern with the idea that the first humans who sinned were in a state of original righteousness has to do with questions about God's justice in also holding *other* human beings, who were not given the supernatural gifts of original righteousness, accountable for sin. As an analogy, imagine that a village of a thousand people decides to raise a billion dollars for a worthwhile charity. The village council passes a law that each person must donate one million dollars, and anyone who fails to do so will be put in jail. A few village members are wealthy enough to give a million dollars; those who can give but don't are justly put in jail. Meanwhile, many village members support the goal of raising a billion dollars and give what they can, but they are simply unable to give a million dollars. We would probably say that the law putting them in jail is unjust. Now suppose that God enabled a few humans in the ancient past, through supernatural gifts, to live in a state of original righteousness. They sinned and lost those supernatural gifts. What about all of the other humans who were alive at the same time? Is it just for God to then declare that all of them are also sinners because they are incapable of living in righteousness, even though they were never given supernatural gifts? However, this theological concern does not necessarily rule out this answer. Perhaps God decided that these first humans who sinned despite having been given the gift of original righteousness were acting as representatives for all humanity, and their actions determined the status of us all. Some theological strengths and concerns about this possibility are discussed later in this chapter. Or perhaps God simply knew that if these first representatives chose to sin despite being given such supernatural gifts, then all other humans alive at that time, if given those same gifts, would likewise choose to sin. If so, then it might even have been an act of mercy on God's part not to make each human go through the same experience as those first sinners, to experience such close fellowship with God and then experience the loss of it. This raises the question of whether or not the fall was, in some sense, inevitable, which is discussed further in the next chapter.

There are reasons to favor the answer that the first humans who sinned were, for a time, in a state of *moral innocence*—not yet able to understand or fulfill all of God's moral law but able to understand and fulfill more limited responsibilities. This was the view of Irenaeus and other theologians throughout church history. Perhaps the moral maturity that God desires in humans can only come through a lifetime of choices, experience, and training.

Because God used evolutionary processes to create our ancestors, they naturally had a mixture of nasty and nice behavioral dispositions. They would not have been able, solely by the power of their own created nature, to avoid sinning. But perhaps long ago, when some of our ancestors were just becoming capable of understanding their moral and spiritual responsibilities to God and one another, God gave some of them gifts of grace and spiritual empowerment. These gifts brought them to a state of moral innocence in which they understood dimly what it meant to sin, but they had not yet sinned and were capable of not sinning—but they still needed to mature.[4] The idea that Adam and Eve needed to learn moral righteousness through a long process of instruction, obedience, and grace goes back to some of the earliest church fathers[5] and has had advocates ever since.[6]

One theological concern with this answer is that it raises the question of how long our ancestors were expected to avoid sinning. Given all the temptations to sin throughout a lifetime, and their own creaturely dispositions toward selfish behavior, is it plausible that they could have avoided sinning for a very long time? If they started in a state of moral innocence rather than original righteousness, it seems at first glance as though it was, in some sense, inevitable that they would sin. However, this theological concern does not necessarily rule out this answer. If humanity's sin was, in some sense, inevitable, then Christ's incarnation and redemption was also God's plan from the beginning. This possibility is explored in the next chapter. But then again, humanity's fall into sin need not be inevitable in this case. We could imagine that our ancestors—given suitable spiritual gifts and instruction from God—might have eventually grown from moral innocence to original righteousness over time without actually sinning along the way. (As an analogy, we could imagine a chess player learning the game and going from beginner level to grand master without ever losing a game along the way, given suitable instruction and suitable opponents at each stage.) Genesis 3 does not give a time limit for how long Adam and Eve were supposed to resist temptation. This has led some theologians throughout the centuries to speculate on what might have happened if they had resisted temptation "long enough" and reached a state in which sin no longer tempted them. Scripture doesn't say, so theologians must hypothesize based on what Scripture does teach elsewhere about God and human responsibility for sin.

Another theological concern with this answer is that it raises the question of how this state of moral innocence was supposed to have spread to all humanity. Imagine that God started with a few individuals who, beginning in a state of moral innocence, eventually developed through obedience to God to

---

4. C. John Collins writes about this possibility in *Did Adam and Eve Really Exist?* (Wheaton: Crossway, 2011), 65: "In fact, this interpretation also helps us to appreciate what is going on in the temptation. In my own work I have argued that the humans were created morally innocent, but not necessarily 'perfect' (so long as 'innocence' does not mean naiveté or moral neutrality). Their task was to mature through the exercise of their obedience, to become confirmed in moral goodness."

5. Theophilus of Antioch, among others.

6. J. Richard Middleton suggests a similar interpretation in "Reading Genesis 3 Attentive to Evolution," in *Evolution and the Fall*, ed. William T. Cavanaugh and James K. A. Smith (Grand Rapids: Eerdmans, 2017), 81–82.

a state of moral and spiritual maturity. What then would be the status of the thousands (at least) of other humans alive at the time, scattered over one or more continents, who had not yet gone through a similar process? However, this theological concern does not necessarily rule out this answer. In the New Testament, the church starts with just a few dozen individuals who were given the Holy Spirit. They were given the Great Commission to make disciplines of all nations. Perhaps, in an analogous fashion, the first humans who became aware of their moral and spiritual responsibilities to God and to one another would have (had they not sinned but instead grown into moral maturity) spread the blessings of fellowship with God to the rest of humanity slowly over time through example and teaching.

There are reasons to favor the answer that the first humans who sinned were in a state of *moral neutrality*. Perhaps already in the earliest moments when our ancestors first began to understand what it meant to be responsible to God and morally responsible to one another, they began to sin. Even without receiving a commandment from God via special revelation, we know (thanks to God's gifts of reason, empathy, and conscience) some things today about how we ought to behave. Perhaps God began to hold our ancestors accountable for their actions from the first moments in which they began to dimly understand the spiritual implications of their actions. In other words, perhaps the first individuals who had developed to the point where they could sin, did sin.

One theological concern with this idea is that it seems to make humanity's fall into sin, in some sense, inevitable. Because God used evolutionary processes to create our ancestors, they naturally had a mixture of nasty and nice behavioral dispositions. None of our ancestors could have been expected to obey God's moral law, even as understood only by general revelation. However, this theological concern does not necessarily rule out this answer. Questions about inevitability are discussed in the next chapter.

Another theological concern with this answer is that it implies that humanity's sinful rebellion goes very far back in time, before our ancestors had developed into fully modern humans. This means that God's creation of humanity and humanity's sinful rebellion were happening, in some sense, simultaneously over hundreds of thousands or millions of years. But this theological concern does not necessarily rule out this answer. Each of us, as individuals, began to sin willfully when we were quite young—much less developed intellectually and socially than we are as adults. By analogy, it should not surprise us if our ancestors began to sin once they reached some threshold of cognitive development, even if they were still less developed than most humans today.

There are reasons to favor the answer that the first humans who sinned were in a state of *legal innocence*. Romans 5:13 says, "To be sure, sin was in the world before the law was given, but sin is not charged against anyone's account where there is no law." Perhaps God allowed our ancestors to advance quite far, cognitively and culturally, before specially revealing his law to some of them and beginning to hold them accountable. The primary concern with this answer is that God's special revelation would have been necessary before any action was considered sinful. This theological concern, and some possible answers to it, were discussed in a previous section of this chapter.

How Did the Entrance of Sin Damage Our Human Nature?

When the first sinners sinned, what immediate damage did it do to them? What damage did it do to them and their descendants in the long run? Chapter 7 noted that theologians throughout church history did not all give the same answers to these questions. The four scenarios for Adam and Eve discussed in this book give similar answers to the types of damage caused by sin but different answers to how that damage spread (next section).

Sin damaged the first sinners spiritually. Sin breaks our proper relationship with God. Genesis 3 depicts Adam and Eve being afraid and trying to hide from God. Throughout the Old Testament, when people are personally confronted by God's presence and holiness, they are afraid because of their sinfulness.

With the benefit of the New Testament, theological reflection throughout church history, and modern scholarship, we can list some other ways that sin damaged our human nature in addition to the theme of alienation from God that we see in Genesis 3.

Sin damaged the first sinners psychologically. Genesis 3 depicts Adam and Eve feeling shame and trying to shift the blame for what they did. We all know the fear, guilt, and shame that result from our awareness of our sin. We know we have harmed our relationships with God and with other people. The psychological scars can run deep and affect us for the rest of our lives. In addition, we know that when we sin, it often becomes easier to sin again and again and again. Repeated sin can become habit, and habit can become something like addiction.

Sin damaged them socially. Genesis 3 depicts a relationship between Adam and Eve no longer governed solely by self-giving love. We ought to love others as we love ourselves. When we fail to do that, it disrupts our relationships.

In addition to these types of damage, which began immediately with the first sin, other types of damage became entrenched or intensified in later generations. Sin damaged them culturally. Genesis 4–6 depicts descendants of Adam and Eve continuing to sin until in 6:5 it says, "The LORD saw how great the wickedness of the human race had become on the earth, and that every inclination of the thoughts of the human heart was only evil all the time." Our behaviors, collectively, help form our culture. We all live today in cultures in which many sins are permitted or even rewarded; this tempts us to sin even more. We all live today in cultures in which sins of the past continue to produce injustice, inequality, and suffering in the present.

It seems likely that sin has, over time, affected humanity genetically. As noted in chapter 4, genes and culture coevolve. Culture affects the social and physical environments in which genetic selection happens. Gene frequencies in the population, in turn, can push cultures in certain directions over generations. It's probably too simple to say that specific genes cause sin. But cultures that tend to reward violence, for example, might over many generations result in populations with greater genetic predispositions toward violence. We are far from understanding the details of how this all works. But it seems plausible that, in the present, our genes and our cultures together push us toward sin in ways that are rooted in the sins of our ancestors.

These psychological, social, cultural, and perhaps even genetic effects of sin—accumulated through generations—could be interpreted as a corruption of human nature. No one today can avoid committing sin. Even infants, who have not yet committed a willful sin, arrive in a broken situation, inheriting a broken nature, surrounded by sinful caregivers and teachers.

In addition, if those who became the first sinners had been given some supernatural gifts so that they started out in a state of original righteousness—or even in a state of moral innocence, with the ability to avoid sinning for a significant period of time—those gifts were lost when they chose to sin. They lost the opportunity for the rest of humanity to be given those gifts. With the loss of those gifts, it became inevitable that all humans thereafter would be sinners. Some theological concerns with this idea, and answers to those concerns, were discussed in a previous section of this chapter.

Did the Damage Caused by Sin Happen Primarily through a Single Act or through an Accumulation of Multiple Acts?

Genesis 3 depicts humanity falling into sin through a single pair of disobedient acts. Many theologians throughout church history taught that several things

changed radically with just those two acts. Adam and Eve lost certain supernatural gifts, or their created human nature was warped, or both. They
changed from being in a state of able-not-to-sin to being in a state of not-
able-not-to-sin. They acquired guilt. All their offspring, apart from divine
intervention, became automatically condemned to be born in this same state.
Genesis 3 by itself does not explicitly teach that all these changes occurred
immediately. These are deductions that some theologians have made on the
basis of all of Scripture. As noted in chapter 7, theologians throughout church
history have disagreed about some of these details.

The theory that all these changes occurred immediately, for the entire
human race as a result of a single pair of disobedient acts, works best if all
humans are descended solely from a single pair of individuals. Today, in light
of the scientific evidence discussed in chapter 4 pointing to the human ancestral population probably never being smaller than a few thousand individuals
at any one time, it is worth considering several other options.

> Perhaps the fall and the damage caused by sin entering the world happened
> primarily through *a single pair of disobedient acts committed by a pair
> of individuals who acted as representatives of all of humanity*. The
> consequences of their disobedience were applied not just to that pair
> but to all of humanity alive at that time and afterward. (This answer
> implies an Adam and Eve scenario of type 1.)
>
> Or perhaps the first humans who sinned, through *a single pair of disobedi-
> ent acts, lost supernatural gifts* that would have enabled them to avoid
> further sin. In doing so, they immediately lost the possibility of their
> offspring or any other humans obtaining such gifts. However, the dam-
> age to human nature and human culture developed slowly thereafter,
> as knowledge of sin and the consequences of sin spread socially and
> perhaps genealogically, over millennia, to the rest of humanity. (This
> answer implies an Adam and Eve scenario of type 2.)
>
> Or perhaps the fall and its most significant consequences occurred through
> *an accumulation of multiple acts within a limited time among a limited
> group of people*. At some point in history, God chose a group of our
> ancestors for a new revelation, a new relationship, and a new com-
> mission. They were morally immature, because moral maturity takes
> time and experience, but their mission from God did not require them
> to be perfect. They should have taken a path of obedience leading to
> greater moral maturity. They repeatedly chose a path of disobedience.
> There wasn't one single act that doomed all of humanity, but there was

a limited time, a probationary period. We don't know exactly when or where this period was or how long it lasted, but it had a definite beginning and end that was known to God, and perhaps known, via special revelation, to the people involved. Once that period was over and humans had decided repeatedly to take paths of disobedience, both individually and collectively, the consequences for humanity were irreversible by human effort alone. Human nature was sinful, requiring Christ's redemptive work to atone. (This answer implies an Adam and Eve scenario of type 2.)

Or perhaps the fall and the consequences of sin occurred *gradually throughout our entire ancestral population over an extended period of time.* Through our ancestors' long history, God gave general revelation and sometimes special revelation to each individual or group as was appropriate for them. Individual acts of obedience or disobedience to God's revealed will happened many times, in many places, over a long history. Of course, there was a historical first sin, but that sin had immediate consequences only for the individual or individuals involved; by itself, it was no more consequential for all of humanity than the historical second or third sins. Each act of obedience pushed humanity toward a closer fellowship with God; each act of disobedience pushed humanity away from God. Eventually, the accumulated spiritual, psychological, and social damage of all the acts of disobedience set humanity irreversibly (by human effort alone) on the path of spiritual separation from God. There was no one specific time we can point to when this irreversible tipping point occurred, but humanity crossed that point long ago. (This answer implies an Adam and Eve scenario of type 3 or type 4.)

There are reasons to favor the answer that the fall and the damage caused by sin entering the world happened primarily through *a single pair of disobedient acts committed by a pair of individuals who acted as representatives of all of humanity.* Genesis 3 portrays the very first sinful disobedience of the first humans as a catastrophic event, significantly changing their relationships with God, each other, and the rest of creation. However, there are some theological concerns with the idea that all these catastrophic consequences befell all humans alive at that time (at least thousands of individuals, spread over a large geographic area) because of the disobedience of this pair of representatives. Some of these concerns, and some possible answers to these concerns, are discussed in the next section.

There are reasons to favor the answer that the first humans who sinned, through *a single pair of disobedient acts, lost supernatural gifts* that would have enabled them to avoid further sin, and that the consequences of sin spread thereafter to the rest of humanity more slowly, socially or perhaps genealogically. Some theological concerns with this answer and some possible answers to these concerns are discussed in the next section.

There are reasons to favor the answer that the fall and its most significant consequences occurred through *an accumulation of multiple acts within a limited time among a limited group of people.* In the Old Testament, God chose the nation of Israel from out of all the nations for a special covenant and a special task, which entailed particular responsibilities. Likewise, during Jesus's life and ministry on earth, he chose, out of all the Israelites, a small group of followers to begin the church and the task of making disciples of all nations. So this answer fits a pattern that we see elsewhere in Scripture of how God sometimes deals with humanity by starting with a small group.

One theological concern with this idea is that Genesis 3 tells a story of sin entering the world, with catastrophic consequences, through just a single pair of disobedient acts. However, this theological concern does not necessarily rule out this answer. Genesis 1 and 2 both tell the story of God's creation of the sun and stars, the earth, and all life on earth, including humanity—processes that took billions of years—in highly compressed narratives. Likewise, Genesis 4 tells of the human development of musical instruments, agriculture, cities, and iron forging—things that archaeology tells us were spread over tens of thousands of years—taking place in just a few generations. So if humanity's rebellion was, in historical fact, a story of multiple sinful acts committed by multiple people over a limited period of time, and Genesis 3 presents this as a theological narrative of just two individuals at a single place and time, this would fit a pattern we see in the other early chapters of Genesis.

Another theological concern with the idea that the fall and its most significant consequences occurred through an accumulation of multiple acts comes from James 2:10: "For whoever keeps the whole law and yet stumbles at just one point is guilty of breaking all of it." James—following the teachings of Jesus—tells us that if we think we can be good enough for God by obeying only *some* of God's laws and living up to only *some* of God's standards, we are deceiving ourselves. God is holy. If we are not holy, we are not "good enough" for God (apart from God's grace in Christ). However, this theological concern does not necessarily rule out this answer. Scripture shows us many times that God is willing to work through long processes to achieve his purpose—in the history of the children of Israel, in the history of the church, and in the slow process of sanctification that God works in each of our lives. Perhaps, at this early stage of humanity's history, God was willing to work through a process to move his creatures toward a state of righteousness because moral and spiritual maturity take time and lived experience.

Another set of theological concerns with this idea has to do with sin spreading from this first group of sinners to the rest of humanity socially or perhaps genealogically. These concerns, and possible answers to these concerns, are discussed in the next section.

There are reasons to favor the answer that the fall and the consequences of sin occurred *gradually throughout our entire ancestral population over an extended period of time.* Perhaps God was willing to work through a long, slow process involving the entire population of our ancestors, with the Holy Spirit guiding and prompting each individual according to his or her abilities. As with the previous answer, this implies that Genesis 3 is a theological retelling of humanity's long process of rebellion in a single, highly compressed story. This answer requires one to accept the view that sin spread from the first sinners to the rest of humanity *developmentally.* Some theological concerns with this idea, and some answers to those concerns, are discussed in the next section.

How Did the Status of "Sinners" Spread from the First Sinners to All Humans?

Every human today is a sinner. That was true in our grandparents' generation, and their grandparents' generation, and so on going back thousands of years (at least).

Scripture does not tell us precisely how sin is transmitted from one generation to the next. As discussed in chapter 7, theologians have offered several theories. Some have said that sin is transmitted from parents to their children. Some have said that it is transmitted culturally, through social interaction and imitation. Some have said that being in a state of sin (as opposed to being in a state of righteousness) is a kind of spiritual status that now applies to all humans and into which every human is therefore born. Some have said that all of the above are true.

When theologians assume that all humans are descended solely from a single pair of individuals, Adam and Eve, these different theories about how sin is transmitted from one generation to the next all amount, functionally, to almost the same thing. They all have the same result. Each generation born after Adam and Eve, up through each child today, is sinful regardless of how sin is transmitted.

Because God used evolution to create humanity, the question of how sin spread from the first sinners to the rest of humanity becomes less academic. We are not all descended solely from a single pair. Even during the narrowest part of the population bottleneck of *Homo sapiens*, our ancestral population was probably composed of at least several thousand individuals spread over a large geographical region.

We can consider several possible answers to the question of how sin first spread.

Perhaps sin spread by *representation*. The first humans who sinned were selected out of a larger population to act as representatives of all humans alive at that time. Because those representatives chose to sin, all humans alive at that time and afterward acquired the status of "sinner." (This answer implies an Adam and Eve scenario of type 1.)

Or perhaps sin spread *socially* from the first humans who sinned to other human groups by cultural contact, imitation, and learning. (This answer implies an Adam and Eve scenario of either type 2 or type 3.)

Or perhaps sin spread *genealogically*, from parents to offspring. As the offspring of the first sinners mixed with other groups of humans who were alive at that time, their children were also under the effects of sin. Eventually, the entire population became genealogically unified in this way, after which all humans born were sinners because they had the very first sinners somewhere in their ancestral tree. (This answer implies an Adam and Eve scenario of either type 2 or type 3.)

Or perhaps sin spread *developmentally*. Only individuals who developed cognitively and religiously beyond a certain threshold were considered sinners. Initially, this might have been isolated individuals or small groups surrounded by many more individuals and groups that had not yet developed to that threshold. Through gene-culture coevolution, the number of individuals and groups who crossed that threshold grew over time. Eventually, the entire population had crossed that threshold and was capable of sinning. Whenever individuals developed the capacity to sin, they chose to sin; no individual chose to lead a sinless life. (This answer implies an Adam and Eve scenario of type 4.)

Regardless of how sin spread after the first sin, all four of these answers lead to the same result: sin spread to all of humanity.

There are reasons to favor the answer that sin spread by *representation*. At some point in history, God might have chosen a pair of individuals (or perhaps a small group) to act as representatives of all humanity. Let's call them Adam and Eve. They were the first to have a new kind of relationship with God. As God later did with Abraham and Sarah, and still later with Jesus's band of followers, God started a new chapter in human history with just a few individuals. Had they maintained obedience and close fellowship with God, they might have opened the way for all other humans to follow. But they sinned. Acting as representatives of all humanity, they closed the way for all. There is precedent in Scripture for times when the action of one individual brings consequences on the entire community. When Achan took plunder from Jericho and kept it against God's command (Josh. 7), the Israelite army was defeated in its next battle. When King David disobeyed God's law by ordering a census (2 Sam. 24; 1 Chron. 21), God punished Israel with a plague. On the positive side, priests represented and could make atonement sacrifices for the entire community. And above all, God's grace comes to many through the righteousness of Christ (Rom. 3:22–26; 5:12–21).

One theological concern with this answer is the spiritual status of all those humans who lived and died in the days, years, and centuries prior to Adam and Eve being selected. If Adam and Eve were chosen very long ago—perhaps a million years ago or more—we might not consider this question very important. The exact intellectual, social, and moral status of our ancestors that long ago is not well known, but they were almost certainly less developed than we are today. However, if Adam and Eve were chosen as representatives much more recently—within the last 100,000 years or so—the question becomes more significant. Were these other humans (nearly identical to us genetically and anatomically) who lived immediately prior to Adam and Eve also image bearers of God? Is there hope for them in terms of Christ's redemptive grace, the resurrection, and life in the new creation? However, such concerns do not necessarily rule out this answer. Scripture tells us what God wants us to know, but it does not answer every question we can think of. Theologians over the centuries have wrestled with related questions (for example, what the spiritual status is of people today—especially children—who never hear the gospel), and theologians have not all come to the same answers. God is the judge of such matters, and we may need to be content with not knowing.

A second theological concern with the idea of sin spreading by representation is that it seems to imply that actions are not sinful until God gives special commands (a version of divine command theory, discussed earlier in this chapter). In the days and years immediately prior to Adam and Eve being chosen as representatives, they and other humans had a mixture of dispositions toward both nasty and nice behaviors. They had God's general revelation. Imagine four of our ancestors living in a small tribe hundreds of miles from Adam and Eve. A few days before Adam and Eve first sin, these four individuals steal something from their neighbor. Their consciences tell them they shouldn't, they know it will harm their neighbor, and they do the theft in secret to avoid shame and punishment from their tribe. But they do steal from their neighbor. It is not considered a sinful act because Adam and Eve have not yet sinned. A few days later, Adam and Eve—after receiving a revelation from God and then acting as the representatives of all humanity—commit humanity's first sins, thereby causing every human to acquire the status of sinner. A few days later, the same four individuals—still living hundreds of miles from Adam and Eve and not in any way communicating with them—commit a similar · theft. Is that act now sinful? Does general revelation now suffice to convict them of sin? Theologically, it seems odd to claim that whether or not an act is sinful depends on the actions of other individuals hundreds of miles away. However, this theological concern does not necessarily rule out this answer. Perhaps once our ancestors reached a certain level of moral and social development, God disapproved of all such acts of theft whether committed before or after Adam and Eve's first sin. God gave them general revelation to guide them to better behavior. But perhaps God graciously withheld judging such acts as sinful until after humanity's representatives chose the path of sin for all humanity.

A third theological concern with this answer is that it seems to imply that most humans alive at the time of Adam and Eve were condemned for an act that they did not commit and over which they had no control. It is true that in the Old Testament, God sometimes punished the entire Israelite community for the sins of some members. But the idea that many individuals might suffer *eternal separation from God* as a result of the wrongdoings of distant individuals is difficult to fit with the biblical picture of God's justice. In Ezekiel 18, God addresses the nation of Israel when the Israelites complain that God is punishing them unjustly because of the sins of their fathers. God declares (especially in verse 20) that he does not impute the guilt of one person's sin on another. As Christopher Hays and Stephen Herring write regarding the Old Testament and the Jewish literature of the intertestamental period,

> The idea of "corporate solidarity" (namely, that a people could suffer the consequences or reap the benefits of the deeds done by their representatives) was common enough, but corporate solidarity focuses more precisely on the way in which a group experiences the effects of another's action, for good or for ill. Nonetheless, Jewish writers shied away from imputing one person's guilt to another, especially when it came to eternal damnation. When Jewish literature talks about the way that the Adamic fall leads to the judgement of subsequent

generations, it invariably includes a middle term: the fall brings sin into the world and, when later generations commit sins, they warrant judgement.[7]

However, this theological concern does not necessarily rule out this answer. Perhaps God justly found the selfish, harmful actions of all humans prior to Adam and Eve to be worthy of condemnation but withheld condemnation and was willing to extend grace and spiritual empowerment to all had Adam and Eve continued in righteous obedience.

A fourth theological concern with this answer has to do with the theological connection between humanity's fall into sin and our concupiscence—our current inability to avoid sinning. In traditional theories of original sin (discussed in chapter 7), the first sin of Adam and Eve resulted in immediate change to them (a withdrawal of spiritual gifts, a change to their created human nature, or both), which left them in a state of *non posse non peccare* (no longer able not to sin)—a state that they then passed on to all their offspring. But now we know that our ancestors, even prior to Adam and Eve, had a mixture of dispositions toward both nasty and nice behaviors developed through gene-culture coevolution. If Adam and Eve were selected as representatives out of a larger population (that was spread over a large geographic area), and if their sin resulted in all humans alive at that time acquiring the status of sinner, there doesn't seem to be any possible (non-miraculous) causal connection between the sin of Adam and Eve and concupiscence in the rest of the population. However, this theological concern does not necessarily rule out this answer. Perhaps their concupiscence simply was their dispositions toward nasty behavior in the absence of supernatural gifts that could overcome those dispositions. Perhaps Adam and Eve had been given such spiritual gifts, but when they nevertheless freely chose to sin, they lost access to those gifts for all humanity.[8]

A fifth theological concern with the idea of sin spreading by representation has to do with the question of whether God could have achieved a different outcome if God had chosen a different pair of representatives. If the answer is yes—if a different pair of representatives chosen out of that larger population might have acted differently than Adam and Eve, choosing not

7. Christopher M. Hays and Stephen Lane Herring, "Adam and the Fall," in *Evangelical Faith and the Challenge of Historical Criticism*, ed. Christopher M. Hays and Christopher B. Ansberry (Grand Rapids: Baker Academic, 2013), 35.

8. Concupiscence in humans today would be due in part to the same things as in our distant ancestors: our evolved dispositions toward nasty behaviors in the absence of spiritual gifts that could overcome those dispositions. But concupiscence today would also include psychological and cultural effects of sin passed on from person to person and generation to generation, accumulated ever since that first sin.

to sin and resulting in an unfallen humanity—then God might be accused of choosing our representatives with poor foresight.[9] If the answer is no—if any representatives chosen out of that larger population would have acted the same as Adam and Eve did, choosing to sin and resulting in a fallen humanity—then we face difficult questions regarding whether the fall was inevitable. However, this theological concern does not necessarily rule out this answer. Questions regarding whether sin was, in some sense, inevitable are addressed in the next chapter.

There are reasons to favor the answer that sin spread *socially* from the first humans who sinned to other human groups by cultural contact, imitation, and learning. At some point in our ancestors' history, God might have chosen certain individuals to have a new kind of relationship with him. They might have been a single pair or a small group in a concentrated historical event (versions of Adam and Eve scenario 2), or they might have been a number of individuals spread out over a longer period of time (versions of Adam and Eve scenario 3). Through obedience to God and the help of the Holy Spirit, these individuals might have spread knowledge about God and sinless relationships with God to the rest of humanity through cultural contact and teaching. But their sin damaged their relationships with God, other humans, and the rest

9. The relationship between God's foreknowledge and human free will is a complicated theological and philosophical issue. Some philosophers and theologians have maintained that God foreknows the outcome of each of his creatures' free choices in any situation. If that is the case, then we could ask why God chose representatives who would freely choose to sin. If God's goal was an unfallen humanity, and God foreknew the outcome of each creatures' choice, God could have chosen representatives who *would* have chosen to remain obedient and not sin. Other philosophers and theologians have argued that when God made creatures with genuine free will, God chose to limit his foreknowledge, so that even God cannot foreknow the outcome of a genuinely "free choice" (although God can foreknow the consequences of either outcome and how to achieve God's ultimate will in either case). In that case, God could not have known for certain that Adam and Eve (or any representatives he chose) would sin until they freely chose to do so. Then the question becomes this: Why didn't God simply kill those first sinners (or, more graciously, allow them to live but isolate them from the rest of the population), start over with another pair of representatives, and keep doing so until God found a pair of representatives who would freely choose obedience, thereby ushering in the beginning of an unfallen humanity? A possible answer to this question might be that God made a covenant with Adam and Eve that, whatever they chose, their choices would stand for all the other humans whom they were representing. Once that covenant was in place, God was bound by God's own word to abide by the outcome. This could be analogous to God's covenant with Abraham, whereby God promised to make a great nation of Abraham's descendants and to bless the whole world through them. Once God made those promises, God was bound by his promise to work through those descendants to achieve his ends, regardless of how obedient or disobedient they were along the way. This answer may be consistent with how we see God working elsewhere in Scripture; however, it requires making additional assumptions about God's relationship with Adam and Eve (a hypothetical covenant that their choices would apply to all other humans alive at the time) that Scripture does not directly teach or imply.

of creation. The social spread of sin could happen as quickly as the spread of any new idea or cultural innovation.

Human children are intensely dependent on their parents and communal caregivers. What children learn from their families, tribes, and cultures shapes their language, empathy, reasoning, and every aspect of their thinking. Adults continue to depend on their tribes for their survival. No individual or family can survive long without tools and training gained from their culture, nor can they survive for extended periods isolated without communication, trade, and cooperation. Because humans are so radically interdependent, once sin entered the world, it seems inevitable that some of the effects of sin would spread from group to group and generation to generation.[10]

Two theological concerns with this answer were discussed earlier. First is the question of the spiritual status of all those humans who lived and died in the days, years, and centuries immediately prior to Adam and Eve being selected. Second, when connected to an Adam and Eve scenario type 2, in which the fall happens in a concentrated historical event, this answer seems to require a divine command theory of sin, implying that actions are not sinful unless God gives special commands against such actions. These concerns, and possible responses to these concerns, were discussed earlier in this section.

A third theological concern with this answer is that, for several centuries after the first sin, our ancestors—while unified by a gene-culture coevolution history going back millions of years—would have been split into two very different *spiritual* categories, depending on how far the social spreading of sin had reached geographically. Imagine two small tribes living about one hundred miles apart, both descended from a single tribe that split a century earlier. They are nearly identical genetically, culturally, and intellectually, but they do not happen to communicate with each other. At this particular moment in history, one tribe has interacted with the cultural spreading of Adam and Eve's sin so that they, too, are aware of their status as sinners and they, too, are considered

---

10. Benno van den Toren, "Human Evolution and a Cultural Understanding of Original Sin," *Perspectives on Science and Christian Faith* 68, no. 1 (2016): 17, writes the following:
This far-reaching dependence on parental and communal care can contribute significantly to our understanding of original sin. If human offspring are so dependent on socialization by their community, they will necessarily inherit both stronger and weaker aspects, both good and bad, or even detestable aspects of the culture in which they are raised. Children are hardwired to trust their educators. This is precisely why parents can do so much good and so much evil in the lives of their children. Growing up as a member of the human species necessarily means being socialized in one particular cultural expression of this culture, with the good and the bad. . . . They therefore inherit both the good and the bad symbolic representations of the world and customs of the particular culture in which they grow up. Sinful ideas and sinful habits are necessarily transmitted from one generation to another.

part of fallen humanity. But the other tribe has not yet had sufficient cultural contact with the spreading effects of sin. For the next few years or decades, they are outside of fallen humanity. What is their spiritual status and their eternal destiny? Are they similar to or radically different from those of the first tribe? It could be argued that this division of our ancestors into two groups with very different spiritual statuses—one fallen, one not yet fallen—is analogous to the distinction between Jews and gentiles in the Old Testament. But this analogy does not hold up. It is true that the Jews were recipients of God's promises to Abraham and subject to the covenant of the Torah while the gentiles were not—two significantly different statuses. However, in Romans and elsewhere, the apostle Paul argues that Jews and gentiles alike are subject to condemnation for their sin for exactly the same reason and that Jews and gentiles alike can be redeemed only by grace through faith in Christ. Scripture does not directly support the idea of two populations among our distant ancestors, one fallen into sin and one outside the distinction between fallen and not fallen (that is, for a few centuries, until such time as the effects of sin had spread socially to all of humanity). This idea would need to be added to Scripture in order to make this scenario work. However, this theological concern does not necessarily rule out this answer. Scripture tells us what God wants us to know, but it does not answer every question we can think of. It may be that Scripture does not tell us about this period of time when sin spread socially, or about the spiritual status and eternal fate of our ancestors from that period, simply because we do not need to know. God is the judge of such matters; we are not. And perhaps we need to be content with not knowing.

A fourth theological concern with the idea of sin spreading socially is this: If God's desire was for an unfallen humanity, why didn't God stop the social spreading of sin beyond Adam and Eve's first sins? God could have prevented sin from spreading by isolating the fallen Adam and Eve from the rest of humanity. This could have allowed God to start over with another pair or group of representatives, similar perhaps to the way God selected David as a new king after the failure of Saul. If it was possible for God to eventually find representatives who would not fall into sin, and whose obedience would allow for all of humanity to eventually join them in an unfallen state, why didn't God do so? On the other hand, if *any* representatives chosen out of that larger population would have acted the same as Adam and Eve did, choosing to sin and resulting in a fallen humanity, then we again face difficult questions about whether the fall was inevitable. Questions regarding whether sin was, in some sense, inevitable are addressed in the next chapter.

There are reasons to favor the answer that sin spread *genealogically*, from parents to offspring. At some point in our ancestors' history, God might have chosen a pair of individuals (or perhaps a small group). Let's call them Adam and Eve. Prior to this, humans engaged in a mixture of nasty and nice behaviors, but—even though they had some guidance from general revelation about how they ought to behave—God did not yet hold them accountable. Adam and Eve received a new revelation and formed a new kind of relationship with God, and God held them accountable. When they transgressed God's commands, they became sinners. This status was not immediately bestowed on the rest of the population, nor did it spread through social contact. It was, however, passed on to their offspring. As the offspring of the first sinners mixed with other groups of humans, eventually after several millennia, the entire population became genealogically unified in this way (as discussed in chapter 4), after which all humans born would include these first sinners somewhere in their ancestral tree. There is some scriptural precedent for this idea, analogous to how the blessings and responsibilities of Abraham's covenant and the law of Moses were passed on genealogically to the children of Israel but not to the gentiles.

Two theological concerns with this answer are similar to concerns with sin spreading socially or by representation. First is the question of the spiritual status of all those humans who lived and died in the days, years, and centuries prior to Adam and Eve being selected out of that population and falling into sin. Second, this answer seems to imply that general revelation was not enough for certain actions to be considered sinful and that such actions were not sinful unless God gave special commands against such actions. Possible answers to these concerns were discussed in previous sections.

A third theological concern with this answer is that for several millennia after Adam and Eve sinned, the ancestral population of humans—while unified by a gene-culture coevolutionary history going back millions of years—would have been split into two very different *spiritual* categories, depending on whether that particular couple was in their ancestral tree. This is similar to the concern discussed previously with sin spreading socially, but it intensifies the problem because of the long timescale for genealogical transmission through many generations. Many people would have lived and died during this millennia-long era of two spiritual categories. This concern becomes especially problematic if Adam and Eve are supposed to have existed in the relatively recent past—say, within the last 10,000 years or so. It is possible (although not certain) that all humans alive since the time of Christ could have, somewhere in their ancestry, a particular couple who lived in Mesopotamia roughly 10,000 years ago.[11] It is possible for sin to have spread genealogi-

11. David A. Opderbeck, "A 'Historical' Adam?," BioLogos, April 15, 2010, https://biologos
.org/blogs/archive/a-historical-adam; Jon Garvey, "Adam and MRCA Studies," *Hump of the*

cally to the entire population during this time. However, this would imply that, for many generations, our species was split into two populations with very different spiritual statuses. One group, which included Adam and Eve in its ancestry, was fallen. The other, which did not include Adam and Eve in its ancestry, was outside the distinction between fallen and unfallen. Other than that, however, these groups had similar levels of linguistic, technological, and social development. Members of both groups had pagan religious beliefs and practices. Given their cultural similarities and their unity as a biological species, is there theological warrant for assigning them such different spiritual statuses based simply on ancestry? This concern becomes less difficult if Adam and Eve are placed further back in history, prior to humanity's cultural developments of the last 10,000 years or so. Some theological concerns remain no matter how far back they are placed. Imagine two young half-siblings of about the same age, raised in the same family and the same tribe. They are similar genetically and intellectually. They share the same language, cultural practices, and religious beliefs. They behave both nasty and nice in similar amounts. One of them has one parent who has Adam and Eve in his or her ancestry; the other does not. In this scenario, one child would be fallen, and the other would be outside the distinction between fallen and unfallen. What is the spiritual status and eternal destiny of the latter child? Is it similar to or radically different from the spiritual status and eternal destiny of the first child? Does such a distinction of spiritual statuses of the two half-siblings fit easily with the rest of Scripture, given what Paul teaches about Jews and gentiles being sinners for the same reason, and being redeemed in the same way? However, this theological concern does not necessarily rule out this answer. As we noted earlier, God is the judge of such matters, and we are not. So we may need to be content with not knowing.

A fourth theological concern with the idea that sin spread genealogically (similar to a concern with the idea that sin spread socially) is the question of why God didn't stop sin from spreading genealogically simply by preventing Adam and Eve from having children. This could have allowed God to start over with another pair or group of representatives who might have been obedient. This concern was discussed earlier in this chapter.

There are reasons to favor the answer that sin spread *developmentally*. As babies today grow into children, we don't know when they become responsible for their actions. It might make sense to talk about degrees of responsibility.

Camel (blog), http://jongarvey.co.uk/download/pdf/AdamMRCA.pdf; S. Joshua Swamidass, "The Overlooked Science of Genealogical Ancestry," *Perspectives on Science and Christian Faith* 70, no. 1 (2018): 19–35; and S. Joshua Swamidass, *The Genealogical Adam and Eve: The Surprising Science of Universal Ancestry* (Downers Grove, IL: InterVarsity, 2019).

Not all children develop at the same rate. Something similar may have happened with our ancestors long ago. Although they were a unified population genetically and genealogically, and tribes interacted with neighboring tribes culturally, throughout their history, they were spread over a large geographical region of at least thousands of square miles (even at the time of the population bottleneck). Some individuals, families, and tribes probably developed higher levels of intellectual and moral responsibility before others did. Eventually, the entire population of our ancestors, collectively, developed past whatever threshold was necessary for moral responsibility. But along the way, God might have held different individuals or groups accountable to different standards, each standard appropriate for the level of development of the individual or group it was being applied to. Although individuals and groups learned to sin from one another, and suffered the effects of one another's sinful acts, no one acquired the guilt of sin from anyone else's actions.

For each individual and each group in this developing population, their God-given gifts of reason, empathy, and conscience counted as general revelation for how they ought to behave. God could have used many different kinds of special revelation, given to many different individuals and groups, to further guide them. There would have been a historical first sin in this population, but trying to identify it is no more important than trying to identify the particular first time in a child's life when they willfully sin. It is a developmental process. There were many occasions when an individual or group knew what they ought to do and could have chosen obedience or disobedience to God's revealed will. There were many occasions of obedience and many occasions of disobedience. No one was ever perfectly obedient. Each act of disobedience took the individuals involved, and humanity as a whole, farther from a right relationship with God.

One theological concern with this answer is that the later parts of humanity's creation and humanity's fall into sin happened simultaneously during overlapping periods of time. Over the last several tens or hundreds of thousands of years, God continued to shape and increase our ancestors' mental and social capabilities using processes we would describe scientifically as gene-culture coevolution. If sin spread developmentally, then throughout this same time period, individuals and groups of humans would have on occasions come to understand, at least in part, how they ought to love God and one another and still disobeyed. The effects of these sinful choices would have accumulated in individuals, families, and cultures. Humanity's sinful rebellion against God would also have been shaping their developing mental and social capabilities, even as God was still in the process of creating and shaping them.

We might worry that this is too much mingling of the distinct theological concepts of God's creation and humanity's sinful rebellion. The distinction between the two keeps us from simply saying, "God created humans sinful," and thereby undercutting divine goodness and human responsibility for sin. However, this theological concern does not necessarily rule out this answer. Consider God's creation and God's providential oversight of nonhuman creation. It is theologically useful to distinguish, as different types of divine action, God's *creation* of the universe and God's *providential oversight* of the natural world. Prior to the discoveries of modern science, most theologians would have assumed that the two are not only theologically distinct but also temporally distinct. They would have said that God's creation of stars, oceans, dry land, and species was accomplished and finished by day 6 of creation, while God's providential oversight has continued ever since. Through modern science, we have learned about the mind-bogglingly long history of the universe. Over *billions of years*, using slow processes, God continued to make new stars, new oceans, new islands, and new species. And God is continuing to make new stars, new islands, and new species today. The theological distinction between God's creative activity and God's providential activity is still useful, but we have learned that both can occur simultaneously over a long period of time. Analogously, God's loving creation of humanity and humanity's sinful rebellion against God are theologically distinct activities, even though both could have been occurring simultaneously over a long period of time.

A second theological concern with the idea that sin spread developmentally is that there would then have been no moment in history when all of humanity was in a state of original righteousness, or even of moral innocence. There would have been no time when humanity as a whole was without sin. It is possible that some individuals, at various times, were briefly in a state of moral innocence prior to sinning, but it seems likely that most of the population would have been in a state of either moral neutrality or legal innocence prior to their first sins. However, this concern does not necessarily rule out this answer. Some pros and cons of each of these four pre-fall statuses were discussed earlier in this chapter.

A third theological concern with this answer is that it requires an interpretation of Adam and Eve that understands the two not as particular historical individuals but as literary and symbolic figures referring to a large number of our ancestors over a long period of time, or to all humans throughout history. Some biblical scholars argue that the best hermeneutical methods suggest that Adam and Eve refer to real historical figures. However, this theological concern does not necessarily rule out this answer. Other biblical scholars argue that the best hermeneutical methods allow or even favor interpreting Adam and Eve as symbolic figures. Some pros and cons of these interpretations were discussed in chapter 7.

A fourth theological concern with this answer is that a developmental spread of sin, while not necessarily requiring that the fall was inevitable, does fit much more easily with the idea that the fall was inevitable. These issues are discussed in the next chapter.

Is the Guilt of Original Sin Passed from One Generation to the Next?

Earlier sections of this chapter discussed the spiritual, psychological, social, and cultural damage caused by sin and how that damage might have spread to the entire human population. What about the *guilt* of sin? Augustine and some other theologians throughout church history argued that the guilt of sin is passed from one generation to the next. So even infants, who have not yet committed any willful sins, not only have a sinful human nature but are also, in some sense, guilty of sin. Not all theologians have agreed with this idea (as discussed in chapter 7).

There are reasons to favor the idea that the guilt of original sin is passed from parents to offspring, or from generation to generation. One traditional argument says that Adam was the "federal head" of all of humanity when he sinned, so his actions justly brought punishment on all of humanity. (This fits most closely with Adam and Eve scenarios of type 1.) A second traditional argument is that all humans share a real, metaphysical unity, so that children are, in some sense, "in" their parents (or in all of humanity) and we are all, in some sense, "in" the first sinners. A third traditional argument comes from the practice of baptizing infants. As discussed in chapter 7, Augustine (and other theologians since) reasoned that one reason the church baptizes infants is to remove their inherited guilt of original sin. (While this third argument, by itself, might not carry much weight in Christian traditions that practice adult baptism, some of those traditions would agree with this much: no one, not even an infant, is righteous apart from Christ; even infants need God's grace through Christ's redemptive work.)

There are also arguments against the idea that the guilt of original sin is passed from parents to offspring, from generation to generation. The most commonly cited argument is that such a transfer of guilt would compromise God's justice. It might be just for God to punish an entire community in this life for the actions of some members of the community, resulting in suffering or even physical death for others in the community. But would it be just for

God to eternally condemn any person for the sins of another? It is difficult to reconcile such an idea with Scripture passages, like Ezekiel 18, that seem to teach that God does not impute the guilt of one person's sin on another. Therefore, if even infants need God's grace through Christ's redemptive work, it must be for some other reason than the inheritance of the legal status of guilt.

Once way to resolve these two strands of theological arguments is to say that an inherited legal status of being guilty of sin is, at its foundation, a recognition of a simple fact: we are not born as pure blank slates. Although infants have not committed willful sins, each inherits a nature that—no matter where or in what culture they grow up—inevitably leads them to sin. No one, not even an infant, is ready for God's holy presence apart from Christ's redemption and the Holy Spirit's sanctifying work.

When Was Humanity Made in the Image of God Relative to the First Sin?

Theories about when humanity was made in the image of God relative to the first sin depend somewhat on what we mean by the "image of God." Chapter 5 described four common theological theories about what is involved in being made "in God's image": (1) our mental, social, and moral *capabilities*, especially ways in which humans are distinct from animals; (2) a pre-fallen state of *original righteousness*; (3) a *personal relationship* between God and humans; and (4) our *commission* to be God's representatives to and stewards of the rest of creation. These are not exclusive theories. Some theologians embrace all four. Other theologians exclude one or more of them in their understanding of the image of God.

Here are four possible answers to the question of when humanity was made in the image of God relative to the first sin:

Humanity's creation in the image of God and humanity's fall into sin both happened developmentally over a long period of time.

Humanity as a whole was designated to be in God's image long before the first sin.

Humanity as a whole was declared to be in God's image shortly before the first sin.

A few individuals were selected out of a larger population of our ancestors at some point in the evolutionary history leading to modern *Homo sapiens*, and only they were designated to be in God's image. They fell into sin shortly afterward. Their status as God's image bearers together with their status as sinners eventually spread socially or genealogically to the entire population.

There are reasons to favor the idea that humanity's creation in the image of God and humanity's fall into sin both happened developmentally over a long period of time. Some pros and cons of this idea were discussed earlier in this chapter.

There are reasons to favor the idea that humanity as a whole was designated to be in God's image either long before or shortly before the first sin—assuming the image of God refers to only our distinctive human capabilities and our commission to be God's stewards of creation. God created humanity's mental, social, and moral capabilities over a long period. At some point in the process, God could have decided that humans had reached a level of development at which they possessed the abilities to act as God's caretakers and stewards of creation. Either shortly afterward or much later, sin entered the world when God chose a few individuals out of a larger population for a special relationship and special revelation. This answer requires that sin spread to the rest of the population by representation, socially, or genealogically. Some pros and cons of each of these ideas were discussed earlier in this chapter.

There are reasons to favor the idea that a few individuals were selected out of a larger population of our ancestors at some point in the history of our species, and that only they were designated to be in God's image. This answer allows the possibility that the image of God, at least at first, included a state of original righteousness made possible by supernatural gifts from God. When these individuals fell into sin, original righteousness was lost and the image of God in them was damaged, but not destroyed. Both the image of God and their status as fallen sinners then spread to the rest of humanity by representation, socially, or genealogically. Some pros and cons of each of these ideas were discussed earlier in this chapter.

What Kind of Death Came through Sin?

As discussed in chapters 3 and 4, the idea that humans were *naturally* immortal prior to sin is not supported by Scripture or by science. Biblical scholars typically interpret Genesis 2–3 as saying that humans were created mortal, while the tree of life symbolically represents a miraculous sustaining provision from God.

Here are two common answers to the question regarding what kind of death came through sin:

The death that came through sin is not physical death but *spiritual death*. Physical immortality has always been something intended for the new creation (Rev. 22). And without the redeeming work of Christ, sin separates us from God in both this creation and the next.

The death that came through sin includes *not only spiritual death but also physical death in this creation*. If the first humans had not sinned, God could have graciously offered miraculous freedom from physical death to sinless humans.

There are theological reasons to favor the answer that sin brought *spiritual death* but is not responsible for physical death. In Genesis 2–3, Adam and Eve did not physically die the same day they sinned. They did lose access to the miraculous tree of life and therefore became doomed to eventually die physically. But they also, on the day of their sin, lost access to God's close presence.

There are theological concerns with this answer, however. In Genesis 3:22–24, God prevents Adam and Eve from reaching the tree of life so that they do not "eat, and live forever" in their disobedient state. And numerous New Testament passages (especially Rom. 5 and 1 Cor. 15) seem to link sin not only with spiritual death but also with physical death.

However, these theological concerns do not necessarily rule out this answer. John Calvin seems to have thought that humans in this life were created for long, healthy lives and graceful deaths (such as described in Isa. 65:20–25). If Adam had not sinned, "Truly the first man would have passed to a better life, had he remained upright; but there would have been no separation of the soul from the body, no corruption, no kind of destruction, and, in short, no violent change."[12] Because of sin, physical death is now a sometimes painful, uncertain, distressing separation of soul from body followed by destruction of the body. It is also possible that the tree of life in the Genesis text is part of God's accommodation to common literary motifs found in other ancient Near Eastern literature—in this case, the motifs of a lost idyllic age and a lost opportunity at immortality. Perhaps God accommodated these common motifs in Genesis 2–3 to teach a theology very different from those of the surrounding Mesopotamian and Egyptian cultures. In Genesis 2–3 (and unlike in the other literature), we learn that the reason humans do not live in

---

12. John Calvin, *Commentaries on the First Book of Moses, Called Genesis*, trans. John King (Grand Rapids: Eerdmans, 1948), 97.

a paradise of close communion with God is because of human sin. In this interpretation, the tree of life in Genesis 2–3 points forward to the resurrection, symbolizing the promise of eternal life in God's presence in the new creation, where it reappears in Revelation 22.

There are theological reasons to favor the answer that sin brought *not only spiritual death but also physical death in this creation*. The most straightforward reading of Genesis 3, Romans 5, and 1 Corinthians 15 is that humans die physically because sin caused our ancestors to lose access to the possibility of living forever, symbolized by the tree of life.

For scenarios in which sin entered the world gradually and developmentally among a large number of our ancestors over a long period of time (Adam and Eve scenario types 3 and 4), it is difficult (but perhaps not impossible) to imagine that physical immortality by God's miraculous provision would have been possible eventually if our ancestors had not sinfully rebelled.

For scenarios in which sin entered the world through particular historical individuals and then spread by representation, socially, or genealogically (Adam and Eve scenario types 1 and 2), it is much easier to imagine that physical immortality by God's miraculous provision would have been possible in this world if our ancestors had not sinfully rebelled.

Blended Scenarios

By mixing and matching the many possible answers to all the questions in this chapter, we can construct many scenarios that would answer the question "When did sin begin?" Early on, we grouped the possible scenarios into four general types:

1. Adam and Eve as particular historical individuals acting as representatives of humanity
2. Adam and Eve as particular historical individuals; sin spread through culture or genealogy
3. Adam and Eve as a highly compressed history referring to many individuals over a long period of time who received special revelation
4. Adam and Eve as symbolic figures referring to many individuals over a long period of time, all who became ready to be held accountable and chose sin

These four types are not entirely exclusive. In fact, they can blend into one another depending on which elements are emphasized in a particular scenario.

For example, if we start with the first type and also postulate that the sin of Adam and Eve did not instantly cause the rest of humanity to become sinners but that, instead, sin spread very rapidly through cultural contact, we end up with a scenario that blends the first and second types. If we start with the second type and assume that the Adam and Eve of Genesis 2–3 refer not to a pair of individuals acting over a few days, or even to a small hunter-gatherer group acting over a few months, but to a socially interacting set of hunter-gatherer groups in a geographic area acting over the course of several decades, we end up with a scenario that blends the second and third types. If we start with the third type and put a high emphasis on general revelation compared to special revelation, we end up with a scenario that blends the third and fourth types. If we start with the fourth type and also see humanity as a whole headed in the direction of sinful disobedience, but we imagine a critical point in history when God chose a pair of individuals for a special revelation, a pair that might through obedience have started down a different path and through God's grace brought the rest of humanity with them, we end up with a scenario that blends the fourth type back into the first or second.

10

Whose Fault Is It?

"IT'S NOT MY FAULT." This is a favorite excuse of many children (and adults) when caught in wrongdoing.

In Genesis 3:11–13, after Adam and Eve sin, they try to shift blame. Adam explicitly blames Eve, and he implicitly blames God for creating Eve. Eve explicitly blames the serpent, and by implication she blames God (who presumably created the serpent and allowed it in the garden). God does not directly contradict or endorse their attempts to shift blame. God tells them the consequences of their disobedience.

The purpose of this chapter is not to try to shift blame. Its purpose is to consider various answers to the question of whether, and in what ways, humanity's sinful rebellion against God was "avoidable" or "inevitable." The words in quotation marks need unpacking.

This is one of the oldest and thorniest theological questions. Augustine was drawn into debates about it, as were many theologians after him. It connects closely to essential truths about God.

If we say that humanity had a significant chance of avoiding the fall, that history could have turned out differently, some theologians object that this is not compatible with God's *sovereignty* and *foreknowledge*. It seems to make Christ's incarnation and redemption of humanity God's plan B—something God had to come up with after humanity thwarted his original plan.

If we say that humanity's fall was (at least in some senses of the word) inevitable, some theologians object that this is not compatible with God's *goodness* and *justice*. It seems to make God too responsible for humanity's sin and to reduce humanity's responsibility too much, calling into question whether it is just for God to punish anyone for their sin.

These old theological debates take on additional significance in light of human evolution. Consider again:

1. Adam and Eve as particular historical individuals acting as representatives of humanity
2. Adam and Eve as particular historical individuals; sin spread through culture or genealogy
3. Adam and Eve as a highly compressed history referring to many individuals over a long period of time who received special revelation
4. Adam and Eve as symbolic figures referring to many individuals over a long period of time, all who became ready to be held accountable and chose sin

Scenario types 3 and 4 are often interpreted as implying that the fall was, in some sense, inevitable. That is one reason (but not the only reason) why some Christians prefer scenarios of type 1 or 2. As we will see, scenario types 3 and 4 do not require that the fall was inevitable, although they do lean in that direction.

Scenario types 1 and 2 are often interpreted as implying that the fall was avoidable. That is one reason (but not the only reason) why some Christians prefer scenarios of type 3 or 4. As we will see, scenario types 1 and 2 do not necessarily imply that the fall was avoidable, although they are often interpreted that way.

Why Doesn't God Stop Sin and Suffering Now?

One proposed answer to the question "Why doesn't God stop sin and suffering now?" often associated in the last century and a half with *process theology*, is that God's power is limited. In this school of thought, God works with his creatures through processes more akin to "persuasion" than "coercion." Since God does not have (or would never use) coercive power, God's creatures can use their own power to act in sinful and destructive ways.

However, in classical Christian theology, God is omnipotent, just, and good; God can—and sometimes does—use "coercive" power. Assuming classical

Christian theology is correct about this, we face a difficult question. Human sins are against God's will. If God can act powerfully to stop sin, or at least prevent the suffering of victims of sinful acts, why doesn't God do so more often?

Scripture speaks about God's will in several different (sometimes overlapping) ways. For example: (1) There are things God decrees. God's decrees cannot be thwarted. (2) There are things God prefers. God takes pleasure in some things and does not take pleasure in others. (3) There are God's precepts. God reveals laws and commandments that we should follow. (4) There may be God's direction for particular times in our lives. We might, for example, perceive a calling to go to a particular place or pursue a particular vocation for a time. (5) There are things God permits. God's decrees cannot be thwarted, but God might permit us to disobey his precepts, to do things he does not prefer, and to do things that do not follow his direction.[1]

When we sin, we disobey God's will, but God permits us to sin. God might at times protect victims of sinful acts from some suffering, but obviously God permits a great deal of suffering. Why God permits sin and the suffering caused by sin is closely related to another of the oldest of theological questions—the question of the "hiddenness" of God. Why doesn't God dramatically prove his existence and power much more openly by, for example, frequently and publicly rewarding good behavior and punishing sin?

Scripture contains a few examples in which many people witnessed dramatic displays of God's power, coupled with teachers who could clearly explain to them the proper understanding. The children of Israel were rescued from slavery in Egypt by many dramatic miracles (Exod. 7–15). The prophet Elijah held a public contest with the prophets of Baal in which God provided miraculous fire from heaven (1 Kings 18:16–45). Jesus performed miracles of healing and other miracles. We might hope that most of the witnesses of these miracles responded with faith and love toward God. But what actually happened? The recently freed Israelites made a golden calf idol. The Israelites at Mt. Carmel did not repent in large numbers and return to worshiping God, and Elijah was soon running for his life. Many religious leaders who saw Jesus's miracles demanded more signs, and then they plotted to kill him.

These examples from Scripture seem to tell us something very unflattering about human nature. If God dramatically proved his existence to all of us, it appears that this would not produce the kind of moral and spiritual growth that God desires for us. It might well have the opposite effect. If God always

---

1. For more on this topic, see, for example, R. C. Sproul, *Essential Truths of the Christian Faith* (Carol Stream, IL: Tyndale, 1992), 67–69.

rewarded good and thwarted evil, we might become more self-interested and calculating, living obediently only in order to earn rewards in this life and the next. Note that this was the accuser's suspicion about Job (Job 1:9–11).

So it may be, at least in part, that God permits sin and the suffering caused by sin because doing so is in the interest of humanity's collective good. For God to do otherwise would change the nature of our relationships with God and one another and might stunt our growth toward becoming the sorts of people that God wants us to become. In *The Problem of Pain*, C. S. Lewis explores the idea of a world in which God always prevents suffering and argues that it would not be good for us.[2] John Hick, in *Evil and the God of Love*, develops the idea that "this world must be a place of soul-making. And its value is to be judged, not primarily by the quantity of pleasure and pain occurring in it at any particular moment, but by its fitness for its primary purpose, the purpose of soul-making."[3]

2. C. S. Lewis, *The Problem of Pain* (New York: Macmillan, 1962), 34, writes:
We can, perhaps, conceive of a world in which God corrected the result of . . . [our abuse of free will] at every moment: so that a wooden beam became soft as grass when it was used as a weapon, and the air refused to obey me if I attempted to set up in it the sound waves that carry lies or insults. But such a world would be one in which wrong actions were impossible, and in which, therefore, freedom of the will would be void; nay if the principle were carried out to its logical conclusion, evil thoughts would be impossible for the cerebral matter which we use in thinking would refuse its task when we attempted to frame them. All matter in the neighborhood of a wicked man would be liable to undergo unpredictable alterations. That God can and does, on occasions, modify the behavior of matter and produce what we call miracles, is part of the Christian faith; but the very conception of a common, and therefore, stable, world, demands that these occasions should be extremely rare. In a game of chess, you can make certain arbitrary concessions to your opponent, which stand to the ordinary rules of the game as miracles stand the laws of nature. You can deprive yourself of a castle or allow the other man to sometimes take back a move made inadvertently. But if you concede everything that at any moment happened to suit him—if all his moves were revocable and if all your pieces disappeared whenever their position on the board was not to his liking—then you could not have a game at all. So it is with the life of souls in a world: fixed laws, consequences unfolding by causal necessity, the whole natural order, are at once the limits within which their common life is confined and also the sole condition under which any such life is possible. Try to exclude the possibility of suffering which the order of nature and the existence of free wills involved, and you find that you have excluded life itself.
3. John Hick, *Evil and the God of Love*, rev. ed. (New York: Harper & Row, 1977), 250. See this quotation in its wider context:
Jesus treated the likeness between the attitude of God to man, and the attitude of human parents at their best towards their children, as providing the most adequate way for us to think about God. And so it is altogether relevant to a Christian understanding of this world to ask, How does the best parental love express itself in its influence upon the environment in which children are to grow up? I think it is clear that a parent who loves his children, and wants them to become the best human beings that they are capable of becoming, does not treat pleasure as the sole and supreme value. Certainly we seek

Suppose that it is sometimes good for our moral and spiritual development that we suffer as victims of another person's sinful actions. And suppose that it is vital for our moral and spiritual development that we see the consequences that sinful actions—our own and others'—have on their victims. Could not God still arrange things differently to reduce suffering? We could imagine, for example, each of us living in something like our own computer simulation. Each of us thinks we live in a "real world," but everyone we encounter is a simulation. We could witness the supposed consequences of sinful acts committed by ourselves and others without any real person (other than ourselves) actually getting hurt. Would that be better? There are at least three theologically worrisome consequences to this proposal. If every person we thought we were interacting with wasn't actually a person, it would mean that God was constantly telling us something false, which seems contrary to God's character revealed in Scripture. Second, it would mean that all the suffering we experienced was coming directly from God (rather than being caused by the actions of God's creatures and permitted by God). Third, when offered a hypothetical choice to live in a pleasant simulation or in the less pleasant real world, people often choose the less pleasant reality rather than the pleasant simulation.[4] We need and desire to be interconnected. People generally want their choices to have real consequences, not only for themselves but also for others.

Moreover, the Gospels (Matt. 16:24; Mark 8:34; Luke 9:23), Pauline Letters (2 Cor. 1:5; Phil. 3:10), and 1 Peter (4:13) all tell us that sharing in Christ's sufferings is part of what it means to be followers of Christ and to participate in his kingdom work.

---

pleasure for our children, and take great delight in obtaining it for them; but we do not desire for them unalloyed pleasure at the expense of their growth in such even greater values as moral integrity, unselfishness, compassion, courage, humour, reverence for the truth, and perhaps above all the capacity for love. . . . And to most parents it seems more important to try to foster quality and strength of character in their children than to fill their lives at all times with the utmost possible degree of pleasure. If, then, there is any true analogy between God's purpose for his human creatures, and the purpose of loving and wise parents for their children, we have to recognize that the presence of pleasure and the absence of pain cannot be the supreme and overriding end for which the world exists. Rather, this world must be a place of soul-making. And its value is to be judged, not primarily by the quantity of pleasure and pain occurring in it at any particular moment, but by its fitness for its primary purpose, the purpose of soul-making. (258–59)

4. See, for example, F. Hindriks and I. Douven, "Nozick's Experience Machine: An Empirical Study," *Philosophical Psychology* 31, no. 2 (2018): 278–98. A great deal of philosophical discussion on this question, and also some empirical studies, have been inspired by Robert Nozick's thought experiment in his book *Anarchy, State, and Utopia* (New York: Basic Books, 1974).

These answers do not satisfy everyone. But they offer a way to understand how the God of classical Christian theology—omnipotent, just, and good—could still permit the suffering that we see in the world today.

Why Did God Create Humans in a Way That Permitted Sin?

The final chapters of the Bible give us images of a new heaven and a new earth (Rev. 21:1), a place where those who are redeemed by Christ will dwell after the resurrection and final judgment (20:11–14). The dwelling of God will be with his people (21:3; 22:4–5). There will be no more death, mourning, crying, or pain (21:4). And, it is usually assumed, God's redeemed people will no longer sin because they have been sanctified and now experience God's close presence all the time.

If God can eventually bring that about, why did God create *this* world in a way that humans could sin, and as a place where there could be mourning, pain, and death?

One possible answer is sometimes called the "aesthetic argument." An artist creating a bright and beautiful painting might make it even more beautiful by including some dark pigments and rough textures in places. By analogy, while any particular sin is against God's will, God might nevertheless consider it better for there to have been some evil that is overcome, and some sinners who have been redeemed, than to have a creation without any evil or sin.

One version of this aesthetic argument is a modified version of the "principle of plenitude"—an ancient philosophical idea that the best possible universe is one that contains every type of being that can exist. Augustine and Aquinas, among others, brought versions of this philosophical argument into Christian theology.[5] An artist, for example, might choose to create sixty

5. Rudi A. te Velde, "Evil, Sin, and Death: Thomas Aquinas on Original Sin," in *The Theology of Thomas Aquinas*, ed. Rik Van Nieuwenhove and Joseph Wawrykow (Notre Dame: University of Notre Dame Press, 2005), 146, summarizes Aquinas:

> The perfection of the created universe, however, requires that there should be a multitude of unequal things, so that every degree of goodness may be realized. . . . It is impossible that one creature alone bears the perfect likeness of God, so as to constitute another God. . . . Because of this, Aquinas argues, plurality and inequality in things are intended by God, so that each creature may mirror God's perfection in its own way and thus contribute to the multiplied way the universe as a whole expresses the goodness of its creator. . . . Because of this inequality, the universe cannot consist only of spiritual creatures, whose nature is incorruptible and who are in an enduring possession of their goodness. Besides the superior degree of spiritual creatures, another degree of good things is required, namely, corporeal creatures, which can fail in goodness and may lose their being. But even corruptible things contribute to the perfection of the universe as a whole, and their existence is therefore required by that perfection. . . .

statues identical in form but each of a different type of metal. The lead and tin statues would, in some sense of the term, be better if they were made of gold—arguably the best metal from which to make a statue. But the artist prefers to have sixty statues each of a different metal rather than sixty identical gold statues. By analogy, God chose to create many kinds of creatures, of many levels of goodness. God may have created many types of creatures superior to humans. He also chose to create humans, who are good in certain ways, but not perfect, and who are capable of sinning.

A second possible answer is that God created humans with the ability to sin because this is an unavoidable consequence of an even greater good that God wants to achieve. One version of this answer is known as "free will theodicy." God wants creatures who can freely choose good. But in giving us freedom, God allows us to sin. Alvin Plantinga articulated the argument this way:

> A world containing creatures who are significantly free (and freely perform more good than evil actions) is more valuable, all else being equal, than a world containing no free creatures at all. Now God can create free creatures, but He can't *cause* or *determine* them to do only what is right. For if He does so, then they aren't significantly free after all; they do not do what is right *freely*. To create creatures capable of *moral good*, therefore, He must create creatures capable of moral evil; and He can't give these creatures the freedom to perform evil and at the same time prevent them from doing so. As it turned out, sadly enough, some of the free creatures God created went wrong in the exercise of their freedom; this is the source of moral evil. The fact that free creatures sometimes go wrong, however, counts neither against God's omnipotence nor against His goodness; for He could have forestalled the occurrence of moral evil only by removing the possibility of moral good.[6]

Perhaps for us to be truly morally good, we must have the freedom to choose evil, and we must grow into goodness through experience. We must learn to have faith and obey God's wishes even when doing so is costly and there is no obvious reward. If we lived in God's clear and immediate presence, as envisioned in the new creation, we could not choose evil, because God's goodness and power would be so clear to us that they would overwhelm our ability to choose against them. Therefore, as Hick argues in *Evil and the God*

And it is in this that evil consists, namely in the fact that a thing fails in goodness. . . . Their corruption is not as such intended by God or by nature, but still, it is likely to happen sooner or later.

6. Alvin Plantinga, *God, Freedom, and Evil* (Grand Rapids: Eerdmans, 1977), 30.

of Love, growing in moral goodness requires some amount of separateness, uncertainty, and independence of humanity in relation to God.[7]

Was the Fall Avoidable, or Was It Inevitable?

If free will theodicy and soul-making theodicy are correct—if they convey at least some of the reasons why God created humanity in such a way that sin was possible—they could be interpreted as implying that the fall was not only possible but also inevitable. Questions about whether the fall was avoidable or inevitable go far back in Christian theology, at least to Irenaeus and Augustine. We must clarify what we mean by these terms. Because this question connects to basic questions about how human freedom and responsibility relate to God's foreknowledge and sovereignty, we must consider it from both a purely creaturely perspective and from one that seeks to account for divine foreknowledge.

From *a purely creaturely perspective*,[8] we could imagine several possibilities. (These don't line up in any particular way with the four Adam and Eve scenario types.) For the first humans who sinned:

1. *Perhaps the fall was avoidable.* God might have raised these first humans into a state of original righteousness through supernatural gifts. Or they might have been in a state of original innocence, and God was ready to work with them over time to increase their maturity and moral discernment. In either case, they had a real, non-negligible chance of obeying God and avoiding sin. Had they done this long enough, through God's grace, they would have reached a state of morally mature righteousness in which sin was no longer a threat. For some Christians, only this first option is theologically acceptable. They would argue that any of the remaining three options makes God

---

7. John Hick, *Evil and the God of Love*, 281, writes:
    In creating finite persons to love and be loved by Him God must endow them with a certain relative autonomy over against Himself. . . . God must set man at a distance from Himself, from which he can then voluntarily come to God. But how can anything be set at a distance from One who is infinite and omnipresent? Clearly spatial distance means nothing in this case. The kind of distance between God and man that would make room for a degree of human autonomy is epistemic distance. In other words, the reality and presence of God must not be borne in upon men in the coercive way in which their natural environment forces itself upon their attention. The world must be to man, to some extent at least, *etsi deus non daretur*, "as if there were no God." God must be a hidden deity, veiled by His creation. He must be knowable, but only by a mode of knowledge that involves a free personal response on man's part, this response consisting in an uncompelled interpretative activity whereby we experience the world as mediating the divine presence.
8. One lacking divine foreknowledge and omniscience.

too responsible for sin and removes too much human responsibility. Some of these arguments are summarized later in this chapter.

2. *Perhaps they began innocent and immature, and no particular sin was unavoidable, but sinning eventually was almost inevitable as they grew to maturity.* The first humans who sinned began in a state of innocence and immaturity. Through special and general revelation, they began to understand that there was such a thing as God's will for their lives. No particular temptation they faced was irresistible. But because of the many choices they faced and the long time that it takes to grow into moral maturity (or because of the large number of humans who started in this state, or both), some of them eventually sinned. With each sin, they took themselves on a path of greater and greater disobedience, further and further from God's will. Eventually, their wills and cultures became so corrupted by sin that it was no longer possible for anyone to live in innocence or righteousness. For some Christians, this option affirms both that humans are responsible for the sins they freely choose to commit and that God could have foreknown that the fall would happen. It also affirms the idea that it takes time and experience for humans to grow toward moral maturity.

3. *Perhaps the fall was not "necessary" but more or less statistically inevitable, given the means God used to create us.* The first humans who sinned began in a state of intellectual, moral, and spiritual immaturity. They were not exactly in a state of moral innocence, because they had a mixture of dispositions toward both nasty and nice behaviors. This mix of dispositions, however, did not automatically make them sinners. Sin is disobedience to God's revealed will. No particular act of sin on their part was unavoidable. But because of the number of people and the number of opportunities to sin, some chose to sin. Because of the large number of times they could have sinned, it was almost inevitable that some of them would sin. With each sin, they took themselves on a path of greater and greater disobedience, farther from God's will. This third option has become more common in the last century and a half. It can be seen as a modification of the previous option prompted in part by what we have learned about the evolutionary means that God used to create humanity.

4. *Perhaps the fall was inevitable because of the way God created us, and God created humanity that way for a reason.* Our ancestors began in a state of immaturity, with a mixture of dispositions toward both nasty and nice behaviors. By the time they began to understand that there was such a thing as God's will, it was inevitable that each would sometimes choose sin. In this sense, both the possibility and the inevitability of sin were part of human nature from the beginning. Some who accept the second or third option would argue that this fourth option goes too far in making God responsible for sin

and that this option is counter to a biblical narrative that includes God's displeasure at human sin. One way to argue in favor of this option is to say that being human fundamentally requires having the freedom and opportunity to grow toward moral maturity in a difficult environment—that there is simply no other way for us to be human. Such growth is necessary to human nature by definition, and that is why God created us using evolutionary processes and why God planned for redemption through Christ from the beginning.[9]

Any of these four possibilities could be made to fit with Adam and Eve scenario types 1 and 2, in which the fall happens over a fairly short period of time. While the latter three possibilities could easily fit with Adam and Eve scenario types 3 and 4, it is difficult but not impossible to make the first possibility (that the fall was avoidable from a creaturely perspective) fit with Adam and Eve scenario types 3 and 4, in which the fall happens over a long period of time involving many individuals. (Perhaps God was willing to work with our ancestors toward sanctification over a long period of time. This possibility will be discussed later in this chapter.)

From *a point of view that seeks to account for divine foreknowledge*, we could imagine several possibilities. (Again, these don't line up in any particular way with the four Adam and Eve scenario types.)

1. *Perhaps the fall was avoidable from a creaturely perspective, and God could not foreknow the outcome.* Therefore, the fall could not be inevitable from God's perspective. According to this view, God foreknows what is foreknowable; but by definition, the outcome of a truly free decision cannot be foreknown.[10] When God gives a creature genuine free will, according to this view, God voluntarily places some limits on his foreknowledge. For some Christians, this option is not theologically acceptable because it reduces God's sovereignty and foreknowledge too much. This option does, however, avoid some of the philosophical challenges faced by later options that affirm both God's foreknowledge and human freedom.

2. *Perhaps the fall was avoidable from a creaturely perspective, and God did foreknow that the fall would happen.* According to this view, God's creatures have genuine free choice, while at the same time God can and does know the outcomes of their free choices before they make them, without logical contradiction.[11] For some Christians, this view ideally preserves God's sovereignty and foreknowledge, on the one hand, while affirming, on the other hand, that

9. Michael Anthony Corey appears to argue this way in *Evolution and the Problem of Natural Evil* (Lanham, MD: Rowman & Littlefield, 2000).

10. According to this particular definition, if the outcome *could* be foreknown, it would not be free.

11. A philosophical/theological school of thought called Molinism, named after the sixteenth-century Jesuit theologian Luis de Molina, is sometimes used to make sense of this view.

God is not responsible for sin—and that God is just to punish sin—because humans had genuine freedom and nevertheless chose to sin. Other Christians wonder if this view actually succeeds in avoiding logical contradiction.

3. *Perhaps the fall was avoidable from a creaturely perspective, and God both foreknew and ordained that the fall would happen.* According to this view, typically associated with some versions of Calvinism and with John Calvin himself,[12] God not only foreknew that humanity would fall but also, in his sovereignty, decreed prior to creation that the fall would happen. Nevertheless, in this view human sin happened by free choice and is therefore justly punishable by God. "Free choice," in this view, is typically seen *not* as a choice that could have been made otherwise by the creature but as a choice that is made voluntarily from the creature's own nature free of external compulsion.[13] For some Christians, that God not only *foreknew* but also *ordained* the fall is implied by a strong doctrine of God's sovereignty.

4. *Perhaps the fall was nearly inevitable from a creaturely perspective, and God foreknew that it would happen.* According to this view, the first humans who sinned had genuine free will, and no particular sin they committed was inevitable. But God foreknew that because of the long time that it takes to grow into moral maturity (or because of the large number of humans in the initial population, or both), they would eventually sin. For some Christians, this view sidesteps any questions about the compatibility, or lack of compatibility, between divine foreknowledge and human free will. Humans have free will, and God nevertheless would certainly have foreknown that the fall would happen because God knew that it would take a long time for humanity to grow into maturity, making the fall more or less inevitable.

5. *Perhaps the fall was inevitable because of the way God created us, and God foreknew this and created humanity that way for a reason.* According to this view, humanity's slow development from amoral animal selfishness to personal moral responsibility and self-giving love, humanity's need for redemption along the way, and God's plan for redemption through Christ were all part of one unified plan from the beginning. Some Christians embrace this option as a logical way to make redemption through Christ God's plan from before the world was created. Other Christians argue that this option (and perhaps the previous option as well) go too far in making God responsible for sin.

Any of these five possibilities could be made to fit with Adam and Eve scenario types 1 and 2. While the latter two possibilities could easily fit with

12. John Calvin, *Institutes of the Christian Religion* 3.21.5; 3.23.6–7 (Beveridge trans.), https://www.ccel.org/ccel/calvin/institutes.
13. See, for example, Jonathan Edwards, *Freedom of the Will* (1754).

Adam and Eve scenario types 3 and 4, it is difficult but not impossible to make the first three possibilities (which include the idea that the fall was avoidable from a creaturely perspective) fit with Adam and Eve scenario types 3 and 4.

Four Theological Reasons for Thinking the Fall Was Avoidable

Four theological reasons are commonly given to support the conclusion that the fall was avoidable:[14]

1. *God permits sin, but God is not the cause of sin.* When we sin, we might want to shift the blame to God. Scripture warns against that. "When tempted, no one should say, 'God is tempting me.' For God cannot be tempted by evil, nor does he tempt anyone; but each person is tempted when they are dragged away by their own evil desire and enticed" (James 1:13–14). And "this is the message we have heard from him and declare to you: God is light; in him there is no darkness at all. If we claim to have fellowship with him and yet walk in the darkness, we lie and do not live out the truth. But if we walk in the light, as he is in the light, we have fellowship with one another, and the blood of Jesus, his Son, purifies us from all sin" (1 John 1:5–7).

Care should be taken not to make too simplistic an argument from this point. There are several Scripture passages in which God is said to ordain or prompt people, for a larger purpose, to take actions we would think are sinful. God prompted the people of Egypt to hate the children of Israel (Ps. 105:25) and hardened Pharaoh's heart several times against releasing them (Exod. 4:21; 9:12). God ordained that Absalom would take his father's wives (2 Sam. 12:11). God at times prompted cruel, violent peoples to wage war against Israel and other nations (e.g., Isa. 10:5; Jer. 1:15; 11:22; Hab. 1:5–11).

And yet, even if God sometimes prompts already sinful people to follow particular sinful inclinations of their hearts as part of a larger plan to bring salvation to the world, we should not conclude that God removes human responsibility for the entrance of sin into the world. Scripture repeatedly proclaims that God is grieved and angered by all the evil that humans do.

2. *God declared from the beginning that creation was "very good"* (Gen. 1:31). Care should be taken not to read our own ideas about "perfection" into this passage. Creation in Genesis 1:31 has the order and function it needs to fulfill its purposes. But there is still plenty in it that humans are commissioned

---

14. This is not a complete list of reasons supporting the conclusion that the fall was avoidable, nor is a complete argument fleshed out for each of the reasons. This is only intended to be a brief summary. These points do not exclude one another. Several or all of them can be true, and they can be mutually reinforcing, each constituting a part of a larger argument for the conclusion that the fall was avoidable.

to "subdue" (1:28). And humans are capable of sinning. Moreover, Genesis 3 depicts a tempter serpent allowed into the garden. All of this is true in a creation that God calls "very good."

And yet, the overall picture of Genesis 1–3 is not one of sin being "built in" to humanity from the beginning. The picture is of human mistrust and disobedience of God leading to sin.

3. *God is just.* Even in our human justice system, we recognize different levels of culpability. To our human sensibilities, it seems as though the fact that the first sinners were punished for their sin implies that they could have done otherwise. And we believe that God is even more perfectly just than we are.

Care should be taken, however, not to make too simplistic an argument from this point. There are, within Christian tradition, those who argue that God foreknew (e.g., Augustine) and even foreordained (e.g., Calvin) that the fall would occur and yet could justly hold the first sinners responsible for their sin because they acted "freely" in the sense that they acted in accordance with their own wills and were not constrained to sin by outside forces. In addition, there are those examples in Scripture noted earlier in which God ordained people, for a purpose, to take actions we would call sinful (e.g., Pharaoh not freeing the children of Israel, violent peoples waging war against Israel) and then punished those sins.

And yet the overall picture of God from Scripture is one of justice. Ezekiel 18, for example, speaks extensively of God's desire to reward the righteous and punish the wicked, each in accordance with his or her own deeds and no one else's. Moreover, while God punishes evil, God's delight is to turn evil people from their wicked ways so that God can extend grace. "'Do I take any pleasure in the death of the wicked?' declares the Sovereign LORD. 'Rather, am I not pleased when they turn from their ways and live?'" (Ezek. 18:23).

4. *The incarnation was not necessarily dependent on the fall happening first.* There is within Christian tradition the *felix culpa* (fortunate fall) idea, which argues that humanity's sin was a necessary precondition for the immense good of Christ's incarnation and redemptive work. The idea has a long history and is connected in particular with St. Ambrose (337–97), who wrote that "sin is more fruitful than innocence" and that the fall "has brought more benefit to us than harm,"[15] and with Pope Gregory (540–604), who wrote that "certainly, unless Adam had sinned, it would not have behooved our Redeemer to take on our flesh."[16]

---

15. Quoted in A. O. Lovejoy, *Essays in the History of Ideas* (Baltimore: Johns Hopkins Press, 1948), 287–88.

16. Quoted in Lovejoy, *Essays in the History of Ideas*, 288–89.

Other theologians, however, have argued that while humanity's sin was a necessary precondition for Christ's *redemptive* work, it was not a precondition for Christ's incarnation. The incarnation was part of God's plan from creation, to dwell with his creatures. H. W. Richardson, for example, writes, "The incarnation proceeds from God's original intention for His creation. God created the world so that the Sabbath guest, Jesus Christ, might come and dwell therein. That is, the world was created for the sake of 'Emmanuel, God with us.' The incarnation is, therefore, not a rescue operation, decided upon only after sin had entered into the world. Rather, the coming of Christ fulfills the purpose of God in creating the world."[17]

Four Theological Reasons for Thinking the Fall Was Inevitable

Four theological reasons are commonly given to support the conclusion that the fall was inevitable:[18]

1. *Several Scripture passages seem to teach that God predestined some to be redeemed through Christ before the world was created.*

> For he chose us in him before the creation of the world to be holy and blameless in his sight. In love he predestined us for adoption to sonship through Jesus Christ, in accordance with his pleasure and will—to the praise of his glorious grace, which he has freely given us in the One he loves. In him we have redemption through his blood, the forgiveness of sins, in accordance with the riches of God's grace that he lavished on us. (Eph. 1:4–8)

> For you know that it was not with perishable things such as silver or gold that you were redeemed from the empty way of life handed down to you from your ancestors, but with the precious blood of Christ, a lamb without blemish or defect. He was chosen before the creation of the world, but was revealed in these last times for your sake. (1 Pet. 1:18–20)

> All inhabitants of the earth will worship the beast—all whose names have not been written in the Lamb's book of life, the Lamb who was slain from the creation of the world. (Rev. 13:8)

17. Herbert Warren Richardson, *Toward an American Theology* (New York: Harper & Row, 1967), 131.

18. This is not a complete list of reasons supporting the conclusion that the fall was inevitable, nor is a complete argument fleshed out for each of the reasons. This is only intended to be a brief summary. These points do not exclude one another. Several or all of them can be true, and they can be mutually reinforcing, each constituting a part of a larger argument for the conclusion that the fall was inevitable.

For I resolved to know nothing while I was with you except Jesus Christ and him crucified. I came to you in weakness with great fear and trembling. My message and my preaching were not with wise and persuasive words, but with a demonstration of the Spirit's power, so that your faith might not rest on human wisdom, but on God's power. We do, however, speak a message of wisdom among the mature, but not the wisdom of this age or of the rulers of this age, who are coming to nothing. No, we declare God's wisdom, a mystery that has been hidden and that God destined for our glory before time began. (2 Cor. 2:2–7)

Care should be taken, however, not to make too simplistic an argument from this point. These predestination passages have been interpreted a number of ways throughout church history. New Testament authors repeatedly urge their readers to choose to follow Christ and not to fall away from faith. Moreover, as noted earlier, there are possible ways to affirm that God's foreknowledge is compatible with real creaturely choice. And yet there is a recurring theme through several New Testament texts about God's plan, including redemption through Christ, going back to before the creation of the world.

2. *God's sovereignty and foreknowledge seem to imply that the fall was inevitable.* God's sovereignty cannot be thwarted by human action. If God's sovereign intention was for a sinless humanity, if it was within God's power to achieve it, then that is what would have happened. Human actions do not force God to come up with a backup plan.

When talking about individual human sins, it seems important to distinguish between things that God directly causes and things that God permits his creatures to do. But if God foreknew, before they were created, that humans would fall into sin, and God created them anyway, that distinction becomes more problematic. Logically, the argument could be made as follows: God foreknew before he created humans that they would fall into sin.[19] If God's desire was for a sinless humanity, and if God could have created humans differently so that they would not have sinned, then why didn't God do that? The fact that God created humans the way he did, foreknowing that they would sin, implies that sinful humans are what God intended.

If "Adam and Eve," the first humans to sin, correspond to real historical individuals selected out of a larger population, then an alternative version of the previous paragraph could go as follows. If God foreknew that the Adam and Eve that he selected would choose to sin, and if God could have selected a different pair who would have instead chosen to obey, why didn't God choose

---

19. There is the possibility, mentioned earlier, that God could not foreknow this, because by definition the outcome of free choices cannot be foreknown. I am discounting that possibility in this section.

differently? God's foreknowledge of their choice implies that God got the result that God intended. The fall appears inevitable. Alternatively, if God would have gotten the same disobedient result no matter who he chose out of the population to be "Adam and Eve," then the fall, again, appears inevitable.

Care should be taken not to make this argument too simplistically. It may seem theologically straightforward to affirm that because God is sovereign, humans cannot force God to come up with a backup plan. But there are places in Scripture where it appears as though God offers humans a choice with consequences, and God expresses a clear preference that they choose one way over another. But when humans choose differently than God's expressed desire, God deals with the outcome accordingly. For example, when the children of Israel demand to have a king like all the nations around them, the prophet Samuel tells them that this is against God's intention, and God even says, "They have rejected me as their king" (1 Sam. 8:7). Nevertheless, God provides them a king and offers to bless that king if he is obedient. Again, God tells Israel that they will remain in the land if they obey him, but they will go into exile if they reject him. They reject God and go into exile for seventy years until God brings a remnant back. Again, God promises to establish King David's descendants as Israel's kings in perpetuity if they follow him faithfully. Many of them do not, and for centuries David's descendants do not reign over the people, until God's promise is fulfilled in a surprising new way through Jesus the Messiah.

It is possible—as Augustine and many theologians since Augustine have done—to affirm that God is not the direct cause of sin, that God created humans with free will, that God foreknew that they would sin, that God permitted the fall and planned for it from before the creation of the world, and that God is nevertheless just to punish sin. And it is possible in this case—depending on how one defines free will—that the fall was freely chosen *from the perspective of the creatures in question*, even though it was foreknown from a divine perspective.

And yet, if the fall was foreknown before humanity was created, and humanity was nevertheless created as it was, it is difficult to avoid the conclusion that the fall was, in some sense, inevitable, even if it was not "built in" to the structure of creation.

3. *The ultimate self-revelation of God is not merely Christ's incarnation but his incarnation and the redemption he worked through the cross.* When Jesus's disciples ask to see the Father, Jesus replies, "Anyone who has seen me has seen the Father," and "I am in the Father, and . . . the Father is in me" (John 14:8–10). Jesus is the ultimate revelation that we can understand of who God is and what God is like. And when we think of Jesus's character,

what stands out most of all is the cross—forgiveness and self-sacrificial love in the face of undeserved evil.

Care should be taken not to make too simplistic an argument from this point. We should be cautious about implying that God's ultimate plan depended on human sin. Perhaps if Christ had become incarnate to an unfallen humanity, God could have used means other than crucifixion to reveal to humanity the height and breadth and depth of self-giving love within the Trinity.

And yet, when we see Jesus offer love and forgiveness in the midst of what he actually suffered—and when we are called to advance Christ's kingdom by participating in Christ's sufferings—the cross remains the symbol of the ultimate self-revelation of God's love for us.

4. *Free will / soul-making /* agape *theodicies might imply that the fall was not only possible but more or less inevitable.* Humanity was created through evolutionary processes as a population. We have some free will. We grow from intellectual, moral, and spiritual immaturity to maturity through a process. We are interdependent; we live and learn in community. This does not mean that sin was "built in" to humanity at its creation. It implies, however, that for a large population of our ancestors over a long period of development, sin would have been almost impossible to avoid. The fall would have been more or less statistically inevitable.

Care should be taken not to make this argument too simplistically. These theodicies are not necessarily correct. They are reasonable theological deductions from what Scripture teaches, but they are not certain. In addition, even if these theodicies are more or less correct, it is possible to combine them with a historical Adam and Eve scenario in ways that could have made the fall avoidable.

And yet these theodicies might be substantially correct, and the simplest interpretations of these theodicies fit with the idea of the fall being more or less statistically inevitable. Some Christians believe these theodicies offer attractive explanations for several interconnected facts: that God chose to create humanity using evolutionary processes, that God chooses to create each new human through a developmental process, that God chooses to sanctify each of us in this life through a process, and that God chooses to advance his kingdom through the work of a community.

A Free Will / Soul-Making / *Agape* Theodicy

Chapter 3 discussed several possible reasons why God's creation included suffering and death prior to the creation of humans. The first half of this chapter discussed several possible reasons why God doesn't stop suffering now and why God created humans in a way that permitted sin. Now we will consider one possible unified theodicy.[20]

Christian Barrigar, in a recent book, describes what he calls an "*agape/probability account*" for God's chosen means of creating humanity.[21] Barrigar defines *agape*-love this way: "It is precisely in the servanthood, suffering, and death of Jesus that we see God's definitive account of what constitutes *agape*-love, namely, *self-giving*—specifically *self-giving to God, and self-giving for the well-being of others, including strangers and enemies*."[22] Regarding God's chosen means of creating humanity, including natural physical processes and biological evolution extending over billions of years, Barrigar writes, "God created the universe to provide the space and conditions for the emergence of habitable bio-niches in which *agape*-capable beings would eventually emerge to live in *agape*-love relationships with God and with others. Earth is one such emergent bio-niche, and *Homo sapiens* are an instance of such emergent *agape*-loving beings."[23]

God thus creates us with a certain amount of free will.[24] We can choose to respond to God and to others with *agape*-love, but we are also free to act in morally evil ways. Such freedom is essential for *agape*-love to be truly self-giving.

To understand the development of our capacity *as a species* for moral choices and *agape*-love, first consider how any individual develops any capacity. Each of us, as individuals, grows from fertilized egg to fetus, infant, child, then adult. As we do, we slowly grow in our capacities to reason, plan, empathize, and practice (or fail to practice) *agape*-love. We do this in community. We start out fully dependent on our caregivers not only for survival but for almost everything we learn. As we grow older, our choices increasingly affect our relationships and shape who we become.

For example, the brains of children are, to a certain extent, hardwired to learn language during a crucial developmental age; however, this happens properly only when they can interact with other language users. Likewise, children's brains are wired to learn physical skills such as walking, running, visual tracking, pointing, throwing, catching, and so on. Observing others

20. Several such theodicies have been published in recent decades. This chapter offers one that combines several of their features.

21. Christian J. Barrigar, *Freedom All the Way Up: God and the Meaning of Life in a Scientific Age* (Victoria, BC: Friesen Press, 2017).

22. Barrigar, *Freedom All the Way Up*, 21.

23. Barrigar, *Freedom All the Way Up*, 21.

24. See quotations by Alvin Plantinga and John Hick earlier in this chapter.

and playing with others are crucial in this process. Children also "naturally" learn the ability to sympathize and empathize with the suffering of others, but proper development depends on interaction with people and teaching from caregivers; when children are raised in socially deprived settings, they are much more likely to grow up deficient in sympathy and empathy.

Now consider your ability to make moral choices: selfish or altruistic, sinful or obedient to God. When you are twenty years old, both your freedom to choose and the choices you make are shaped by your history. That history started with things beyond your control, such as your genetics and prenatal environment. It was heavily shaped by your parents, teachers, caregivers, and friends. It was also shaped by the choices you made, again and again, as you grew up. Every time you made a choice, you shaped your own developing brain. Your choices in turn affected the way that your parents, teachers, caregivers, and friends interacted with you, which further affected your development.

This process, in which each person is incredibly dependent on a community for survival and learning but their own choices also shape who they become and in turn shape their community, is how God chooses to create each new human being today. And because God used evolutionary processes to create our ancestors, this appears to be how God chose to create each new human being throughout history.

For our ancestors, as for us today, this development happened in a world where there is pain and suffering and "natural evil." It happened in a world where actions have consequences. It happened in a world where our ancestors could foresee the short-term benefits of acting in selfish ways that hurt other people and the short-term costs of acting out of *agape*-love toward others. They had dispositions toward both kinds of actions, and they had some freedom to choose.

George Murphy, in *Models of Atonement*, asks us to imagine our ancestors when they were just becoming aware of the moral and spiritual significance of these abilities.

> Let us imagine the earliest hominids—we do not have to decide where or when they lived, how many there were, or if they were a single group—who had evolved to the point of self-awareness and linguistic ability. The evolutionary processes by which this condition was reached was one in which God was at work through natural processes. These humans had developed abilities to reason and communicate and were able in some way to receive and at least faintly understand God's Word, to trust in that Word, and obey God's will for them. We don't know in what way that expression of God's will may have come to them or what may have corresponded to the prohibition of the tree of

knowledge in Genesis. It might have concerned the way in which people should live together harmoniously, but about that we can only speculate. These first humans were at the beginning of a road along which God wanted to lead them and their descendants to fully mature humanity and complete fellowship with God. In principle they could follow that road, but it would not be easy. They had inherited traits that enabled their ancestors to survive and pass on their genes. And those traits, as we have seen, would predispose them to some extent toward selfish behavior and away from the community—with God, one another, and all creation—which God intended for them. Such behavior was not hardwired into them, but tendencies toward it were very strong. They could refuse to trust and disobey what they knew of God's will for them. In the language of Reinhold Niebuhr, sin was not "necessary" but it was "inevitable."[25]

Michael Corey argues that God chose to create each new human, and humanity as a whole, through these processes so that each person participates as much as possible in their own moral development.

This is the sense in which we can say that the various evils of our world are both necessary and contingent *simultaneously*. They are contingent because they depend on the nature of our individual moral choices and other factors, which themselves could have been otherwise. However, they are also indirectly necessary at the same time, since these same contingent events are only possible because of the specific structural parameters of this world, which are themselves necessary for the existence of bona fide humans. . . .

Human beings must possess a significant degree of behavioral freedom during the initial stages of their developmental journey. They must also be given the underlying potential for developing an optimal degree of freedom throughout their lives, along with various opportunities for maximizing the breadth and scope of this freedom to the greatest possible extent. . . .

The property of free will itself, however, doesn't appear to be an all-or-nothing phenomenon, since it can be expressed in a variety of different "strengths," depending on the relative degree of its ontological "completeness" (which itself corresponds to the individual's overall state of ontological wholeness). This being the case, it makes sense to suggest that God would have wanted us to develop the greatest degree of freedom that is humanly possible, even to the point of designing our world in such a way as to ensure the greatest possible development of this all-important property. . . .

According to this way of thinking, the robustness of our freedom is directly proportional to the degree to which our cognitive programming has been self-acquired. Part of the reason for this has to do with the underlying nature of our

25. George L. Murphy, *Models of Atonement: Speaking about Salvation in a Scientific World* (Minneapolis: University Lutheran Press, 2013), 65.

volitional center, because agents who play an active role in their own cognitive programming also help to determine the nature and content of their own sense of volition as well.[26]

A Free Will / Soul-Making / *Agape* Theodicy without Inevitability

The simplest interpretation of this theodicy is that, eventually, at least one of our ancestors would sin—because they had the freedom to do so, because they had a mixture of dispositions toward both selfish and altruistic behavior, and because there were so many of them. And because humans are so interdependent, once sin entered the world, it would spread.

If we believe it is theologically important to do so, there are at least two ways to affirm most of this theodicy and yet have the fall be avoidable.

First, it's possible to add to this theodicy one of the scenarios in which the Adam and Eve of Genesis 2–3 refer to real, historical individuals (scenario types 1 and 2). At some critical point in history, God might have specially selected a pair or small group out of a larger population for a special revelation and a special relationship. Perhaps God even gave them the supernatural gifts to bring them into a state of original righteousness. Or perhaps God was willing to work closely with them so that they could gain moral and spiritual maturity through a process of faith and obedience over a period of time. Had they continued in this way long enough, perhaps sin would have ceased to be a temptation for them, and they could have brought the blessings of this close relationship with God to the rest of humanity.

Second, it's possible to imagine an avoidable fall in scenarios in which the Adam and Eve of Genesis 2–3 refer to a large population of our ancestors over a long period of time (scenario types 3 and 4) if God was willing to work with our ancestors through a long period of sanctification. Several analogies might be helpful. In each of our lives, God sanctifies us through the work of the Holy Spirit through a process that continues our whole lives and that relies on our cooperation. In the Old Testament era, God worked through the children of Israel in a process lasting centuries before they and the world were ready for the Messiah to appear. Since Pentecost, God has worked through the church in a process lasting still more centuries to advance Christ's kingdom on earth. So it would not be out of character for God to have been willing, at the dawn of humanity, to work with a large population of our ancestors over a long time to lead them toward greater faith and obedience. But God also gave them

---

26. Michael Anthony Corey, *Evolution and the Problem of Natural Evil* (Lanham, MD: University of America, 2000), 189, 197–98.

freedom. Just as the children of Israel chose idolatry and disobedience again and again, leading to the exile, so our ancestors chose disobedience again and again, leading them down a path away from God. Perhaps that path was not inevitable, but they followed it past a point where only redemption through Christ could turn things around again.

11

Difficult Questions for Each Type of Scenario

CONFRONTED WITH NEW SCIENTIFIC DATA pointing to human evolution, Christians have found multiple ways of responding. This book describes four general types of scenarios, each of which seeks to preserve the core doctrine of original sin:

1. Adam and Eve as particular historical individuals acting as representatives of humanity
2. Adam and Eve as particular historical individuals; sin spread through culture or genealogy
3. Adam and Eve as a highly compressed history referring to many individuals over a long period of time who received special revelation
4. Adam and Eve as symbolic figures referring to many individuals over a long period of time, all who became ready to be held accountable and chose sin

This book has also briefly considered a few specific scenarios. For example: humans created miraculously and *de novo* without common ancestry with

251

other animals, but with the appearance of common ancestry in the genetics;[1] Adam and Eve as a single pair who are the sole progenitors of all humans;[2] Adam and Eve created *de novo* amid a larger population of *Homo sapiens*, whose offspring then mixed with that larger population;[3] and humanity created by God using evolutionary processes in which the fall was necessarily

1. A significant theological concern with God creating all humans *de novo* in this way is the appearance of false history. Chapter 4 describes multiple, independent, detailed, and mutually reinforcing lines of scientific evidence indicating an evolutionary history including common ancestry between humans and animals. Most Christians conclude that God creating humans *de novo* but making it appear to every scientific study as if there was an evolutionary history is inconsistent with God's character revealed throughout Scripture.

2. Chapter 4 mentions multiple lines of evidence (allele diversity, linkage disequilibrium, and patterns of incomplete lineage sorting) in the genetic diversity of the human population today. These data are most consistent with our ancestral population being at least a few thousand individuals going back millions of years. As a footnote in chapter 4 notes, at the time this is being written, a recent analysis argues that the allele diversity data could also be consistent with (but not prove) all humans today having descended solely from a single pair, provided that pair lived more than half a million years ago. A similar reanalysis of the linkage disequilibrium and incomplete lineage sorting data remains to be done. The preponderance of genetic and archaeological evidence strongly favors the current scientific consensus that our ancestral population was at least as large as a few thousand individuals going back several million years. For that reason, this book focuses on discussing scenarios that affirm that consensus.

3. A recent publication, S. Joshua Swamidass, *The Genealogical Adam and Eve: The Surprising Science of Universal Ancestry* (Downers Grove, IL: InterVarsity, 2019), suggests a scenario in which Adam and Eve were created *de novo* amid a larger population of *Homo sapiens* and their offspring then mixed with that larger population. This could potentially avoid the theological problem of the appearance of false history *in the human genome today*, because nearly all DNA in the human population today would come from the larger population of *Homo sapiens* rather than Adam and Eve. A few concerns remain. For their offspring to be able to interbreed with those of the surrounding population, the ordering of genes on Adam and Eve's *de novo*–created chromosomes would need to have matched that of the surrounding populations (whose genomes were created through evolution and common ancestry with animals). Moreover, the body of a typical person who grows from fertilized zygote to fetus, infant, child, and adult includes many features that record evidence of that history (e.g., a belly button, teeth with wear patterns, scars, ultraviolet damage to eye lenses, a genetic chimeric pattern in the cells of the body that retains a history of mutations that occurred during development, an immune system that retains memory of diseases encountered, an internal biome of gastrointestinal organisms gained from the local environment and family members). The brain of a typical adult has a wiring that records evidence of knowledge and skills learned over years of interaction with other humans and the environment (e.g., language skills, physical skills such as walking and throwing, survival skills, facial recognition, empathy and sympathy, and moral reasoning). The bodies and brains of an Adam and Eve created *de novo* would presumably *not* show evidence of such developmental history (in order to avoid the appearance of false history) but still be functional. In particular, their brains would need language skills and moral reasoning skills that would not make them too different from the surrounding population of evolved *Homo sapiens* so that they could, in a sense, represent them before God and so that their offspring could mix with the larger population. However, their brains would have wiring for these skills not by means of ordinary development but by the *de novo* miraculous creative action of God. The theological implications of this proposal are unclear and have yet to be worked out.

built in to human nature apart from human choice, with the reality of sin and God's plan for redemption simply revealed to humanity at a later time.[4] Concerns with these scenarios were addressed earlier in the book and are summarized in footnotes here. These scenarios are not the focus of this book, but they are mentioned here to give an overview of some additional specific scenarios that others could consider.

This chapter summarizes the most challenging theological questions facing the four types of scenarios that are the focus of this book.

Six Difficult Questions for Scenarios with Adam and Eve as Historical Individuals (Scenario Types 1 and 2)

1. *What was the spiritual status and eternal destiny of the surrounding population immediately prior to Adam and Eve's sin?* This question was explored in chapter 9. One possibility is that the entire population was already considered to be created "in God's image"; however, even though they were not morally perfect and sometimes behaved in nasty ways toward one another, they were not yet held accountable for sin. If so, we have questions about their eternal destiny (although, of course, God is the ultimate judge of these things and might simply choose not to tell us). Another possibility is that only Adam and Eve, at first, were considered to be "in God's image." In that case, questions about how sin spread to the rest of the population (question 4 below) become even more important, because both sin and the status of being God's image bearers were spreading simultaneously.

2. *Why didn't general revelation "count" prior to Adam and Eve's sin, but it did count afterward?* This question was explored in chapter 9. In Romans 2, Paul argues that gentiles, who do not have the law, need Christ's atonement because they have the law "written on their hearts" (v. 15). Humans today are accountable not only for whatever special revelation they receive but also for what they can discern from general revelation. God gave our ancestors gifts of empathy, conscience, and reason so that they could understand what they did when they hurt other people. Was general revelation unimportant before Adam and Eve? Did the importance of general revelation change dramatically after Adam and Eve sinned? If so, how and why?

---

4. There are significant *theological* challenges with the idea that sin and the fall were simply "built in" to humanity because of the means God used to create us. Throughout Scripture, sin is portrayed as a power that destroys us and is at odds with God's will. God is angry with human sin. God is said to be just in punishing sin. Sin is portrayed as entering into human history through human choice. It seems difficult to reconcile these teachings of Scripture with the proposal that human sin was *necessarily* built in to human nature by God, apart from any human choice.

3. *In addition to giving Adam and Eve special revelation and initiating a special relationship with them, did God miraculously transform them in some way?* This question was explored in chapters 5 and 9. Does the proposed transformation include a significant increase in their mental capabilities? If so, is there a God-of-the-gaps theological problem to worry about? If not, what exactly is the proposed transformation, and why was a miracle necessary? Did the proposed transformation happen to the entire population or just to Adam and Eve, and what are the theological consequences of either answer?

Also, did God give Adam and Eve supernatural gifts to bring them up to a state of original righteousness for a while—gifts that they subsequently lost after sinning? Or was God planning to raise them from a state of moral innocence and immaturity into a state of maturity over time? What are some theological implications of either answer?

4. *How did sin spread from Adam and Eve to the rest of the population?* This question was explored in chapter 9. Did everyone immediately become sinners because Adam and Eve acted as their representatives (scenario type 1)? If so, how do we answer questions about God's justice in condemning some people for the actions of another over whom they have no influence? Or did sin spread culturally or genealogically over time (scenario type 2)? If so, in the generations after Adam and Eve, when sin was in the process of spreading to the entire population, why would two individuals in neighboring tribes or families potentially have very different spiritual statuses simply because sin had spread to one tribe or family but had not yet reached the other?

5. *Did Adam and Eve have a real chance of choosing differently? And if so, might God have gotten a different result by choosing a different set of individuals out of the larger population to act as "Adam and Eve"?* This question was explored in chapter 10. Saying that God could have gotten a different result seems troubling, because then it seems as if God chose Adam and Eve poorly. Saying that God could not have gotten a different result no matter who God chose seems to make the fall inevitable (although not directly caused by God). What are the theological implications of either answer?

6. *Assuming God's desire was for a sinless humanity, then immediately after Adam and Eve sinned, why didn't God isolate them from the rest of the population and start over?* This question was explored in chapter 10. If Adam and Eve would have sinned no matter who God chose out of the larger population, and God foresaw this, then it seems once again that the fall was, in some sense, inevitable (although not directly caused by God). If the fall was avoidable and Adam and Eve had a real chance of choosing obedience over sin, then the question remains as to why God didn't isolate them after they

sinned (so that their sin did not spread to the rest of humanity) and choose new individuals with whom to work.

Six Difficult Questions for Scenarios with Adam and Eve as Figures Representing Many Individuals over a Long Period of Time (Scenario Types 3 and 4)

1. *How should we interpret Paul's use of "one man, Adam" in Romans 5 and elsewhere?* This question was explored in chapter 6. Many New Testament scholars argue that the mere fact that Paul, in Romans 5 and elsewhere, assumed that Adam was a real historical individual would not, by itself, require us to believe so. However, Paul seems to have used that assumption as a basis for explaining a vital piece of theology about how one person, Christ, can bring forgiveness of sins to many. Should we consider Paul's use of Adam to be another example of the Holy Spirit accommodating inspiration to the limited knowledge of the human author, or something else?

2. *What role, if any, did special revelation play in the entrance of sin into the world?* This question was explored in chapters 5 and 9. General revelation through empathy, reason, and conscience tells us some things about how we ought to behave. But special revelation can give us clarity about important things such as the fact that there is one God (instead of many gods) and that we should love our enemies (rather than love our neighbors and hate our enemies). How might we imagine our ancestors becoming aware of sin based only or primarily on general revelation (scenario type 4)? Or if special revelation plays an important role in the fall, but humanity's fall happened among many individuals over a long period of time (scenario type 3), what forms might that special revelation have taken?

3. *Was the fall, in some sense, inevitable?* This question was explored in chapter 10. If the fall happened through the sinful rebellion of many individuals over a long period of time, then it seems as if there was virtually no chance that humanity could have avoided the fall. If the fall was more or less statistically inevitable, what sort of theodicy should we use to justify God creating humanity in that way? Alternatively, if the fall was avoidable, how do we imagine it might have been avoided over such a long period of time?

4. *What should we make of the tree of life in Genesis 2–3 and Paul's apparent belief that physical death was a result of the fall?* This question was explored in chapter 9. If the fall happened through the sinful rebellion of many individuals over a long period of time, it is difficult to imagine how physical

death for humans could, in any sense, have been caused by the entrance of
sin into the world. How then should we interpret those passages?

5. *In what sense was creation "very good" and sin something that entered
the world through human choice?* This question was explored in chapters 9
and 10. In these scenarios, the final stages of humanity's creation via gene-
culture coevolution—including the stages in which humanity's most advanced
mental and social attributes developed—were happening simultaneously, over
a long period of time, with humanity's sinful rebellion against God. Can
we continue to think of the creation of the world and of humanity as being
"very good," in some sense, prior to the entrance of sin? If so, how? If not,
how should we think about it?

6. *In what sense is God not "too responsible" for human sin?* This question was explored in chapter 10. This connects back to the third question of
whether the fall was inevitable. If the fall was, in some sense, inevitable, then
how much responsibility do we humans have for sin, and in what ways is God
just for judging human sin?

How These Scenario Types Agree with One Another

We should embrace difficult questions. Many important church doctrines
underwent centuries of intense discussion before the church reached sufficient
consensus to write those doctrines into creeds. On some important doctrines,
such as the nature of the divine inspiration of Scripture, the church maintains
a range of theories. On some important doctrines, such as the atonement, the
church is concluding that multiple theories are needed to do justice to the full
range of scriptural teaching. By wrestling with difficult questions, we learn.
As we debate these issues within the church, it is easy to focus on how much
we disagree with one another. In order to do this work in a God-glorifying
way, we must also remember the ways in which we agree with one another.

The different types of scenarios considered in this book agree on several
important points:

1. Scripture is inspired by God and authoritative. Scripture is redemptive
in nature. Scripture refers to historical events. Sometimes Scripture includes
straightforward information about history or the natural world. Sometimes
Scripture says things that might sound at first, in our modern cultural context, like straightforward statements about history or the natural world but
really are not. The church benefits from the work of biblical scholars who
work collaboratively using sound hermeneutical methods and follow the lead
of the Holy Spirit.

2. Science doesn't dictate theology or interpretations of Scripture. On occasion, science—along with other fields of human study such as philosophy, archaeology, sociology, and linguistics—alerts us to theological difficulties with certain interpretations that were not obvious to us earlier. Theology, taking into account these new considerations as well as older considerations, ultimately decides which interpretations are viable or best.

3. Scripture in many places teaches that God is good, just, and holy. Sin is a rebellion against God's revealed will. The earliest acts of sinful disobedience by our ancestors had consequences for them and their descendants. All humans today are prone to sin and incapable of not sinning. The incarnation, life, death, and resurrection of Jesus Christ are central to God's atonement for human sin.

Conclusion

God's Answer Is Still Christ

SIN WOULD KEEP US AWAY from God eternally without God's rescue.

We want to know what God is doing about sin. Through Scripture, in stories with a great deal of historical detail, God tells us what he is doing. God worked with the children of Israel over centuries. God gave them the law of Moses, poetry, and wisdom literature. God gave them prophets, kings, and priests. In the written history, we see stories of defeat and exile and stories of deliverance and restoration. All of this led to just the right time in history when the Son of God, the Second Person of the Trinity, came to earth and became incarnate as a human. God's ultimate revelation was not a set of laws or a theological theory, but a person. He himself lived among us. Christ taught and healed and lived in front of many eyewitnesses. Christ suffered and died and rose again in front of many eyewitnesses who recorded the stories and passed them on to the church. God continued to work in history through the church. God continues that work today.

We also want to know when God will bring the world to an end and usher in a new reality without sin. We want to know all sorts of details about exactly what will happen and when it will happen. God doesn't give us all those details. God gave us the book of Revelation. Its prophecies are open to many interpretations and, as church history shows, many misinterpretations. God has told us what God wants us to know. God has not told us everything we would like to know.

We also want to know exactly how God created the world. In an age of science, many of us want to know with scientific and historical detail. God didn't give us all those details in Scripture. Instead, God gave us Genesis 1,

Psalm 104, and other passages that speak about God's creation of the world in ways that the original ancient Near Eastern audience could understand. These passages speak about God creating a firmament above a flat earth, with primeval waters above the firmament and below the earth. Through those Scriptures, God told the original audience what he wanted them to know. Through the same Scriptures, he tells us today what he wants us to know. God has not told us the answer to every question we might want answered. God does, however, enable us to learn many historical details by scientifically studying his creation.

We might be worried that God will put an end to sin here on earth by using miraculous power to kill all sinners. In part to answer that worry, God inspired the flood story of Genesis 6–9. The story seems to tell of the entire earth being destroyed by a flood with only eight human and several animal survivors. But by studying God's world scientifically, we have learned that, while there were many local floods throughout history, there never was such a global flood. Through archaeology, we have learned that Genesis 6–9, like Genesis 1, makes use of literary styles and cultural assumptions of the ancient Near East. We would like to know the exact historical details behind Genesis 6–9, but God doesn't give us all those details. Through those Scriptures, God told the original audience what he wanted them to know. Through the same Scriptures, he tells us today what he wants us to know. God has not told us the answer to every question we might want answered.

We want to know when sin began. The different scenarios presented in this book disagree about the *history* of how sin entered the world and spread, but they all agree about the *fact* of sin. The fact of sin is more important than its history. Throughout church history, there have been multiple theological theories about the history of sin; in the end, all such theories have relied on a certain amount of speculation.

The problem we face now is *not* that there are no scenarios that harmonize the scientific evidence for human evolution and the doctrine of original sin; rather, there are too many scenarios, and we are finding it difficult to decide which one is best.

We want to know exactly how and when sin started. Perhaps we want to blame other people for our sin, like Adam did in Genesis 3:12. Perhaps we want to blame other parts of creation for our sin, like Eve did in Genesis 3:13. Perhaps we want to try to shift as much of the blame as possible onto God, as Adam and Eve implicitly did.

Perhaps our motives are better. Perhaps we want to know more historical details so that we can construct a useful systematic theology of how sin damages us, or of how sin spreads. We have learned that Genesis 2–3 tells us important things about our relationship with God, but it does not tell us many historical details. God told the original audience what he wanted them to know. He tells us today what he wants us to know. God has not told us the answer to every question we might want answered.

We work with what God has given us. We have Genesis 2–3, Romans 5, and the rest of Scripture. We have everything we can learn from studying the natural world scientifically. We have everything we can learn from archaeology. We have everything we can learn from studying human nature and culture through philosophy, history, and the social sciences. And as we learn more, the Holy Spirit might occasionally prompt us to make some adjustments in our doctrinal theories. We can do this work well, or we can do it poorly.

Above all, God gave us Jesus Christ. His words and actions show us how we should live in a world where there is sin. His life, suffering, death, and resurrection show us the full extent of God's self-giving love. Whatever we might learn about how and when sin began, and whatever mysteries might remain, we know what God is doing about the problem. We know that God's victory is assured. Christ is God's ultimate answer.

Scripture and Ancient Writings Index

Subject Index